Policy Studies Institute

THE EFFECTIVENESS OF SOCIAL CARE FOR THE ELDERLY

Policy Studies Institute

THE EFFECTIVENESS OF SOCIAL CARE FOR THE ELDERLY

An overview of recent and current evaluative research

E. Matilda Goldberg and Naomi Connelly

Heinemann Educational Books · London

Heinemann Educational Books Ltd
22 Bedford Square, London WC1B 3HH

LONDON EDINBURGH MELBOURNE AUCKLAND
HONG KONG SINGAPORE KUALA LUMPUR NEW DELHI
IBADAN NAIROBI JOHANNESBURG
EXETER (NH) KINGSTON PORT OF SPAIN

First published 1982

British Library Cataloguing in Publication Data

Goldberg, E. Matilda
   The effectiveness of social care for the
   elderly. – (Policy studies institute series)
   1. Social work with the aged – Great Britain
   1. Title   II. Connelly, Naomi   III. Series

   ISBN 0-435-83353-7
   ISBN 0-435-83354-5 Pbk

Typeset by Inforum Ltd, Portsmouth
and printed by Biddles Ltd, Guildford, Surrey

Contents

Acknowledgements

Many people have helped in this enterprise. The Joseph Rowntree Memorial Trust made it possible with their generous funding. The Director, Robin Guthrie, gave us a great deal of encouragement and support throughout. We are particularly grateful to many research colleagues who shared their as yet unpublished findings with us so generously. We owe a great debt to our Advisory Committee who raised many searching questions and issues with us, often bringing fresh perspectives to our, at times, tedious papers!

We greatly mourn the loss of two of our advisers, Jack Tizard and Philip Abrams, in the mid-stream of their activities. We had been looking forward to discussing the final drafts of our work on residential care with Jack Tizard and on neighbouring with Philip Abrams as they had contributed so much of the seminal thinking to these two fields.

Robin Huws Jones did not only act as a wise Chairman but he carefully read and commented on the final drafts of all the chapters, which proved immensely helpful to us.

Last but not least, we want to thank our administrative secretary to the project, Rosemary Lewin, whose help extended far beyond her immaculate, accurate and uncomplaining typing and retyping of drafts. She helped to read and summarise some of the literature, dug out statistical information for us: in short, as far as time allowed she acted as a competent research assistant.

The Advisory Committee

Chairman: **Robin Huws Jones**, formerly Consultant, Joseph Rowntree Memorial Trust

***Professor Philip Abrams**, Department of Sociology and Social Administration, University of Durham

Peter Barclay, Chairman, National Institute for Social Work

Dr David Fruin, Senior Research Officer, National Children's Bureau

Robin Guthrie, Assistant Director (Planning and Research), Social Work Service, Department of Health and Social Security (to 1979); Director, Joseph Rowntree Memorial Trust

Stephen Hatch, Head, Voluntary Organisations Research Unit, Policy Studies Institute

Lord Seebohm

****Professor Jack Tizard**, Director, Thomas Coram Research Unit, University of London Institute of Education

Peter Westland, Under-Secretary (Social Services), Association of Metropolitan Authorities

Professor John Wing, Professor of Social Psychiatry and Director of the Medical Research Council Social Psychiatry Unit, Institute of Psychiatry, University of London

Priscilla Young, Director, Central Council for Education and Training in Social Work

* died October 1981
** died August 1979

1 Introduction

Social work and social care

In the late 1970s the Joseph Rowntree Memorial Trust suggested that the time was ripe to bring together the results of studies and thinking on the effectiveness of social work, to discover what had been established so far, to identify emerging trends for practice and policy, and – if possible – to indicate possible future directions.

It became clear from an exploration of the social work literature of the last two decades that the concept of social work remained fairly circumscribed in the 1960s, the decade in which a number of important evaluative studies were carried out. Most professional social work was in fact *casework* directed towards the amelioration of psycho-social problems of individuals and families. Social work consisted of relatively small-scale enterprises dealing separately with the social needs of fairly well defined client groups: children deprived of 'normal' home life, disturbed children and delinquents, the mentally ill and mentally handicapped, the physically ill and handicapped, the elderly in need of residential care and so on. Most of these client groups were looked after by specialised social workers.

Since the reorganisation of the social services in 1971, social work has become big business. The boundaries are ever expanding; they range from psychotherapy to social planning. The new departments in England and Wales are (rightly) called departments of social *services* and not departments of social *work*, the term used in Scotland. Social workers spend much of their time on routine administration, screening activities, citizens' advice bureau type of information, liaison and advocacy with other agencies, and surveillance of vulnerable or 'at risk' groups, rather than on casework. Indirect social work roles – putting clients in touch with other services, mobilising resources of all kinds on clients' behalf, co-ordinating services, acting as advisers to partially trained workers or volunteers – are growing, as are roles as community workers and community organisers. On the other hand, counselling functions are being assumed more and more by volunteers or semi-professionals. There are school counsellors, marriage guidance counsellors, bereavement counsellors and so on. Indeed, the roles and tasks of social workers have become so diverse and diffuse that the Department of Health and Social Security found it necessary in 1980 to appoint a working party to consider the functions and tasks of social workers (Working Party on Roles and Tasks of Social Workers 1982).

The term 'social care', meaning 'the social as distinct from the economic ways in which people look after each other, directly or indirectly' (Barnes and Connelly 1978), seems to convey more adequately these recent developments in the personal social services. The concept embraces not only social work and other statutory personal social services but also all kinds of voluntary activities as well as self-help and mutual help. It seemed to us more appropriate therefore to address ourselves to the effectiveness of social *care*, of which social work constitutes only one element. This idea raised another difficulty: it would prove impossible to review the much wider territory of studies and current evaluative projects relating to the effectiveness of social care across all client groups. Hence we decided to confine ourselves to a single group exemplifying and indeed demanding the wider social care approach, and thus posing new challenges. Preferably it should be a client group attracting a fair amount of evaluative and innovative action research over a range of social care activities – social work, domiciliary services, volunteer efforts, mutual help schemes, day and residential care. The broadening field of social care for the elderly comes nearest to meeting these criteria.

We hope however that the ways in which we have looked at overlapping service boundaries and cross-cutting issues will have relevance to evaluation of social care activities generally, taking the elderly as a case in point. Indeed, in our methodological chapters we deliberately quote illustrative examples from a wide field of social care.

Aims of the enterprise

The first aim of this book, then, is to draw together the main strands of recent and current research and demonstration projects which seek to evaluate some aspects of social care for the elderly. The research we have considered ranges from small-scale descriptive studies by individual researchers in social services departments, through sophisticated experiments testing the outcomes of innovative social care, to large-scale investigations comparing a number of services or institutions. We have also occasionally taken account of new developments in social care of the elderly where as yet little evaluation has taken place. Some of the material discussed in this book remains unpublished or has had only a limited circulation in such journals as *Clearing House for Local Authority Social Services Research*.

We hope therefore that this overview will enable other researchers and those commissioning research, as well as teachers, to discover what has been done, with what results, what gaps exist, and what seem to be critical issues for further investigation.

The second aim of this study is to conduct an illustrated exploration, as it were, of the process of evaluation at different levels; evaluation carried out under different auspices (in-house or independent research organisation), with different perspectives in mind (the consumer, the caregiver, the independent observer) and concerning different types of activities in the spectrum of social care – from voluntary neighbourhood care to residential care.

Last but not least we hope that this review will convey a clear picture to practitioners and policy-makers of the state of the art in the evaluation of social care for old people: what has been established on fairly firm evidence, what practices appear to work and why, and what policy issues emerge.

Is such an exercise necessary?

The doubts and criticisms that have been expressed about the effectiveness of social work and the statutory social services during the last decade and beyond are too well known to be rehearsed here once more. The continuing retrenchment in expenditure on social care brings the topics of accountability and cost-effectiveness to the fore. At the same time there is a nostalgic euphoria in the air about recreating something which probably never existed in an industrial society, a 'caring community' in which the statutory services provide a 'safety net' for those who cannot be looked after by their own informal networks, the services' main function being to 'enable the community to care' for their own members.

One hypothesis underlying these notions is that in the recent past the all-embracing statutory social care has tended to undermine the community's ability to take care of their own members by doing things *for* people, taking decisions out of their hands rather than stimulating their resourcefulness, self-help and mutual help capacities. Certainly some evidence can be adduced that long-term casework with some types of chronically disorganised families has probably provoked and perpetuated dependency; that providing meals on wheels routinely to recently bereaved widowers is not the best way of encouraging self-help or mutual neighbourly help; and that over-cautious physical care proffered to old people in residential homes can encourage passivity and dependency. In general, however, there is no evidence to show that organised social care saps initiatives, encourages families to abdicate responsibilities for their dependants, or discourages mutual helpfulness. Evaluative studies known to us rather point the other way: that domiciliary and skilled social support to very frail people and their carers can lift morale and helpfulness (Challis and Davies 1980, Power and Kelly 1981) and can stimulate activity and enterprise (Goldberg *et al* 1970).

Moreover, Parker (1981), in a recent symposium, has made a formidable case for a realistic appraisal of demographic and social trends which will affect the resources needed and available for looking after the very old and physically disabled in our midst. He has acknowledged that there are strong economic and social incentives to shift the balance away from expensive state provision towards the family and the local community, but the scale of what is needed will make that change difficult to achieve without further distorting the distribution of caring roles which places additional expectations upon some – especially women – and not others. White (1981), in the same symposium, reminded us that many of our present services exist as a result of public awareness that individual effort, community concern and voluntary activity cannot by themselves fulfil the aims of consistent and equitable services throughout the country. At the same time, many commentators agree that more thought needs to be given to the optimal balance and distribution of functions as between the statutory, voluntary and private sectors. A consensus is also developing that more decentralised and locally responsive patterns of social care delivery are desirable, without abandoning the important considerations of equity and accountability.

In this climate of contradictory philosophies of social care and uncertainties about roles and functions of paid professionals and volunteers, it is important to establish what empirical evidence exists about the effectiveness of different forms of social care, ranging from family or neighbourhood support to a variety of statutory services. Such a critical appraisal will be all the more essential in the field of old age since social and demographic trends (in particular the steady increase in the number of the very old within the next two decades) indicate that 'more of the same', in services or opportunities already available, will be inadequate – even assuming that resources will be available for such increases.

The elderly and social care

Inevitably in our subsequent discussions on the attempts to evaluate the processes and outcomes of different forms of social care the emphasis will be on services and care activities for groups of people often lumped together as 'the elderly' or 'old people'. But we want to stress that we are acutely aware that 'old age' as defined in our society can stretch over a life span of 30 years or more – longer than childhood and adolescence put together. We also try to remind ourselves throughout this volume that 'the old' are as different from each other in personalities, life experiences and expectations as other age groups. This raises the question: why make a special 'need' or client group of them? However, there is no denying that, especially at the very elderly end of the distribution, say from the age of 75 or 80 onwards, this group shares many characteristics, needs and life experiences (for example, loss), and any civilised society will think in terms of support and caring arrangements for this potentially vulnerable group of citizens.

It is also worth remembering that the phenomenon of large numbers of very elderly people in our midst, many of them frail, both physically and mentally, nearly half of them living alone, is comparatively new. While child care is accepted as a social obligation, 'aged care' is not as yet so firmly established, and is also considered less rewarding and hopeful. Thus as a society we are still groping our way towards satisfactory answers. We want older people to remain independent and able to care for themselves as long as possible, living as 'normal' lives in the community as possible, yet we want them to be sufficiently supported by networks of family and friends, or by more formal services, not to suffer unnecessary physical or mental hardship. This is clearly a difficult balance to achieve.

The question then arises: what are the strategies and technologies that are being developed to help old people to live as comfortable and as normal lives as possible, and how effective are they? The last decade has seen a rapid growth of research and demonstration projects, ranging from transport facilities to the treatment of dementia. But in the enthusiastic development of formal and informal caring arrangements and in subsequent attempts to evaluate their effectiveness there lurks another danger: it is that many tend to think, especially of the very old, as passive recipients of services or care who can be slotted into various appropriate care arrangements rather than as people with individual life experiences who have the right to choose and to have a say in the way they live. We want to assure our readers at the outset that when we talk in terms of aggregated categories of both users and services without appearing to pay attention to individual differences in 'take-up', collaboration and attitudes of satisfaction or dissatisfaction, this is because we cannot qualify every statement, and not because of insensitivity to the all-important elements of individual differences and the 'fit' between service or caring activity and the recipients with their particular needs.

The boundaries of the study

Although we are adopting the broad concept of social care our study has narrower limits than we might have wished. Originally we intended to encompass the pre-retirement, the early retirement and the later stages of increasing dependency. However, pre-retirement measures, including courses and other means of preparation for retirement, though growing in number and importance, are only just beginning to be evaluated (Phillipson 1981). So we shall have very little to say about this phase although we recognise the importance of exploring the effects of increasing unemployment among older people, of retirement policies, life styles, and informal and formal preparation, in relation to adjustment to old age.

Similarly our material on the 'young olds', the immediate post-retirement stage up to the middle seventies, is sparse, partly because this is a reasonably healthy and vigorous age group requiring relatively few supportive services or other forms of social care, and partly because the psychological and social needs arising during this phase and their fulfilment have been little studied. As we shall show, certain pointers are emerging about the 'young olds' as a reservoir for volunteers, active members of mutual help networks and pressure groups. But, as yet, studies are lacking which indicate whether, for example, participation in social clubs, mutual aid networks and the like contributes to more fulfilment and less isolation and loneliness later, with easier acceptance of support services when needed.

Thus most of the material we shall consider is related to the very elderly, who are of course the group most in need of social care – formal and informal. Many evaluative studies are concerned with an examination of these various services and helping activities and their effect on the well-being of the very old. In view of the demographic trends and the philosophy of enabling people to live as 'normal' a life as possible, the emphasis of many experiments in this and other countries is on how to support even very frail elderly people in the community so as to delay or eliminate altogether the necessity for permanent residential care. Hence a good deal of space will be devoted to studies evaluating developments in domiciliary services, day care, neighbourhood support and so on.

There are other boundaries which we had to establish. While one can argue that an evaluative examination of social care for the elderly must be based on all the social services, from income maintenance through housing, health, personal social services to transport, we have focused mainly on the personal social services. Otherwise this enterprise would have become unwieldy and diffuse and certainly would have transcended our own experience and knowledge. Inevitably we shall touch on the health dimension in relation to primary health care and day hospital care. Although housing in general is not included, we shall consider evaluative studies of special types of accommodation for the elderly such as sheltered housing, assisted lodgings, and residential care in old people's homes.

Within the field of the personal social services we have aimed to be as comprehensive as possible, ranging from studies of informal networks of care and mutual help through formal statutory and voluntary services to residential care.

Methods of study

We have pursued our explorations in a variety of ways. Our main sources of information are completed published and unpublished studies. We have also kept in touch with a number of current projects and studies. Thirdly, we have tried to become aware of promising innovative projects, even if no evaluation had, as yet, been built into the project. Lastly, we have carried out a small pilot study among social workers dealing with elderly clients, to gain some idea of what social workers consider to be their specific contribution to the care of the elderly.

During the time of our study the volume of evaluative research among the elderly has grown steadily. Although we have attempted to keep abreast of research developments, clearly by the time this book appears it will already be out of date. But we want to emphasise once more that the purpose of this overview is not merely a literature review but a more general attempt to use the results of research and demonstration projects in the field of social care of the elderly to ask: what are the ways in which the effectiveness of formal services and of informal supports are being assessed? What is the state of the art? What are the issues emerging if we apply a fairly consistent framework of evaluative analysis to social care activities for the elderly in terms of their needs, responses to these needs, and what impact these responses have as seen by the various actors – the elderly themselves, the caregivers, the community, and the independent researchers? And what are the implications for policy, especially for the most promising use of resources?

The plan of the book

The first part of the book is concerned with the theory and methods of evaluation. Having set out the arguments for evaluation we demonstrate with examples from field studies extending to different client groups the various methods which can be used to assess the effectiveness of social care activities, from analytic description through monitoring to controlled field experiments.

After a short chapter describing recent developments and the present framework of social care services for old people, we shall examine the results and implications of evaluative research in the social care of elderly people living in their own homes. We shall be looking at domiciliary services, the contribution of social work, the role of day care and voluntary and informal social care.

The third part of the book will be concerned with special accommodation for the elderly, including sheltered housing, assisted lodgings and residential care.

In the final section we shall try to draw together the emerging issues and discuss possible directions for future research and for the development of practice and policy.

References

Barnes, J. and Connelly, N. (eds) (1978) *Social Care Research*, London, Bedford Square Press.

Challis, D.J. and Davies, B.P. (1980). A new approach to community care for the elderly, *British Journal of Social Work 10*, 1–18.

Goldberg, E.M., Mortimer, A. and Williams, B.T. (1970) *Helping the Aged: A field experiment in social work*, London, George Allen and Unwin.

Parker, R. (1981) Tending and social policy, in E.M. Goldberg and S. Hatch (eds) *A New Look at the Personal Social Services*, London, Policy Studies Institute.

Phillipson, C. (1981) Pre-retirement education: the British and American experience. *Ageing and Society 1*, 393–413.

Power, M. and Kelly, S. (1981) Evaluating domiciliary volunteer care of the very old: possibilities and problems, in E.M. Goldberg and N. Connelly (eds) *Evaluative Research in Social Care*, London, Heinemann Educational Books.

White, T. (1981) Recent developments and the response of social services departments, in E.M. Goldberg and S. Hatch (eds) *A New Look at the Personal Social Services*. London, Policy Studies Institute.

Working Party on the Roles and Tasks of Social Workers (1982) *Social Workers: Their Role and Tasks*, London, Bedford Square Press.

Part One
The Methodology of Evaluation

2 What is Evaluation – Why Evaluate?

Aims

What exactly do we mean when we talk about evaluating the effectiveness of an activity or a service? Evaluation is in some sense a matter of assessing the value or worth of an activity or an object, but if this is accepted it inevitably follows that there is no objectivity in evaluation: 'value' and 'worth' are essentially subjective judgements which will vary from individual to individual, from group to group and according to the roles and functions and points of view the evaluators occupy. For example, the value the general public or service providers attach to providing domiciliary help for the elderly or support to a deprived family may differ from the value the receiver or the potential user of a service may attach to the service. A woman on probation said: 'I wanted immediate help when my Giro did not arrive in time, but they don't give money. I wanted understanding, but I did not get it'. And the probation officer said: 'My aim was "passive resistance", not to rush around and do things for the client but get her to stand on her own feet and deal with the authorities herself'. A home help organiser recently referred to the application for cleaning help by an almost totally disabled elderly woman as 'low priority'. For her, household cleanliness had a lower priority than personal care and maintenance of morale and emotional well-being. For the elderly woman, however, a home help to do her heavy household chores was something to which she gave the highest priority.

In these examples the conflicting aims of clients and service providers are quite obvious. However, the contradictory aims and expectations and hence the values attached to both the type of help required and the desired outcomes are seldom made explicit. Hence an old person who has received practical help (for example, advice about her entitlement to a special grant or an aid to daily living) may be pleased with this outcome, while the social worker bemoans the fact that she only managed to mobilise practical resources rather than to deal also with the underlying feelings of isolation and depression this client seemed to experience.

The best known examples of unexpressed and unrealised contradic-

tory expectations and outcomes are to be found in Mayer and Timms'
study *The Client Speaks* (1970). Some clients were puzzled about what
the social workers were driving at in their psycho-dynamic casework
approach, which aimed at 'insight' as a positive outcome; these clients
were dissatisfied since they did not get the material help and practical
advice they had expected.

Thus the first point to consider in any evaluation process is what aims
are being pursued, and secondly whose values and expectations are
embodied in these aims – and which of these we are evaluating.

Needs

Aims and objectives in social care are designed to meet a variety of
needs. So the next step is to consider needs for social care. But human
needs beyond the basic ones for shelter, food and warmth are exceedingly difficult to define and categorise. As Bradshaw (1972) has
expounded in his well known article on the typology of needs, we
should be clear what definition of need is being considered. An operational definition of need may be based on validated measures of incapacity developed by experts, for example Townsend's personal incapacity
measure (Townsend and Wedderburn 1965). Or the definition of need
may be based on the felt need of individual people. This can vary from
person to person and will largely depend on their experiences and
expectations. Thus an elderly person scoring high on the experts'
incapacity measure but with a fierce sense of independence and a great
deal of ingenuity may not feel the need for a home help, while someone
with a moderate degree of disability but of a dependent and anxious
disposition may feel acute need for help. Thirdly, need may be defined
more administratively and equated with expressed demand as exemplified by the number of applicants for particular services. Such administrative indicators may miss those who do not know of existing services
or are unaware of their entitlement to such benefits. Finally, definition
of need may be based on ideas of comparative equity which postulates
that people with similar characteristics, disabilities and living circumstances should be entitled to similar kinds of help. Ideally an assessment
of need would take all these aspects into account – a systematic assessment of functioning, the subjective perceptions of the individual, the
strength of entitlement, as well as the comparative perspective. In
practice these ideal conditions are rarely fulfilled, as we shall see in
subsequent discussions.

Other elements enter into the picture of need. For example, defini-
tions of need change over time; who would have thought even 20 years
ago that bereavement counselling would now be perceived by many as
meeting a recognised social need in our society? Currently, we are
witnessing a gradual shift in needs as perceived by home help service

providers away from a 'chore' service towards a home and personal care service, partly generated by the needs of the growing number of very old and frail people for diverse personal services. Administrative perception of needs, and hence provision, can and does vary from area to area – for example, in relation to day care for the under-fives. One authority may consider comprehensive day care for this age group a high priority while another authority will consider this an 'extra', leaving it to the initiative of the Pre-School Playgroups Association to set up voluntary arrangements. As already noted, there can be profound differences in perception of needs as between clients and service providers or 'experts': the probation client felt she needed practical and emotional support – the probation officer thought she needed to learn to stand on her own two feet. The needs and hence the action required can conflict between members of the same family. The needs of a daughter in danger of breaking down under the strain of caring for her aged and frail mother may conflict with the mother's felt need to live close to her family. Whatever the complexities, the evaluation of a service or caring activity presupposes a careful specification of the needs or problems it has been designed to meet, as well as who has defined and recognised them.

Means
The third component in any evaluative process is the means chosen to tackle specified needs or problems, in order to achieve desired objectives. Here again, as we shall see in subsequent discussions, many difficulties arise, since social care constitutes a whole spectrum of activities from simple one-off information or informal voluntary help through practical services to a complex amalgam of practical help, emotional support and collaboration with other helping agencies, or to various forms of residential care. Not only is it difficult to specify the type of input which seems to be required to meet defined needs and achieve certain ends, but it is just as difficult to determine in retrospect exactly what factors in the intervention process have contributed to an observed outcome. Indeed, it is often hard to assess whether it is the social care input or some other influences which are responsible for any changes in circumstances or attitudes. One of the questions most hotly debated in a recent workshop on evaluative research (Goldberg and Connelly 1981) is how to separate the effect of the method of intervention from the influence of the person giving the help, particularly in the sphere of counselling or casework. We shall presently consider research methods designed to overcome some of these difficulties.

The complexities are compounded if we want to evaluate the impact of a whole programme rather than a specific treatment or care activity. For example, how do we ascertain which elements or what combination of different elements is responsible for any changes that may occur in a juvenile crime prevention programme which introduces special precautions in supermarkets, additional police controls, school discussion groups and additional play facilities?

Outcome
The final question with which evaluation needs to be concerned is how to recognise success or failure – by what criteria can we measure it? If objectives are concrete and visible, such as a clean house, a job, an aid to mobility, or more regular school attendance, measurement of 'success' is comparatively easy. However, if the objective is greater contentment, a happier marital relationship, acceptance of a handicap, or even easier acceptance of death, then achievement is more difficult to assess. For instance, if an emaciated, confused woman is safely settled in an old people's home and is in much better physical and mental health, yet is pining away for her budgerigar, her filthy flat and the pile of old newspapers she has always been going to read, is this success or failure? We hope to explore these questions further in our discussions of evaluative research projects.

Perhaps the question 'what is evaluation?' can best be summarised in Suchman's definition: it is 'a method for determining the degree to which a planned programme achieves the desired objective. Evaluative research asks about the kinds of change desired, the means by which this change is to be brought about, and the signs according to which such change can be recognised.' (Suchman 1967)

Why evaluate?
Why should we want to engage in this difficult process of evaluation, strewn with a variety of pitfalls?

Public accountability
Until recently, rapidly increasing public resources were invested in the personal social services, but few questions were asked whether and how services were improving and what was being achieved with the increased resources. Accountability is aided by information and monitoring systems capable of giving an ongoing account of who gets what, at what cost – not only to government, but to the service providers, to the recipients and last but not least to the public at large.

In the next chapter we will discuss in more detail the creation and use of monitoring devices enabling the social services to be more accountable to their public as well as to government.

Deployment of resources
Secondly, the monitoring type of evaluation can tell us how resources in

capital and running costs, manpower and skills are deployed among different need groups, different sections of the community and in different geographical locations. Do those in greatest 'need' get the largest share of the cake? Several studies to be discussed later have shown that even in such a comparatively practical service as the home help service, it has proved impossible to establish an unequivocal relationship between apparent 'needs' as indicated by the client's personal capacity and circumstances of living, and the amount of service offered. In several locality studies the amount of home help received seemed to depend far more on where the client lived than on her circumstances. Other studies in the personal social services have pointed to an inequitable distribution of skilled staff as between different client groups. Thus the great majority of trained social workers are deployed in work with children and families and very few among such groups as the aged or the mentally handicapped. Hence scrutiny of the deployment of resources is essential if we aim at achieving a measure of territorial and social justice.

Effectiveness

The most basic and important reason for evaluation is to determine what impact a particular service or caring activity has on the well-being of its users – are they any better off for having received the service? Although this is such an obvious aim of evaluation, yet evaluative research throwing light on outcomes is comparatively rare. There are many reasons for this, perhaps the most potent being the difficulties in establishing agreed and clear criteria of what constitute positive outcomes in the field of social care, as we have already indicated.

Even in relatively concrete domiciliary services it is not easy to establish criteria of success. How should we judge, from whose point of view – the point of view of the users, how satisfied they are? Or by the relief brought to others close to them in their environment? Should we take into account the assessments of the service providers and their satisfaction? Or is it possible to measure outcomes more objectively, by determining the extent to which previously identified needs have been met: for example, the floors now washed regularly, the place dusted, the shopping done. Or should we give more weight to the measurement of subjective feelings and attitudes: does the client feel more comfortable, more hopeful, more cared for, although the surroundings may still be fairly dusty and untidy? Answers to these questions will become more manageable if needs and aims are defined carefully at the beginning of the helping process.

Is it sufficient to ensure that those who are in need of a service according to defined criteria of impaired functioning, environmental circumstances and felt need receive the service? While coverage is an important element in evaluation, it is an input or 'effort' variable rather than an outcome one. People can receive regular home help or ready-cooked meals which are only marginal to their needs, and which reinforce dependency rather than self-help and may thus be disabling rather than enabling. Such considerations also apply to the provision of aids: success cannot be judged by the delivery of the aid alone, it is its use which will determine its effectiveness. A bath aid still in its original wrapping at the death of an old person must be judged as a negative outcome, despite successful coverage and delivery. The response to and the take-up of an offer of service is an important intermediate variable often overlooked in evaluative research.

When we come to more personalised help, such as counselling or social casework, the measurement of effectiveness has proved still more difficult, as numerous studies have shown. This has been partly because of rather vague and global aims, such as 'improving inter-personal relationships' or 'social functioning' or 'ego strength'. Often there have been no acknowledged aims apart from self-exploration designed to afford people more insight into the possible bases for their behaviour and attitudes.

Recently, aims of casework or counselling have become more modest and specific and hence are proving more amenable to outcome evalua-tion. However, in becoming more and more specific there is also the danger that we measure what we *can* measure, for instance, changes in behaviour in simulated situations, rather than in the world outside, which is the real test (Reid and Hanrahan 1981).

Cost effectiveness
Especially at a time of retrenchment in the personal social services it is essential not only to determine whether the services offered are actually taken up and if taken up whether they meet the needs of clients, but also at what cost. For example, the famous field experiment *Brief and Extended Casework* carried out by Reid and Shyne (1969) showed that, at the most conservative estimate, brief casework intervention restricted to 8 interviews in families experiencing disturbed relation-ships had at least as beneficial results as open-ended treatment with an average of 20 interviews with similar families. Clearly on cost grounds alone (400 interviews compared with some 1500) short term interven-tion should be the treatment of choice in similar problem situations.

Or consider the field experiment carried out by Goldberg and her colleagues (1970) which showed that trained caseworkers achieved better results in some areas of psychological and social functioning among the elderly than untrained welfare officers. However, in many other respects there were no significant differences in the outcomes brought about by the two types of worker. A legitimate question arising from these findings is whether it is worth the cost of additional training and reduced caseloads to substitute fully trained caseworkers for less trained welfare officers in the social care of the aged. As we shall show later the study itself pointed to a cost effective answer: namely the differential deployment of different types of social helpers based on initial accurate assessments, since only a small proportion of elderly clients appeared to need the help of trained caseworkers.

Safeguard against 'the new'
Hard-headed assessment of effectiveness measured by relevant criteria is particularly necessary when new treatments or organisational arrangements are pushed with great enthusiasm as though their useful-ness had already been proven beyond doubt. Experience in a wide range of fields has shown that some methods of 'prevention' or 'cure', of building design, or of care, heralded as being superior in effectiveness compared to existing methods, are found not to be so once they have been in use over time, or after they have been tested experimentally. An example of a new enthusiasm is that for patch-based delivery of per-sonal social services, whose key features are the functioning of the service within a small geographical area (population size 5,000 to 10,000) and employing community-oriented methods of work. It is suggested that this method of organisation means that a higher propor-tion of those at risk will be helped, that help will be provided earlier and that there will thus be fewer crisis interventions, that long term support in informal ways within the community will be more common, and that there will be fewer admissions to residential care than in the more traditional forms of service delivery. In a wave of enthusiasm, a grow-ing number of area offices are adopting the patch system but luckily serious empirical evaluation research is afoot to test some aspects of its effectiveness before it becomes the new panacea of service delivery.

Similarly in the field of residential care for the elderly we find a great wave of enthusiasm emerging in favour of the group living principle, where small numbers of old people live together in quasi-domestic units doing as much as possible for themselves and for each other, preserving a reasonably active and independent life. Careful evaluation of the pros and cons of this form of organisation is needed before this type of living arrangement is adopted as a general principle in preference, for exam-ple, to a hotel or boarding-house model which may suit the needs of certain people more than enforced intimate contact and support in small groups.

We hope that these five sets of arguments will convince our readers that attempts at evaluating the process and outcome of social care activities is essential if we are in earnest about meeting people's needs as effectively as present knowledge and wisdom gained in practice allow. This obligation holds true even though the political decision-making process may at times reject the rational results of evaluative research.

We conclude that whatever the difficulties inherent in the process of evaluating the outcome of a helping act or a service, it is essential at least to clarify needs, means and ends, and at the very best to arrive at a valid assessment of outcome.

References

Bradshaw, J. (1972) A taxonomy of social need, in G. McLachlan (ed.), *Problems and Progress in Medical Care*, Seventh series, London, Oxford University Press for Nuffield Provincial Hospitals Trust.

Goldberg, E.M. and Connelly, N. (eds.) (1981) *Evaluative Research in Social Care*, London, Heinemann Educational Books.

Goldberg, E.M., Mortimer, A. and Williams, B.T. (1970) *Helping the Aged: A field experiment in social work*, London, George Allen and Unwin.

Mayer, J. and Timms, N. (1970) *The Client Speaks*, London, Routledge and Kegan Paul.

Reid, W.J. and Hanrahan, P. (1981) The effectiveness of social work: recent evidence. In Goldberg and Connelly (eds), op. cit.

Reid, W.J. and Shyne, A.W. (1969) *Brief and Extended Casework*, New York, Columbia University Press.

Suchman, E.A. (1967) *Evaluative Research*, New York, Russell Sage Foundation.

Townsend, P. and Wedderburn, D. (1965) *The Aged in the Welfare State*, London, G. Bell and Son.

3 How to Evaluate – From Description to Field Experiment

Most of the evaluative research in social casework in the 1960s and early 1970s foundered partly because input was largely unspecified – that is, 'casework' or 'group work', or comparatively recently, in a probation experiment, 'situational treatment' (Folkard *et al*. 1976). Casework is an amalgam of many different approaches to problem exploration and problem solving, ranging from the highly practical to the most intensely psychological, from a sharply focused task-centred approach to an open-ended exploratory approach. Similarly with group work – it can be structured around certain tasks or activities, it can have an educational bias, a mutual help emphasis, it can be an open-ended therapeutic group in which interactions between participants are explored, and so on.

The early investigations lacked straightforward descriptions capable eventually of forming categories of what social workers actually do with and for their clients. Also lacking were 'hunches' or hypotheses about what kinds of activities or approaches seemed to 'work' with what kind of clients in what kinds of situations. Lastly, as already mentioned, aims (if they could be wrung out of social workers) were so vague and global that it was hard to translate them into operational terms so that it was possible to know when the goal had been reached.

In the absence of systematic studies of clients and their problems, the nature of the social work input and the goals pursued, the early American field experiments which attempted to assess outcome of casework among different client groups proved disappointing. Could one expect so-called 'multi-problem families' in New York State who were chronically dependent on welfare services and who had developed hopeless and negative attitudes to respond positively to sudden attempts at intensive casework? (Brown 1968). In any case, was an exploratory casework approach relevant in the absence of much-needed material and social resources? Was it surprising that adolescent girls with incipient behaviour problems and poor achievement at school showed little change in behaviour or attitudes as a result of weekly counselling sessions which they had not sought, in the absence of any attention being paid to the girls' environment – their families, peer groups, and their school work (Meyer *et al* 1965)?

The lesson to be drawn from these early failures to show any effect of social casework is not necessarily that all kinds of social casework are generally ineffective (although this may be so), but that indiscriminate application of one type of treatment to almost any kind of problem is like dispensing aspirin for all ills.

The second lesson to be learned is that sophisticated approaches towards evaluating outcome of any type of intervention, without the necessary groundwork which describes and defines relevant variables in relation to problems, input and postulated outcome, is wasteful. Reid has referred to such ventures as 'bad marriages between tight design and loose programmes'.

Description

Hence the first step in evaluation is good descriptive studies of specific clients, the help or services they receive and how these are organised. Such studies can give information on who is there – the age, sex and living circumstances of the clients served; why they are there, that is to say what are the problems or needs which occasion contact with the service; how they came to be there – their referral route, what they obtain in the way of services or help when they get there, how much, how often, for how long; and finally what appears to be the outcome – did they receive the advice or the service for which they came, did they vanish, never to appear again, did the agency get rid of them with the label 'low priority', were they referred to another facility?

Such quantitative descriptive studies can give an account of a service programme or of an institution at a certain point in time or during a short circumscribed period. However, such data can also be collected continuously as a monitoring process over a longer period, making it possible to learn a great deal more about the flow of clients in and out of the service system, the use of material and skill resources in relation to different types of clients over time and so on. Let us first look at an example of descriptive snapshot studies.

Relatively straightforward descriptive accounts are particularly useful as a preliminary to evaluating new services that have sprung up haphazardly, often under different auspices, and whose potentialities need to be assessed before policy decisions can be made about their future development. One such service is day care for the elderly which has come into being relatively recently, has grown fast and unevenly and ranges from day hospitals providing maintenance and rehabilitative therapy to lunch clubs and drop-in centres providing social facilities for fairly fit and mobile clients.

Four major descriptive studies – three local ones exclusively concerned with day care for the elderly and one national one dealing with adult day care including the elderly – were carried out in the mid-1970s (Bowl *et al* 1978, Clegg 1978, Carter 1981, Fennell *et al* 1981). These descriptive day care studies provide an overview of the distribution, the auspices, the nature and the broad aims of different types of day care services, their staffing, and the type of clientele they serve. Some of these studies also evolved useful ways of classifying styles of management, activity patterns and client characteristics which will enable future researchers and policy makers to make cross-sectional comparisons between different day care facilities – a further step in the evaluative process which we will discuss later. These descriptive methods (although they included some interviews with users) were not designed to assess the effectiveness of different types of day care in relation to different types of need but by clarifying different aims, types of activities and management styles and users' reactions to them, these surveys raise pertinent questions for evaluative studies. For example, what types of activity, what dosage of day care, and what management styles are appropriate and helpful to what kinds of clients? Similarly, a burning question which description and observation can illuminate, but which needs experimental approaches in order to assess more precisely the impact on both users and staff, is whether to segregate or to mix various types of disability, different age groups or different type of provision, for example, day care within residential care (Edwards and Sinclair 1980).

On the other hand, some of the gaps and discontinuities the descriptive studies discovered hardly need any further sophisticated techniques of evaluation before policy decisions can be made. One example is the issue already pinpointed in 1970 by Brocklehurst, that the purpose of day hospitals for the elderly may be achieved but the good may be lost if there is no outlet to a day centre at the completion of treatment. Equally, the lack of transport becomes evident as a basic problem as soon as the availability of day services for those very isolated and disabled people who need them most is examined.

Monitoring social care

If, instead of carrying out an *ad hoc* study at one point in time, an ongoing descriptive system can be developed which enables service providers to monitor their social care activities, we move closer to an evaluative exercise. Such a system called the 'case review system' (CRS) was developed in an area office of a social services department, and was designed to monitor social work activities with all types of clients, including the elderly (Goldberg and Warburton 1979). Such a method of evaluating practice can be adapted to any kind of social care – domiciliary services, day or residential care. A general monitoring system necessitates an agreement by the service providers to adhere to a pre-coded recording method which minimally indicates client characteristics, problems tackled, and types of help provided. Ideally such a system should embody objectives and action plans as well as present and past helping activities. For example, the CRS asks social workers to look back at what they have done in the past review period and forward to what they wish to achieve within the next period and how. Hence, the instrument goes beyond monitoring of who is there, and who gets what – important though these elements are – towards evaluation, enabling practitioners and management to compare problems, plans and actual achievement on an individual or an aggregated basis by client groups, referral sources and routes, geographic areas, reasons for closure and so on.

A good monitoring system can thus discover typical patterns of resource distribution in relation to need groups. It can help to answer such questions as who are the clients who get 'one-off' advice and are then 'closed', who are the ones who come back again and again, and who are those who stay for ever on the books of social services departments? Do clients with similar demographic characteristics, circumstances of living and apparent problems receive similar or different 'treatment' in generic or specialised teams? Do clients from certain areas make more demands on services than those residing in other areas, and what may be the reasons in terms of demographic characteristics, distance from area office and so on? What are the seasonal variations in demands for service? What is the explanation of the growing number of re-referrals to social services departments, which in some areas amount to more than half the intake? Is any increase in re-referrals due to better recording methods, or have closing procedures changed over time?

Thus, regular monitoring can help to put the whole social service operation into a wider social and community context. The questions just raised cannot possibly be answered either by individual case studies or by snapshot-type descriptive studies. Almost all the findings of the descriptive studies of the home help service to be discussed in Chapter 5 relating to maldistribution of resources between areas could have been discovered through simple monitoring devices.

It is clear that any client-oriented monitoring system requires the active collaboration of service givers, since if they do not fill in the recording instruments the whole operation is null and void. Service providers need to be convinced that the categories developed (say for describing problem situations or caring activities) are appropriate and reflect as accurately as possible what they are doing and aiming for. Above all, they will need feedback in a form that gives them comprehensible and interesting information about their work and achievements, and stimulates them to ask questions about any kind of discontinuities or contradictions revealed in caring arrangements or mismatches between aims and achievements. We shall see in the following chapters that lack of systematic reviewing is one of the major causes of maldistribution of services in domiciliary and other services.

Finally, monitoring devices need not be confined to the service givers' perspective alone; they can include the clients as active participants in reviewing progress. Such combined reviews have been found illuminating and helpful in task-centred casework, where the final interview is devoted to a review of the problems tackled, the tasks undertaken, and the achievements as seen by both the social worker and the client. Shared reviews could also be carried out in day and residential settings either individually or in groups, but such active participation by clients will not always be advisable or feasible – for example, with very confused elderly people, or with clients who only reluctantly accept statutory surveillance.

Monitoring systems based essentially on service providers' data and judgements can also be linked to regular consumer or user surveys, and compared for congruence or discrepancies with the assessments of service providers. In one area, for example, such comparisons suggested that social workers tended to underestimate what they were achieving, particularly on the practical level, compared with the clients' views, and this applied especially to the elderly (Glampson and Goldberg 1976).

In summary, then, a general monitoring system is capable of elucidating trends in client characteristics, problems presented, help requested, service responses and achievement of objectives. However, it cannot test with any certainty the effectiveness or efficiency of specific intervention programmes. The monitoring exercise already referred to (Goldberg and Warburton 1979) highlighted sharply the extent to which social services departments have become providers of information and signposts to other agencies and services. The issue then arises as to whether these functions are best carried out by the social services departments; if so, how should they be organised? Would strengthening advice bureau services be a more effective solution? These questions can only be answered by empirical experimental studies which examine alternative ways of providing information, either within the context of the social services department or based outside it, for example in the voluntary sector. Similarly, the organisation of effective gate-keeping functions emerged as a vital issue from this monitoring exercise. Again, further evaluative studies are needed comparing the effectiveness of alternative physical locations and organisational arrangements for screening and assessment. Or take an example from the field of mental illness: the monitoring device of case registers has indicated the slow build up of a new long-stay population in psychiatric hospitals despite the revolution in discharge policies (Wing 1981). The question was then asked: are the psychiatric hospitals the most appropriate environments for these patients? An experimental study is now taking place comparing progress and outcome of a group of patients in a specially designed facility (a hostel in the grounds of a psychiatric hospital) with the progress of a similar group of patients remaining in hospital. Thus data derived from monitoring systems can provide base lines for further operational research and outcome studies, and most importantly they can suggest areas in which these studies are vitally necessary for the development of soundly based policies.

Monitoring community work

So far we have discussed monitoring as a type of evaluative action research with the individual client and his immediate family as the unit of analysis. What about action research designed to monitor and evaluate work with community groups? If social workers are reluctant to specify aims and commit themselves to a plan in relation to individual clients, aims are even more difficult to pinpoint among activists whose objective often is for the community groups to define their own needs. If social workers find it difficult to categorise problems and type of social work input and to keep a record of their contacts with other agencies, this becomes even more problematic in the context of the multiple problems and purposes of community development: for example, goals in the life of a tenants' association may be dictated by unforeseen political developments. Even if community workers do agree to specified monitoring procedures, all that may be realistically possible is independent observation and clarification of processes set in motion and their apparent outcomes. These processes may not be susceptible to quantitative analysis. But it may still prove instructive for action-oriented workers to become more analytic about their tactics and the relationship of these to outcome. Thus Butcher and his colleagues (1980) in assessing the achievements of a senior citizens' action group and other community action projects have developed a useful evaluative tool – not dissimilar to the case review form – which asks questions about aims, needs, inputs and outcomes in the practice of community work.

Lees (1975) suggests that 'if the exploratory nature of community initiative is acknowledged, evaluative research can in this way contribute to the community development process and help to refine community work skills'. He also suggests that the contribution of research monitoring could be to show how the existence of a problem comes to be recognised and how individuals and groups decide what is to be done. Such monitoring case studies could elucidate whether and how people become involved in community concerns. From this point of view it is important to have on record how decisions are made, how much information is necessary, who influences the outcome the most, how disagreements are resolved, what procedures are used, and in particular what is the effect of community initiative on the way choices are made.

In addition to the detailed monitoring of processes, it is at times possible to assess success or failure of community action by external indicators: for example, improved standards of housing repair, decrease in vandalism, increase in take-up of social security benefits and so on.

In the field of social care for the elderly, community work has been slow to develop. The main initiatives can be found in the formation of neighbourhood care groups whose characteristics, activities and achievements have been described by Abrams and his colleagues (1981 and 1982). This research will be considered in more detail in Chapter 8. Pensioners' action groups with largely political aims of improving the conditions of old people are also making themselves felt, and have received some attention in descriptive case studies (Buckingham *et al*. 1979).

In both individually-based and community-based social care, descriptive studies and monitoring data are important and necessary steps in the evaluative process elucidating 'who is there' and what happens, but throwing relatively little light on the impact of social care activities on users of services, participants in community action and the community at large.

How then can we find out whether any specific caring activities have had any beneficial effects?

Consumer studies

One idea which will occur to most people is – 'ask the customer'. Strangely enough this has rarely been attempted until recently. Even now with consumerism flourishing and much lip-service being paid to clients' rights to self-determination and participation, well designed consumer studies are relatively few and far between. The reasons are various.

First of all most people realise that follow-up studies undertaken by the helpers themselves would hardly be viable, since clients might not feel free to express their true feelings to the people who have tried to help them, and on whose goodwill they may have to depend in the future; helpers might also be biased in interpreting answers. Secondly, some interventions (particularly in the realm of counselling) are regarded as intensely personal and confidential; there is considerable resistance on the part of helpers and therapists to outsiders exploring such transactions and their impact. There is an understandable reluctance on the part of service givers (like all of us!) to expose themselves to criticism. User surveys on the effects of razor blades or the crunchiness of biscuits are relatively impersonal, at the worst exposing some failures in raw materials, manufacturing processes or marketing, while examination of the outcome of human services inevitably draws attention to the technical and social skills of individual service providers.

Thirdly, and very importantly, up to fairly recently the social service field was imbued with the paternalism which Barbara Wootton so ferociously attacked in her famous article in *Twentieth Century* entitled 'Daddy Knows Best' (Wootton 1959). Clients were often held not to know what the 'underlying' reasons for their malaise were; negative reactions to intervention were commonly interpreted as 'resistance', ready acceptance of advice as 'dependence' and quick improvement as 'flight into health', hence client opinions were not taken at face value or thought worth serious consideration.

Rudolf Klein in his stimulating study *Complaints against Doctors – a study in professional accountability* (1973) has widened the 'Daddy Knows Best' perspective, pointing out that much professional practice is based on judgements; hence professionals have argued that only their peers can judge their work, and evaluate this elusive quality of judgement. In the Maria Colwell inquiry (Colwell Report 1974), Olive Stevenson took this line in her Minority Report in which she as a social worker felt better able than her colleagues on the inquiry to evaluate the quality of the judgements on which many of the basic decisions in this case had rested. This case also demonstrates that in most professions, certainly in medicine and social work, judgements of professionals may differ, and to quote Klein 'differences of opinion how various illnesses should be treated at various stages may occur. There may be differences about the degree of risk that can be taken in a specific situation, decisions have to be taken on inadequate evidence, since collecting all the facts required to make an ideally rational decision is beyond the capacity of the doctor'. Clearly this relates to social care activities as much as to medicine. He continues: 'in effect the GP is engaged in calculating the odds. If he calculates them accurately he will be successful, if he calculates them inaccurately he will have failed in his professional obligation.' This statement can be applied to social work without any change in wording at all. How one might ask, then, can the client judge the quality of decision-making, or treatment, if the state of the art is such that there is no objective evidence or agreement as to what are the right decisions in specific circumstances?

Klein raises another important point: we talk rather glibly about 'consumers', of social or medical services. But 'a consumer' normally implies that someone has freedom of choice, that he has the information required to exercise that choice rationally, and that finally he can refrain from buying a particular product. The consumer of medical or social services is rarely in such a position. Indeed, the more he is in need of the service, the more acutely ill or the more acute the social problems are, the less choice he may have, and this applies as much to social services, now highly concentrated in local authority social services departments, as it applies to medicine.

Thirdly, there is the growth of professionalism, which to a large extent is a process of monopolising technical know-how and excluding the layman. Hence one might argue that it is the professionals' duty to give the customer not what he wants but what he ought to have.

What are the contributions that consumer or user studies have made or are making to the evaluation of the effectiveness of social care? The best known exploratory study remains the one by Mayer and Timms (1970), who interviewed a small sample of clients of the Family Welfare Association in London. Most of the limelight has been concentrated on that half of the study which is concerned with the dissatisfied client and little is heard of their equally interesting analysis of the satisfied client. What stands out clearly in relation to the dissatisfied clients is that they failed to obtain the help which they sought, and that there were serious misunderstandings and misconceptions between clients and social workers. What is more, neither clients nor social workers were aware that they operated on different premises about the springs of human behaviour and the ways in which it might be altered. In particular, the clients were puzzled by the social workers' exploratory techniques which often paid little attention to the client's definition of his problems and his immediate needs. They also resented, and could not understand, why the social worker focused on them and their possible contribution to any problem rather than on the person who, in the client's opinion, was at fault, namely the daughter, the husband or the neighbour. It seems that the social workers made few efforts to familiarise their clients with the assumptions underlying their approach. Clients who received the material help they sought and also gained a good deal of relief from unburdening themselves and getting support and direction from the social worker were satisfied.

Rees, examining client and social worker perspectives in their transactions in a social services department in Scotland, also found a good deal of misunderstanding between client and social worker (Rees 1974). He suggests that social workers are not familiar enough with the clients' orientations to problem solving and often are insufficiently explicit about premises on which they are working. He also thinks that if social workers were clearer and more open about the kind of situations in which they could not help rather than raising expectations which cannot be fulfilled, there might be fewer disappointed and dissatisfied clients.

There have been very few published consumer or user studies based on sufficiently large representative samples of social services department clients to draw reliable conclusions, and those reported by

Glampson and Goldberg (1976) so far remain the only ones of their kind. In these studies some 300 clients of the social services department in a southern town were interviewed in order to explore their expectations, feelings of satisfaction and views on the services they had received and to gain a picture of their knowledge of the functions of the social services and their perceptions of social workers. At the same time, all the social workers dealing with these clients were also given an opportunity to convey their views. These studies, too, revealed discrepancies in social worker and client perspectives which are mirrored in subsequent client/social worker studies. While the social workers thought that clients expected most of all to be able to discuss personal problems and to receive advice, sympathy and information, less than ten per cent of the consumers said they expected help of this kind, although they greatly appreciated the caring elements in the relationships with social workers. The majority of the consumers were reasonably satisfied with the services they received, partly because they expected in the main practical help and advice. The two client groups who received this type of help in large measure – the elderly, and those with predominantly material problems – turned out to be the most satisfied. Social workers, on the other hand, often felt frustrated that they were only able to offer practical services and advice and were aware of the functions they were not able to fulfil: those of the caseworker attending to the emotional problems of their clients. Accordingly, they expected their clients to be equally dissatisfied and to voice more complaints than they actually did. These consumer studies – like the exploratory study of Mayer and Timms – suggest that clients turn to social workers for the solution of practical problems more often than social workers think, and that they derive considerable satisfaction from having these practical needs met.

However, there are indications in other user research that the picture becomes more ambiguous in longer term contacts with social workers when either undue dependency develops, with the social worker acting as a kind of 'maintenance drug' and moral support, or uncertainty and mixed feelings become evident about the lack of clarity, aims and purpose of the social work contact. These findings become evident in several studies which examine users' and social workers' subjective perspectives as well as more objective outcomes for specific client groups: families who are recipients of long-term social work (Sainsbury *et al* 1982), parents of disabled children (Glendinning 1981) and clients suffering from mental ill health (Fisher *et al* 1981). These indications will be discussed in greater detail in the chapter on social work.

Studies of elderly clients' satisfactions and preferences are also being attempted in residential homes and, as will be demonstrated in Chapter

10, it is proving very difficult to obtain candid views from people who are mostly very frail and dependent on the care and goodwill of the residential staff and who have hardly any alternative choices left for different kinds of living arrangements.

Recent trends in social work and in the social care field generally towards greater specificity and open negotiation between client and helper about the problems as perceived by the clients, ways of tackling them and aims to be pursued, and the setting of time limits, may lead to a clearer understanding of social care tasks and objectives on the part of clients as well as of the caregivers. This has been demonstrated in recent studies of task-centred casework, in which many clients in their follow-up interview with an independent assessor were able to give a clear picture of the problems and tasks they had agreed to work on with their social workers, the part they themselves and the helpers had played in tackling these tasks, and what had been achieved (Goldberg *et al* 1982).

In summary, then, it seems that the clearer clients are about what needs or problems social service providers can help with and what to expect from their intervention, and the more they can participate in the process, the better informed their judgements about the helpfulness or otherwise of the intervention can be. This is not to deny the subjective element compounded of past and present experiences that enters into any kind of helping relationship and colours personal judgements of its worth. For instance, it has often been stressed that one should regard with caution the high degree of satisfaction with any kind of help usually expressed by the very old, since the hardships they have experienced may well have conditioned them towards very modest expectations. Perhaps one should also be wary of the feeling of emotional support and 'recognition' expressed by people with chronic and seemingly intractable emotional problems who regard their social workers as a kind of permanent friend who sorts out their environmental problems from time to time, but never really tackles any of the sources of their disturbances or aims at any changes, a process which social workers themselves have despairingly recognised as 'being rewarded for having problems' (Fisher *et al* 1981).

In view of the many complex issues affecting consumer evaluations of social care, how much weight should be attached to user studies? There are two separate issues here. First, as has already been discussed, the client's own view is only one subjective though important element in the constellation of factors that need to be taken into account in judging effectiveness. Second, follow-up data alone are of little use, if they cannot be compared with the state of affairs at the start of the intervention. As we all know, memory, especially among the elderly, can be faulty. Thus an elderly widow who on referral to a social services department was depressed, forgetful and isolated, eating and sleeping poorly, may say after six months of contact with a volunteer and attendance at a day centre that she is no better than she was on referral, since her life remains pretty empty and pointless without her lifelong companion. Yet observation and information from friends and neighbours indicate that this client is now more active, has made some friends at the day centre, eats and sleeps better and is less forgetful. Thus on more objective measures she is functioning better and getting more out of life, but she has forgotten how low and miserable she was on referral six months ago and the underlying feeling of having lost what she valued most in life is still with her and will probably remain with her. Unless her present state can be assessed not only on her subjective feelings but also on behavioural criteria, and can be compared with her state on referral, and unless one has a realistic conception of what social help can hope to achieve in her particular circumstances, such a case could easily be judged a failure on the basis of a follow-up study alone.

'Before and after' studies which make base line assessments before clients receive help and independent assessments after help has been terminated, on both observable functioning and behaviour and subjective feelings and attitudes, bring us a good deal closer to a reliable evaluation of outcome. Recent studies exploring the effectiveness of task-centred casework in social service and probation settings used this design (Goldberg *et al* 1983). But although many interesting insights were gained into the processes and the impact of this particular method of casework, the 'before-and after' design could not tell us whether other forms of intervention or no intervention at all would have produced similar results.

Experimental studies

So let us return to our widow. How can we find out whether it was the help she received, rather than merely the passage of time, that led to her physical and mental improvement? Suppose that we could produce an exact duplicate of this widow with identical life circumstances, but not offer her any social service help, and then, on comparing her state at the end of six months with that of our client, we find that the duplicate widow had not changed at all in her behaviour and attitudes. In this case we could reasonably conclude that it was the help that had been responsible for the change in our client. In other words, if we could control all the personal and environmental factors in the lives of these two elderly women so that their circumstances were identical and only vary *one* influence, namely the extra social care one of them receives, then we could postulate a cause and effect relationship.

The above hypothetical example represents the essence of an experimental test which consists in comparing the 'before and after' state of two equivalent subjects or groups of subjects, one of whom has been subjected to a specified form of experience while the other has not. Given a large enough sample, we can then postulate that any random intervening events would affect both 'experimental' subjects and 'control' subjects in a similar fashion, and that the only consistently varied experience was the specified intervention. Any differences emerging between the two subjects or groups at the end of such an experiment could then be reasonably attributed to the particular intervention rather than to other random influences both may have experienced in the intervening period.

Such experimental conditions can be created in nature without too much difficulty: we can treat one half of a field with a certain weed-killer and not the other, and watch the results. Similar conditions can also be created in the animal world but this already introduces more complexities. We can breed identical strains of rats, keep them under similar conditions in adjoining cages and treat one group with a certain drug and not the other, and at the end of the experiment be reasonably certain that any difference in behaviour, physical or psychological condition in the treated group must be because of the effect of the drug since all other conditions from their genetic make-up, through diet and housing to temperature and inter-rat relationships have remained similar in the two groups of rats. The snag is, of course, that with human beings such a measure of genetic and environmental control is not possible, and all we can hope for is to approximate very roughly the principles governing these experimental axioms.

First of all, since we cannot produce identical pairs of clients we can try to match pairs as closely as possible in those characteristics that we think essential in relation to our test. For an elderly person we might aim to match age, sex, social class, marital status, living circumstances, housing conditions and – much more difficult – nature and severity of disability and social interactions such as contacts with children and neighbours. Even this crude type of matching may involve a great deal of effort and time. Hence a more common, cheaper and more reliable method is randomly to assign the target population on which we want to test our method of intervention (say, married couples seeking advice from a marriage guidance council, or delinquents referred to a probation officer) to an experimental group which will receive the type of intervention to be tested, and to a control or comparison group which will not receive this type of intervention. If the assignment is truly random, usually the two groups emerging turn out to be similar in most important respects. Of course the researcher will have to produce evidence that this is so before the experiment starts. Thus Reid and Shyne (1969) in their experimental study of brief and extended treatment showed that the 120 families which were randomly assigned to brief and open-ended treatment were similar in all the aspects that were thought essential for the test, namely age band, ethnic origin, family composition, social class, ratings of family functioning, problems presented and so on.

Similarly, Goldberg and her colleagues (1970) randomly assigned newly referred clients of a welfare department to an experimental group who were to receive help from trained social workers and to a comparison group who were to remain under the care of untrained welfare officers. They showed that the two groups were similar in relation to a large variety of background, social and medical variables, but that there was a difference just above the five per cent level of statistical significance in the number of men in the special and comparison group. (This means that if the whole procedure of random allocation had been carried out on 100 different samples of old people, a similar result with more men in the special group would have occurred in five samples.) Still, it was a difference to be reckoned with and it was up to the researchers to explore whether or not this difference in sex ratio between the special and the comparison group was likely to introduce any distortion into the results.

The second difference between rigorously controlled laboratory experiments and so-called 'field experiments' is that it is not always possible or ethically defensible to withhold treatment from the control group. For example, having assessed the 300 elderly welfare clients for their needs it would have been invidious to leave half of them without any help. However, it is possible to carry out studies in which patients or potential clients on a waiting list can be randomly assigned to an experimental treatment group and to a waiting list group who await their turns in the usual way. The most common solution to this dilemma is to test the *relative effectiveness* of two different types of intervention. For instance, in the experiment with the elderly welfare clients social work carried out by trained social workers with the 'special group' was compared with social work carried out by untrained welfare officers in a 'comparison' group. In the study experimenting with brief and extended casework, short-term casework lasting up to eight interviews was compared with open-ended casework lasting up to 18 months; in a recent probation experiment 'intensive situational' treatment by probation officers carrying small caseloads was compared with ordinary probation supervision by officers carrying much larger caseloads (Folkard et al 1974 and 1976). In a recent experiment in task-centred casework, an experimental group of people who had attempted suicide by self-poisoning and who were receiving short-term task-centred casework were compared with a control group of similar patients receiving routine services available in the area (Gibbons 1981). Figure 3.1 gives a diagrammatic presentation of experimental design.

Figure 3.1 Flow chart of an experimental design to evaluate a health or social work treatment programme

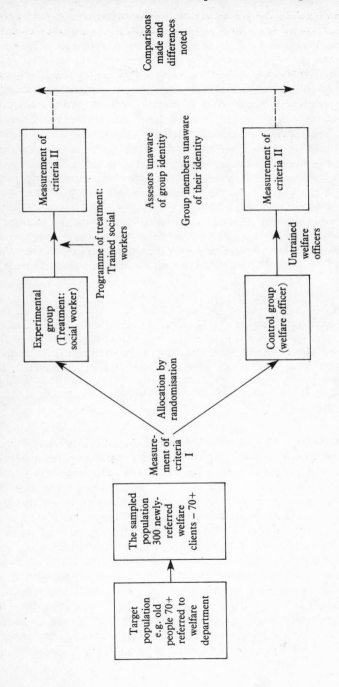

Adapted from B. G. Greenberg and B. F. Mattison (1955), The whys and wherefores of program evaluation, *Canadian Journal of Public Health 46* p. 298

However, it is worth stressing that particularly in circumstances in which the 'natural' course of the disease or the condition to be studied is not known, comparing two different types of intervention or treatment which show few and small differences in outcome (which is often the case in social intervention experiments) still does not answer the question whether any intervention or treatment is better than none. It should also be remembered that in a situation of shortages of services of all kinds, opportunities may present themselves, particularly in the voluntary sector, for one experimental extension of a service which then would allow comparison between those receiving the new service and those not yet reached. But in most problem situations calling for some form of social care, the question usually is what kinds of help or support are the most appropriate, rather than whether any help should be offered at all.

So far then we have established two necessary conditions in order to ensure that any outcome of an intervention – favourable or unfavourable – is due to the intervention rather than to a myriad of other events in the clients' lives which may have nothing whatever to do with social care.

(i)   We need two samples of clients which are as similar as possible and at the same time representative of the kind of population we wish to study. This equivalence is usually achieved by randomly assigning the chosen population to an 'experimental' and a 'control' or 'comparison' group.

(ii) The treatment to be tested will have to be administered to the experimental group and a recognisably different form of intervention to the control or comparison group. In this way the relative effectiveness of different treatments will be put to the test.

Three further conditions will have to be observed:

First, we need to specify the treatments or types of intervention which are being evaluated. In other words, we need to know what it is we are evaluating, otherwise it will not be possible to replicate the experiment, let alone to generalise from it. We have noted that in the early experiments there were no such specifications. Recently attempts have been made to break down social work and social service activities into their major components, including the hitherto ignored elements of co-ordinating activities, of mobilising resources and of advocacy (Goldberg and Warburton 1979). Reid and his colleagues have developed typologies of casework techniques based partly on Hollis' work (Hollis 1967 a and b, Reid and Shyne 1969) which can be coded by listening to tape recorded interviews. Behaviour modification techniques, now gaining ground in social service settings, are the most standardised and hence the easiest to describe, categorise and measure. Generally, in the more recent social services experiments it has been possible to specify interventions to a much greater extent than in the early experimental studies. The inputs in residential care are even more difficult to specify, although here, too, progress has been made in describing different kinds of regimes, care practices and living arrangements.

These developments towards greater specification of intervention have not yet been able to capture in any successful way the impact the personality characteristics of the helpers have on outcome. Recent research in both institutional and community settings has established clear relationships between worker styles and outcome (Sinclair 1971, Goldberg et al 1983). But how these personality variables are related to technical skills in the helping process needs much further elucidation.

Despite these shortcomings it was possible to show in the experiment *Helping the Aged* that the amount, content and 'mix' of social work activity differed significantly in the special and comparison groups. Similarly Reid and Shyne demonstrated that the emphasis given to different modes of intervention differed in the short-term and open-ended treatment groups.

Secondly, the definition of criteria in an experimental design is essential for the successful outcome. These can range from subjective feelings and attitudes such as the degree of depression or satisfaction with life felt at the moment, through measures of physical and social functioning (mobility, capacity for self care, activity patterns, contacts with relatives and friends) to external conditions such as changes in income, housing and so on. Sometimes indicators purporting to be reflectors of outcome, such as number of re-admissions to a hospital for chronic schizophrenic patients or number of children in foster homes restored to their natural parents, are used, rather than direct behavioural or situational criteria. Such indicators are popular since they are usually easily measured, but they need careful scrutiny, since they may not be indicative of successful outcome: good social community care of a schizophrenic patient may result in early re-admission to a hospital before a crisis blows up; restoration to natural parents may be the worst thing that can happen to a happily placed foster child, and so on. Criteria of success can also be established in the form of specific objectives for each individual client, and outcome would then be measured according to the degree to which these objectives have been achieved as measured by a rating scale.

Thirdly, chosen criteria of change should be measured in both groups in as unbiased a fashion as possible before and after intervention. Ideally, the persons carrying out these assessments and measurements should be independent of the helpers and unaware of the kind of intervention that has taken place, and if possible also unaware of who is in the experimental and control groups. While such 'double blind' trials are possible in drug therapy, this is hardly ever achievable in social care field experiments, since the assessors can often discover in their interviews who was in the experimental group and what kind of 'treatment' was received.

Although the randomised experiment or at least an approximation to it is the most powerful tool to detect whether a certain type of intervention is responsible for any effects produced, it is used comparatively rarely in the evaluation of social care. The method has been criticised on various grounds such as:

(a) random assignment of clients to an experimental and a different type of comparative treatment within the same organisation, for example, an area office, inevitably leads to 'contamination', since practitioners will talk to each other, clients can exchange notes and so on;

(b) practitioners are inclined to sabotage random assignments, being often unwilling for their clients to be in a comparison group since they are convinced that the experimental treatment is the treatment of choice;

(c) practitioners are prohibited from learning and adapting their practice in the course of an experiment, as feedback of intermediate results is usually avoided since it will tend to alter practice methods;

(d) experimental methods can only compare two types of intervention rather than a variety of methods;

(e) an experiment can detect whether a certain method of intervention brings about change but it cannot say *why*.

Some of these objections can be overcome by careful preparatory work with the practitioners who are going to participate in the experiment. The reasons for success or failure can be established within the context of an experiment by exploring associations between client characteristics, worker characteristics, inputs and outcomes. Other objections are more difficult to meet, such as the danger of 'contamination', and the lack of feedback.

Quasi-experiments
In some situations, particularly when outcomes of whole programmes rather than well defined specific types of treatment are to be evaluated, random assignment or matching procedures within the same target population are not feasible. In such circumstances, experimentals and controls are often drawn from socially similar populations residing in different areas which have similar demographic characteristics. While such a procedure avoids the danger of 'contamination', it introduces other elements of uncertainty, since a host of uncontrolled factors can enter the situation. For example, a factory can shut down in one area and a great deal of unemployment ensue, the political composition of

the social services committee may change, medical facilities may alter in one area and not in another and so on. One well known project in which the quasi-experimental design is being used is the Community Care Project (Challis and Davies 1980, Davies and Challis 1981) whose aim is to improve community services to very frail elderly clients who are on the margin of need for residential care, so as to enable them to remain in the community if they wish to do so. The second aim of this project is to introduce greater cost-effectiveness in deploying resources by delegating budgetary control to field social workers. Clearly it would be exceedingly difficult to introduce such a novel and complex service on the basis of random assignment to experimental and control services within one and the same area office. Hence the project is being carried out in two demographically similar areas within the jurisdiction of the same social services department. An implementation team of three social workers carries out the experimental project in one area office, while the comparison group of clients, also on the margin of needing residential care in the control area, receive the ordinary run of social services.

For the rest, the procedures are similar to those in randomised experiments, that is to say, clients in both the experimental and comparison groups are assessed before and after intervention; input, which in this project does not only consist of direct social work intervention but in employing and supervising a variety of paid and unpaid helpers, is specified and as far as possible categorised, measured and costed; the assessor is independent of the helpers, but since the clients' addresses denote whether they are in the experimental or comparison group the assessor will be even less 'blind' than in a randomised experiment.

Two other quasi-experiments in the field of social care for the elderly have been recently completed and will be considered in more detail in other sections of this book. One project in Weston-super-Mare asked how far local volunteers can work in effective partnership with health and social services to provide reliable and systematic support to elderly neighbours. In this case, the experiment was located in a group general practice and the study population consisted of the registered patients aged 75 and over. A volunteer scheme was established in one part of the town and offered to those patients who wanted to avail themselves of this service, while no such scheme was organised in other parts of the town. The entire study population was assessed before and 18 months after the introduction of the volunteer scheme, and the help given by the volunteers was monitored throughout the period. The authors of this study (Power and Kelly 1981) explain convincingly why they chose a quasi-experimental design:

> This quasi-experimental design of contrasting areas was chosen because random allocation of cases within one area did not seem

feasible. Ordinary people volunteering might accept a research component and help in a monitoring exercise, but would find it hard to
accept that they could help one nearby neighbour, but not another.

The other quasi-experiment is the Coventry Home Help Project (Latto
1980 a and b, Latto 1982) in which home help hours were almost
doubled in one district of the city but not in the others. This increase in
provision was accompanied by various enrichments of the home help
service, such as more administrative and clerical support to the organiser, increased training for home helps, enhanced payments for certain
difficult tasks and the introduction of specialised home helps. A sample
of home help recipients in the experimental district was compared with
a sample of home help clients in other districts at the beginning, at
mid-point and at the end of the experiment which lasted for three years.

In all these quasi-experiments a large variety of outcome measures
were used, ranging from assessments of depression and 'morale'
through physical and social functioning to such criteria as numbers
admitted to residential care, extent of use of other services and cost.
How meaningful and successful these outcome measures were will be
taken up elsewhere.

Cross sectional designs
It will be noticed that in all the experiments and quasi-experiments
quoted the researchers themselves introduced a new ingredient or a
new service into the social care field (trained casework, brief casework,
task-centred casework, decentralised budgets, a volunteer service, an
enriched home help service) and then proceeded to test their effectiveness compared with the usual services.

If one wants to find out which of a variety of approaches already in
existence works best, a cross sectional comparative design is often used,
particularly in the context of residential care (Sinclair and Clarke 1981).
In other words, the researchers compare outcomes in a variety of
natural situations without deliberately changing anything, and then
relate these outcomes to a variety of factors in the hope of explaining the
different outcomes. For example, Sinclair (1971) compared the absconding rates in 23 probation hostels for young men and found that the
proportion of boys leaving prematurely as a result of absconding or
further offending, varied from 14 per cent to 78 per cent. He then
related the different leaving rates to a host of background, personal,
location and regime factors. He found that a considerable amount of the
variation could be accounted for by the way the warden and his wife ran
the hostel and that the wardens with the lowest rates of absconding were
those who ran a strictly disciplined hostel but who expressed warmth
towards the boys and were in agreement with their wives about how the
hostel should be run.

This type of cross sectional design has been used to good purpose in studies of vandalism in housing estates (Wilson 1978), studies of residential nurseries (Tizard and Rees 1975) and in studies of ordinary secondary schools (Rutter *et al* 1979). Sinclair and Clarke have argued (1981) that while random allocation experiments enable one to be certain whether an effect has taken place they leave one uncertain how it is achieved: the study of a number of institutions makes it possible to pick out the most successful and then by correlational techniques look for the explanation. However, as is well known, significant correlations are not necessarily indicative of cause and effect and the question remains whether *all* the possible competing explanatory factors have been put into the equation. On the other hand, as Sinclair and Clarke suggest, a combination of monitoring designs and cross sectional analysis could advance our knowledge substantially as to what 'works' under what circumstances – provided, we would add, that satisfactory outcome measures can be developed. Information derived from monitoring devices could be compared in relation to outcome as between different methods of intervention, different types of care givers involved, different client groups and so on. A small beginning was made by Goldberg and Warburton (1979) comparing very crude criteria of outcome in different client groups in relation to type, length and intensity of help given and type of worker involved.

Summary
In this and the previous chapter we have introduced our readers to the process and rationale of evaluative research and to methods of evaluating outcome, pointing to their respective strengths and weaknesses. The evaluative process starts with the identification of aims, goes on to the definition and assessment of needs, the description and monitoring of input and moves on finally to the measurement of outcome. We have identified the main methods of evaluation as description, monitoring, experiment (and quasi-experiment) and cross-sectional comparisons.

In the subsequent explorations of evaluative research into the effectiveness of social care we shall use the framework of aims, needs, input and outcome and where appropriate refer to the methods employed. It will soon become apparent that the vast majority of studies which seek to evaluate some aspects of social care for the elderly are of the descriptive kind and that more powerful experimental designs geared towards the evaluation of outcome are the exception rather than the rule.

References
Abrams, P., Abrams, S., Humphrey, R. and Snaith, R. (1981) *Action for Care: A Review of Good Neighbour Schemes in England*, London, The Volunteer Centre.

38   *Social Care for the Elderly*

Abrams, P., Abrams, S., Humphrey, R. and Snaith, R. (1982) Patterns of Neighbourhood Care: End of Project Report, University of Durham Rowntree Research Unit, Unpublished report to DHSS.

Bowl, R., Taylor, H., Taylor, M. and Thomas, N. (1978) *Day care for the Elderly in Birmingham* (2 vols), University of Birmingham Social Services Unit, Unpublished.

Brocklehurst, J.C. (1970) *The Geriatric Day Hospital*, London, King Edward's Hospital Fund.

Brown, G.E. (ed) (1968) *The Multi-Problem Dilemma: A social research demonstration with multi-problem families*, Metuchen, NJ, Scarecrow Press.

Buckingham, G., Dimmock, B. and Truscott, D. (1979) *Beyond Tea, Bingo and Condescension*, Stoke-on-Trent, Beth Johnson Foundation.

Butcher, H., Collis, P., Glen, A. and Sills, P. (1980) *Community Groups in Action: Case studies and analysis*, London, Routledge and Kegan Paul.

Carter, J. (1981) *Day Services for Adults: Somewhere to go*, London, George Allen and Unwin.

Challis, D. and Davies, B. (1980) A new approach to community care for the elderly, *British Journal of Social Work 10*, 1, 1–18.

Clegg, P.E. (1978) *Day Care for the Elderly in the Metropolitan Borough of Kirklees*, University of Bradford, Unpublished.

Colwell Report (1974) *Report of the Committee of Inquiry into the Care and Supervision Provided in Relation to Maria Colwell*, London, Department of Health and Social Security.

Davies, B. and Challis, D. (1981) A production relations evaluation of the meeting of needs in the Community Care Projects, in Goldberg and Connelly (eds.), *op. cit.*

Edwards, C. and Sinclair, I. (1980) Debate: segregation versus integration, *Social Work Today*, 24 June.

Fennell, G., Emerson, A.R., Sidell, M. and Hague, A. (1981) *Day Centres for the Elderly in East Anglia*, Norwich, University of East Anglia Centre of East Anglian Studies.

Fisher, M., Newton, C. and Sainsbury, E. (1981) Social work support to people suffering mental ill-health and to their families, University of Sheffield Department of Sociological Studies, Unpublished report to DHSS.

Folkard, M.S., Fowles, A.J., McWilliams, B.C., Smith, D.D., Smith, D.E. and Walmsley, G.R. (1974) *IMPACT. Intensive Matched Probation and After-Care Treatment. Volume I: The design of the probation experiment and an interim evaluation*, Home Office Research Study No. 24, London, HMSO.

Folkard, M.S., Smith, D.E. and Smith, D.D. (1976) *IMPACT. Intensive Matched Probation and After-Care Treatment. Volume II: The results of the experiment*, Home Office Research Study No. 36, London, HMSO.

Gibbons, J. (1981) An evaluation of the effectiveness of social work intervention using task-centred methods after deliberate self-poisoning, in Goldberg and Connelly (eds.), *op. cit.*

Glampson, A. and Goldberg, E.M. (1976) Post Seebohm social services: (2) the consumer's viewpoint, *Social Work Today*, 9 November.

Glendinning, C. (1981) *Resource Worker Project Final Report*, University of York Department of Social Administration and Social Work, Social Policy Research Unit, Unpublished report to DHSS.

Goldberg, E.M. and Connelly, N. (eds.) (1981) *Evaluative Research in Social Care*, London, Heinemann Educational Books.

Goldberg, E.M., Mortimer, A. and Williams, B.T. (1970) *Helping the Aged: A field experiment in social work*, London: George Allen and Unwin.

Goldberg, E.M. and Warburton, R.W. (1979) *Ends and Means in Social Work: The development and outcome of a case review system for social workers*, London, George Allen and Unwin.

Goldberg, E.M., Gibbons, J. and Sinclair, I.A.C. (1983) *Problems, Tasks and Outcomes: The evaluation of task centred casework in three settings*, London, George Allen and Unwin.

Hollis, F. (1967a) Explorations in the development of a typology of casework treatment, *Social Casework 48*, 335–341.

Hollis, F. (1967b) The coding and application of a typology of casework treatment, *Social Casework 48*, 489–497.

Klein, R. (1973) *Complaints against Doctors: A study in professional accountability*, London, Charles Knight.

Latto, S. (1980a) Help begins at home, *Community Care*, 24 April.

Latto, S. (1980b) Help begins at home, *Community Care*, 12 June.

Latto, S. (1982) *The Coventry Home Help Project – Short Report*, Coventry Social Services Department.

Lees, R. (1975) The action-research relationship, in R. Lees and G. Smith, *Action-Research in Community Development*, London, Routledge and Kegan Paul.

Mayer, J. and Timms, N. (1970) *The Client Speaks*, London, Routledge and Kegan Paul.

Meyer, H.J., Borgatta, E.E. and Jones, W.C. (1965) *Girls at Vocational High: An experimental study in social work intervention*, New York, Russell Sage.

Power, M. and Kelly, S. (1981) Evaluating domiciliary volunteer care of the very old: possibilities and problems, in Goldberg and Connelly (eds.) *op. cit.*

Rees, S. (1974) No more than contact: an outcome of social work, *British Journal of Social Work 4*, 255–279.

Reid, W.J. and Shyne, A.W. (1969) *Brief and Extended Casework*, New York, Columbia University Press.

Rutter, M., Maughan, B., Mortimore, P. and Ouston, J. (1979) *Fifteen Thousand Hours: Secondary Schools and their effects on Children*, London, Open Books.

Sainsbury, E., Nixon, S. and Phillips, D. (1982) *Social Work in Focus*, London, Routledge and Kegan Paul.

Sinclair, I.A.C. (1971) *Hostels for Probationers*, Home Office Research Studies No. 6, London, HMSO.

Sinclair, I.A.C. and Clarke, R.G.V. (1981) Cross-institutional design, in Goldberg and Connelly (eds.), *op. cit.*

Tizard, B. and Rees, J. (1975) The effect of early institutional rearing on the behaviour problems and affectional relationships of four-year-old children, *Journal of Child Psychology and Psychiatry 16*, 61–73.

Wilson, S. (1978) Vandalism and 'defensible space' on London housing estates, in R.V.G. Clarke (ed.) *Tackling Vandalism*. Home Office Research Studies No. 47, London, HMSO.

Wing, J. (1981) Monitoring in the field of psychiatry, in Goldberg and Connelly (eds.) *op. cit.*

Wootton, B. (1959) Daddy knows best, *Twentieth Century*, October 1959, No. 166, 248–261.

Part Two
Evaluating Care in the Community

4 Recent Trends in Community Care

Before exploring in some detail what we can learn about the effectiveness of social care for old people from recent and current evaluative research, it may be helpful to review briefly recent trends in 'community care'. Such care, hailed as a new concept for the care of the disabled and the mentally disordered in the 1960s, has always been the main support of most elderly people. That is to say, they were and are being looked after more or less adequately by family, friends and neighbours as they become frailer and more dependent. No more than 6 per cent of the population over 65 live in residential or hospital accommodation (Hunt 1978), although this figure increases to 8 per cent for those between 70 and 80 and to 21 per cent for those aged 85 and over. Thus the vast majority of old people go on living in their own homes until a terminal illness may necessitate hospital admission.

How much, in what ways, and with what effect 'the community' cares for old people is a topic we shall explore throughout this book. As Walker has reminded us (1981), as far back as 1958 the then Minister of Health stated that the 'underlying principle of our services for the old should be this: that the best place for old people is their own homes, with help from the home services if need be.' And the report on *Health and Welfare* (Ministry of Health 1963) described the needs of the elderly in the following terms:

> elderly people living at home may need special support to enable them to cope with their infirmities and to prevent their isolation from society. As their capabilities diminish they will more often require such services as home help, laundry service, meals cooked ready for eating, and chiropody. Loss of mobility brings the need for friendly visiting, transport to social clubs and occupation centres, and arrangements for holidays. When illness is added to other infirmities, they need more home nursing, night care and help generally in the home. In terminal illness, an elderly person may for a limited period need considerable help from many of the domiciliary services.

This is as comprehensive a statement on the kinds of community services needed by the elderly as has been uttered in the 18 years which followed.

The gradual building up of a framework for the provision of domiciliary services makes an interesting study of a continual interplay between practical experience, systematic investigation and policy formation, with the voluntary sector playing an ever-changing role in these developments. It took the second world war, which prevented many people from looking after their elderly parents, to draw attention to the plight of elderly people, just as the evacuation experience had aroused people's consciences about the deprivation experienced by many children. In the field of the social care of the elderly the war experiences led to the formation of the National Old People's Welfare Council (NOPWC – the forerunner of Age Concern) and the establishment by the Nuffield Foundation under the chairmanship of Seebohm Rowntree of the Survey Committee on the Problems of Ageing and the Care of Old People, which in turn led to the setting up of the National Corporation for the Care of Old People, renamed in 1980 the Centre for Policy on Ageing (CPA). Both Age Concern and CPA remain vigorous and dynamic voluntary organisations influencing practice, research and social policy with respect to the older population of Britain.

In the statutory field one of the first postwar Acts to give local authorities powers to provide domiciliary services by employing home helps was the National Health Service Act 1946. It also gave very general powers for the care and after-care of persons suffering from illness and for preventive measures relating to health, which made such services as chiropody possible. Another major postwar social care measure, the National Assistance Act of 1948, enabled local authorities to make arrangements for 'promoting the welfare' of people who were disabled or substantially handicapped and to make contributions to the funds of voluntary bodies providing meals or recreation for old people. Most important, the Act laid a duty on local authorities to provide accommodation for all persons 'who by reason of age, infirmity or any other circumstances are in need of care and attention not otherwise available to them'. Aneurin Bevan, the then Minister of Health, when introducing this Bill to Parliament visualised that for the elderly the workhouse would be replaced by special homes for up to 30 residents; these would be run by welfare authorities for the 'type of old people unable to do the housework, the laundry, cook meals and things of that sort' (Hansard 1947–48). Clearly Bevan did not anticipate the very great expansion of domiciliary services which in many localities now enables even very frail and dependent old people to live in their own homes if they wish. But he did have the ideal of a much smaller residential home than we have yet been able to achieve for the majority of residents.

The voluntary sector played a very important part in the development of meals services, particularly the Women's (now Royal) Voluntary Service, which as the threat of bombing and invasion receded became involved in providing services for the elderly population, including mobile hot meals. Similar developments were promoted by the Red Cross, and the NOPWC encouraged the formation of local voluntary councils which could co-ordinate these efforts and also stimulate activities such as old people's clubs, visiting schemes and chiropody facilities. These voluntary efforts continued to flourish, even after the introduction of the National Assistance Act 1948, since this Act empowered local authorities to provide grants to voluntary agencies rather than to provide direct domiciliary services themselves. The statutory sector, on the other hand, always had the power to provide home help services, although the desirability of supplementary and complementary contributions by volunteers were referred to in every Ministry of Health circular. Aids to daily living, the third important arm of the domiciliary services, were not specifically mentioned in either the National Health Service Act or the National Assistance Act, and as there was no obligation on welfare departments to provide them progress was slow in this sphere until the Chronically Sick and Disabled Persons Act of 1970.

Throughout the 1950s and early 1960s the Ministry of Health annual reports made frequent references to the need to develop domiciliary services as a means of enabling elderly people to remain in their own homes, and to accept admission to hospital or for residential care as the right course 'when an old person himself accepts the necessity for this and when he has reached a point when the community services are no longer sufficient' (Ministry of Health 1961). The Ministry of Health remained 'confident that an increased number of able and reliable voluntary workers can be forthcoming' (Circular 7/62) and that there was therefore little point in extending the legal powers of the local authority. In contrast, many local authorities did see a need to become directly involved in the provision of domiciliary support services and to demand a greater say in the running of the voluntary services, especially the Old People's Welfare Committees. But it was not until 1962 that local authorities were empowered to provide direct meals services, partly because the voluntary agencies were anxious to maintain their supremacy and partly because the County Councils Association opposed a service which was to be paid for out of the general rate. The final decisive influence was probably the evidence produced in Harris's survey of *Meals on Wheels for Old People* (1961), which highlighted the patchiness of existing meals provision over the country as a whole and which revealed that two-fifths of the recipients received only one meal a week.

Means, in his description of the development of the meals services (1981), shows that the multiple and somewhat ambiguous aims which adhere to the meals on wheels service to this day are longstanding. One member of Parliament in discussing the 1962 amendment to the 1948 Act claimed that 'it brings to the homes of old people not only a meal, which they may be unable to cook for themselves, but also *friendliness*', and someone else felt that 'we shall be bringing them into *contact with life* and showing them that they are not neglected', and thirdly it was maintained that regular contact with the isolated elderly through a meals service would enable a *check* to be kept on their health and social needs (our emphasis). Edith Pitt, the Parliamentary Secretary to the Ministry of Health, also pointed out that whoever called with a meal would be able to put the recipient in touch with other branches of the social services if there was need (Hansard 1962). These comments clearly put as much emphasis on the social dimension of the meals service as on the purely nutritional aspects.

Since the amendment to the 1948 Act in 1962 there has been substantial expansion of meals provision and tighter control over the voluntary agencies, until towards the end of the 1970s more than half of all local authorities provided meals services directly, although the voluntary agencies still played a very important part, particularly in the rural areas.

Increased commitment to care in the community on the part of the state was also reflected in the Health Services and Public Health Act 1968 and the Chronically Sick and Disabled Persons Act 1970, both of which considerably increased the powers of local authorities to provide domiciliary support services. Thus the former made it a duty to provide a home help service adequate for the needs of the area and the latter placed a duty on local authorities to find out the numbers of disabled people in their area, to publicise the services available, and to establish the need for such services.

Completing the framework for community care services was the Local Authority Social Services Act of 1970 which integrated the hitherto separate children's and welfare departments and transferred certain important functions such as the home help service from the local authority health departments to the new social services departments. Since 1971 the three basic domiciliary services for old people (the home help service, the meals service, and aids and adaptations) have been the responsibility of the social services departments, offering great potential scope for the interweaving of these services with the residential, counselling and advisory facilities also available in these departments. (In the case of adaptations, responsibility is shared with housing departments. DHSS Circular 78/14.) As we shall observe when examining evaluative studies of these separate functions, the road towards practical integration, which requires broad problem-oriented client assessments, skilled case management and co-ordination of services for its success, has proved a difficult one. Theoretically, integration of services at the statutory level should make collaboration with the voluntary agencies simpler and more effective. But here, too, in practice fruitful and well-planned collaboration is beset by administrative, political and philosophical obstacles, as we shall see later on in this book.

Research and policy

Two further points are well worth considering: the first is the cross-fertilisation between research, practical experience and policy guidelines which is so clearly evident in the 1960s and early 1970s. The expansion of the home help and other domiciliary services owes a great deal to the evidence produced in Townsend and Wedderburn's classic survey of *The Aged in the Welfare State* (1965) and to the results emanating from the Government Social Survey report on *The Home Help Services in England and Wales* (Hunt 1970). Many of the provisions contained in the Chronically Sick and Disabled Persons Act 1970 were derived from Harris's study of the *Handicapped and Impaired in Great Britain* (published in 1971), which showed that only a very small proportion of even severely handicapped people had come to the attention of the local authority welfare services. As for policy guidelines, DHSS Circular 53/71 contains many suggestions about the organisation and practice of home help and related domiciliary services which are still regarded as 'innovative' in some quarters: for example the Circular stresses that home help is a service to a household, rather than to an individual; it points to the need to assist relatives caring single-handed for elderly relatives and to the many ways in which home help services could be diversified; it urges the need for imaginative consideration of alternatives, such as improving the environment, good neighbour schemes, and the many complementary jobs that could be carried out by volunteers, while reminding authorities about payment of out-of-pocket expenses and the possibility of 'small honoraria' for voluntary help. Similarly, the often quoted Circular on the meals services (5/70) is full of suggestions based on examination of practices in various areas. These are still of great relevance, stressing as they do the need to be alert to desirable alternatives and providing perceptive observations on the organisation, nutritional aspects and cost control of the meals services. A later Circular (52/73) passed on promptly the results of a survey of meals services produced in a number of kitchens in different parts of the country and made fairly detailed recommendations based on these findings.

In contrast, the most recent survey on *The Elderly at Home* carried out on behalf of the DHSS by Hunt (1978), though revealing certain gaps in services particularly in relation to the very frail and very elderly and resulting in a DHSS-sponsored seminar, has not yielded similar forward-looking policy guidelines. Instead we have been presented with a very general document, *Growing Older* (DHSS 1981a). Apart from restating in less concrete forms than previous documents the aim of community care as enabling old people to lead an independent life in their own homes for as long as possible, the report shows a change in philosophy. Instead of the state assuming fairly and squarely the main responsibility for the equitable distribution of services and resources – in collaboration always with the voluntary sector – there is a shift towards wanting to make the community itself responsible for the support and care of elderly citizens. *Growing Older* says:

> Whatever level of public expenditure proves practicable, and however it is distributed, the primary sources of support and care for elderly people are informal and voluntary. These spring from the personal ties of kinship, friendship and neighbourhood. They are irreplaceable. It is the role of public authorities to sustain and, where necessary, develop – but never to displace – such support and care. Care *in* the community must increasingly mean care *by* the community.

This is more in the nature of a declaration of faith than of realistic guidelines for practice. For we know that there will be a sharp increase of very old people in the next decades and far fewer daughters and practically no single daughters to care for them, and that the majority of these women will be either at work or well into retirement age themselves (Moroney 1976, Eversley 1982). Thus, as Parker has pointed out (1981),

> not only will the demand for tending increase, therefore, but the traditional source of supply will be reduced for demographic reasons. Add to this the reduced likelihood that kin will be living locally and the possibility of more regular tending being provided by female relatives must be put in question.

The realisation that the expectation of a welfare state providing comprehensive care from the cradle to the grave is Utopian has also led to more positive developments: the rhetoric about inter-weaving informal, voluntary and statutory care is in some areas being replaced by vigorous experiments. Possibilities of new forms of 'contracting out' by statutory authorities to voluntary and private agencies are being explored, as an alternative to direct provision by the authorities themselves. Such developments may be accompanied by changes in the roles of statutory personnel into those of case managers and co-ordinators and resource persons to a variety of services, as is discussed in later chapters.

Expansion of services

Although there has been a considerable expansion of domiciliary ser-vices for old people and particularly the very old, this has not kept up with growing needs and has not resulted in as equitable a distribution of resources as one would have hoped for. However, important strides have been made. Thus Bebbington (1979), comparing Townsend and Wedderburn's survey *The Aged in the Welfare State* carried out in 1962 with Hunt's national survey, found that by 1976 about twice as many elderly people received home help, meals on wheels and domestic nursing as in the 1960s. The extra services had gone to the very elderly: 30 per cent of those over 80 received a home help in 1976 compared with 22 per cent in 1962. Bebbington also estimated that in 1976 only 1.3 per cent of the elderly in the severe incapacity grade (some 80,000 individu-als in the United Kingdom) had no help with essential household tasks compared with nearly five per cent in 1962. Further, while in 1962 very few of the elderly were receiving more than one domiciliary service, by 1976 one in three of the elderly in receipt of services had more than one. However, Bebbington also warned that the real gains might not be quite as dramatic as suggested, mainly because of increasing needs, both physical and social, among the over-eighties: 58 per cent of this age group were judged to be moderately or severely incapacitated in Hunt's survey compared with about 46 per cent in the earlier study. Among them are found increasing numbers of seriously demented old people who need a great deal of sensitive supervision. Over two-fifths were living alone by the mid-1970s compared with only a quarter in the early 1960s and fewer saw their relatives frequently. There is also evidence that the services, though reaching more people, are more thinly spread. In the recent survey, just over two-fifths of the elderly had home helps more than once a week, compared with nearly two-thirds in the early 1960s.

More recent statistics (DHSS 1981b) show that the expansion of services continued during the late 1970s, although at a slower rate. The number of those aged 65 and over receiving home help rose from 570,000 in 1975/76 to 645,000 in 1978/79, representing an increase per 1,000 population aged 65 and over from 85.5 to 94.9, or nearly one in ten of those in the age group. The number of meals served in the homes of recipients increased from 24.3 million in 1975/76 to 27.0 million in 1979/80, representing a growth rate from 371 meals per 100 persons aged 65 and over to 391. The cuts in public expenditure brought expansion to a halt before many of the authorities had approached the guidelines for domiciliary services laid down in 1976 in the DHSS document *Priorities for Health and Personal Social Services*. This retrenchment makes it more than ever necessary that available resources should be distributed as rationally and equitably as possible.

Variations in services and differences in 'needs'
Bebbington and Davies (1980b) have examined variations in expenditure on social service provision for the elderly across the country. They estimate that 'current expenditure on the elderly in 1977/8 was less than £25 for each person aged over 65 in Devon and the Isle of Wight, while in the London Boroughs of Camden and Islington it was about £137'. As they suggest, persisting variations of this magnitude must be considered in terms of 'historical factors, local political ideologies and policies, relative costs, and availability of alternative services' but 'of paramount importance' is the question of whether differences in provision reflect differences in needs. Moreover, the researchers point out that this range of variation has scarcely decreased since it was first described and examined a decade earlier.

Although costs are higher in certain parts of the country, and particularly in Greater London, the statistics show that variations are primarily of *volume* of services. Thus the number of home helps (whole time equivalents) provided per 1,000 population aged 65 and over in England in 1977/78 ranged from 3.2 (in Dorset and Kingston upon Thames) to 16 in Hackney. The variations also indicated differential coverage: for every 1,000 people aged 65 and over in England on average 91 received home help, but this ranged from 38 in Sutton to 194 in Doncaster. Furthermore, where the service is least well provided it is typically also spread most thinly, ranging from an average of 20 cases per home help per annum in poorly provided areas to about 12 cases per home help in well provided areas (Bebbington & Davies 1980b).

Even greater variations are found in the meals on wheels services, where the number of meals served at home per 1,000 people over the age of 65 varied in 1978/79 from around 1,000 in Sheffield to well over 14,000 in Tower Hamlets (DHSS 1980a). Again we observe the phenomenon of greater intensity of service in the well provided areas: not only does Inner London serve the largest percentage of elderly people with meals on wheels, but while the regional averages of meals per week per person ranged from 1.8 to 3.0 in 1978, the average for Inner London was 5.3 per person. (DHSS 1980b). Or to take aids and adaptations: among the metropolitan districts in 1977/78 Wakefield topped the list for aids with 20,475 (net expenditure £197,403) whereas Calderdale, also in West Yorkshire, supplied only 375 aids (net expenditure £26,893) (CIPFA 1979). These figures must, however, be seen in the context of other local sources of supply, as the NHS and voluntary organisations such as the Red Cross are more important sources in some areas than in others. Great variations obtain in the provision of day care places also, as we shall see in the chapter on day care.

To what extent are these variations related to the need for services among the elderly population of an area? This is a fundamental question that we have to consider in any discussion of effectiveness of services. Bebbington and Davies (1980 a and b) have made an attempt to relate variation in volume of services and expenditure to needs for services of individual elderly people as well as to political and social conditions in different areas of the country. They note that since services for the elderly were established so recently and developed so quickly it is not surprising that their distribution is now uneven; they also point out that these services have undergone massive reorganisations and have often been administered by people who were comparatively inexperienced in administering services for the elderly.

The authors argue that in previous studies 'need' has been inadequately conceptualised and measured. They postulate that an essential criterion of a good 'need indicator' is that it should be clearly linked to judgements about the use of resources. In order to arrive at their needs indicator, the researchers defined a number of 'target groups' among the elderly: those in moderate need, in considerable need, and in severe need. Using a variety of sources, they then estimated the numbers in the different target groups among the elderly in each social services authority, and they estimated expenditure requirements for packages of social services, taking into account labour and other cost variations. (Details of the methods and sources used for the calculations are outlined in Bebbington and Davies 1980a.)

These calculations enabled the authors to compare apparent need, as represented by the need indicator for each area, with actual recurrent spending by social services departments on services for the elderly. They concluded that 'the current pattern of provision shows considerable responsiveness to the pattern of need, but is still a long way from our conception of territorial justice'. The authors are aware that other factors apart from the needs elements influence the volume of provision. These are the general level of social conditions and the cost of providing services; that is to say those authorities which face above average manpower and other costs spend disproportionately more on the elderly. This phenomenon may in part be related to the way the rate support grant has been calculated in the past, which linked level of spending in one year with allocation in the next. Certain political factors also influence the levels of spending. Spending is relatively high in areas of high Labour Party representation on local councils and is low in areas where the domestic ratepayer is responsible for a relatively large proportion of any change in the rates bills.

Thus Bebbington and Davies's work suggests that while the growth of social care services for old people has been uneven and there are large variations in both coverage and intensity, these variations bear some relationship to differential needs for services, to political values and to relative cost. But we are still a long way off achieving 'territorial justice'.

Having looked at the broad recent developments and distribution of social care in the community, we will now turn to more detailed examination of particular types of social care and attempts at evaluating their effectiveness.

References

Bebbington, A.C. (1979) Changes in the provision of social services to the elderly in the community over fourteen years, *Social Policy and Administration 13*, 111–123.

Bebbington, A.C. and Davies, B. (1980a) Territorial needs indicators: a new approach, Part II, *Journal of Social Policy 9*, 433–462.

Bebbington, A.C. and Davies, B. (1980b) *Patterns of Social Service Provision for the Elderly: Variations between local authorities of England in 1975/6, 1977/78, and as forecast in 1979/80*, Discussion Paper 162/2, University of Kent Personal Social Services Unit.

CIPFA (Chartered Institute of Public Finance and Accountancy) (1979) *Personal Social Services Statistics: 1977–78 Actuals*, London, Chartered Institute of Public Finance and Accountancy.

Department of Health and Social Security (1970) *Organisation of Meals on Wheels*, Circular 5/70.

Department of Health and Social Security (1971) *Help in the Home: Section 13 of the Health Services and Public Health Act 1968*, Circular 53/71.

Department of Health and Social Security (1973) *Meals on Wheels*, Circular 52/73.

Department of Health and Social Security (1978) *Adaptations of Housing for People who are Physically Handicapped*, Circular (78)14.

Department of Health and Social Security (1976) *Priorities for Health and Personal Social Services in England: A consultative document*, London, HMSO.

Department of Health and Social Security (1980a) *Meals Services 1978–79: England*, Personal Social Services: Local Authority Statistics, Table B.

Department of Health and Social Security (1980b) *Meals Services during 7 Days: England 1978*. Personal Social Services: Local Authority Statistics, Table B.

Department of Health and Social Security (1981a) *Growing Older*, London, HMSO.

Department of Health and Social Security (1981b) *Report of a Study on Community Care*.

Eversley, D.E.C. (1982) Some new aspects of ageing in Britain. In T.K. Hareven (ed.) *Ageing and the Life Cycle Course in a Cross-cultural and Interdisciplinary Perspective*, New York, Guilford Press.

Hansard, Parliamentary Debates, House of Commons, 1947–48, vol. 444, columns 1063–1718. London, HMSO.

Hansard, Parliamentary Debates, House of Commons, 1962, vol. 657, column 845, London, HMSO.

Harris, A. (1961) *Meals on Wheels for Old People*. London, National Corporation for the Care of Old People.

Harris, A. (1971) *Handicapped and Impaired in Great Britain*, OPCS: Social Survey Division. London, HMSO.

Hunt, A. (1978) *The Elderly at Home*, London, HMSO.

Hunt, A. assisted by Fox, J. (1970) *The Home Help Service in England and Wales*, London, HMSO.

Means, R. (1981)*Community Care and Meals on Wheels: A study in the politics of service development at the national and local level*, Working Paper 21, University of Bristol School for Advanced Urban Studies.

Ministry of Health (1961)*Report of the Ministry of Health for the year ended 31st December 1960, Part 1: The Health and Welfare Services*, Cmnd 1418, London, HMSO.

Ministry of Health (1962) *Development of Local Authority Health and Welfare Services: Co-operation with voluntary organisations*, Circular 7/62.

Ministry of Health (1963) *Health and Welfare: The development of community care*. Cmnd 1973, London, HMSO.

Moroney, R.M. (1976)*The Family and the State: Considerations for social policy*, London, Longman.

Parker, R. (1981) Tending and social policy, in E.M. Goldberg and S. Hatch (eds.) *A New Look at the Personal Social Services*. Discussion Paper No. 4, London, Policy Studies Institute.

Townsend, P. and Wedderburn, D. (1965) *The Aged in the Welfare State*, London, G. Bell and Sons.

Walker, A. (1981) When there's someone to help you, there's no place like home, *Social Work Today*, 20 January.

5 Domiciliary Care

As we saw in the previous chapter, the aim of government policy for elderly people has been and still is to keep them 'active and independent in their own home' (DHSS 1978) – an aim which is generally held to express the desires of most elderly people themselves. The role of the domiciliary services is obviously critical in working towards this aim, but, like all very generalised aims, its implications must be spelled out in some detail in order to be of practical use in exploring the effectiveness of particular domiciliary social services. In their 1981 document *Growing Older* the DHSS make two important further points: that the community services should not be regarded as a panacea for all problems and that successful community care rests on collaboration between services – statutory and voluntary, formal and informal.

Social care for the elderly in their own homes takes a variety of forms. The most essential are the home help service, providing basic cleaning but in many cases also help with shopping, cooking, laundry and personal care, developing increasingly into a more comprehensive home care service; and meals on wheels – the provision of a ready-cooked or ready-to-cook meal in the elderly person's home. Many other forms of care can provide further support. Some of these have developed as supplements to the home help service. There are, for example, various forms of 'good neighbour' schemes, carrying out brief but regular tasks such as getting an elderly person up in the morning, lighting coal fires, popping in to make the odd cup of tea, or just making sure that a very frail housebound person is all right. At the other extreme are intensive care schemes (frequently following hospitalisation) involving much more flexible and concentrated help than the two to four hours per week of a home help's time generally available. Some areas also provide day sitters and night sitters, heavy cleaning and gardening squads, surveillance and visiting schemes including street wardens and peripatetic wardens, alarm systems, laundry services for the incontinent, and others.

Community health care services are often closely interwoven into a package of domiciliary support for an individual elderly person: health visiting, district nursing and chiropody being the main provisions. The 'aids to daily living' and 'aids to home nursing' provided by social services departments, health authorities and voluntary organisations also function as part of the support service, as do adaptations to dwellings, responsibility for which is shared by social services and housing departments.

In this chapter we concentrate in the main on the home help service and its offshoots, on meals on wheels, and on aids and adaptations. Studies concerned with developments in intensive community care for the very frail elderly under the direction of social workers, and studies of voluntary neighbourhood schemes, both of which make a substantial contribution to domiciliary care, are considered in the chapters on social work and voluntary support respectively.

The studies
Altogether we have reviewed some 60 to 70 recent studies on the domiciliary services, most of them carried out by local authority researchers in response to policy questions (Goldberg and Connelly 1978, Connelly and Goldberg 1979). They are largely descriptive in character, one-off surveys rather than action research or experiments. Nevertheless, they address evaluative questions such as the distribution of services in relation to 'need', how to discover unmet need and plan for a more equitable distribution of resources, how satisfied users are with the help they receive and how they are affected by different charging policies, what care-givers think of the services and what satisfaction they gain from their work, and how the organisation of the service is related to effective functioning. Two major studies, one on the home help service carried out by Coventry Social Services Department (Latto 1982) and the other on meals services by Johnson and his colleagues (1981) at Leeds University, have some quasi-experimental features built into them. The Coventry study, discussed from a methodological point of view in Chapter 3, sought to compare the effects (including cost effectiveness) of an enriched home help service in one area of the city with the ordinary home help services in the rest of the city, and the Leeds study attempted to assess the acceptability, nutritive value and cost of three different food options: frozen meals, long life food and raw food packs.

In the following discussion of attempts at evaluating the effectiveness of domiciliary services for elderly people we shall adhere to the framework sketched out in Chapter 2. First we will consider the aims of the services, next try to clarify what needs they are designed to meet, and how these are assessed, then examine how the services operate in relation to resource and skill inputs and with regard to their organisational frameworks, and finally consider what emerges about outcomes.

Aims
Many investigators discovered considerable lack of clarity about objectives, even in such practical services as home help and meals on wheels.

Although the home help service was originally instituted as a domestic help service, the multiple needs of the very frail elderly who form an increasing proportion of the home help clientele are raising new questions about aims and functions. Is the primary aim to provide a general domestic cleaning service for those who can no longer carry out these chores, or should it develop into an intensive personal care service taking on a multitude of tasks (often performed by caring relatives) for very frail and dependent elderly people, especially those who live alone? Should the teaching of coping skills be among its aims? Does the meals service aim mainly at the provision of a hot, nourishing meal or is the aim of providing social contact and surveillance of equal importance?

It is instructive that a study carried out by the Bradford Social Services Department into the ways in which the home help service was being used concluded by spelling out recommended aims and priorities (Hurley and Wolstenholme 1979). This was thought to be essential because, as in other studies, the researchers found that clients living in different parts of the district experiencing apparently similar needs and circumstances received very different allocation of hours. Furthermore, in the more generously provided areas many clients had help with tasks they could do for themselves. Since the aims and priorities articulated in the Bradford study reflect the shift in thinking about objectives of the home help service, it is worth quoting them in some detail.

The broad general aim was to assist old people to live in the community as long as possible, thereby delaying the need for entry into old people's homes and geriatric hospitals. Three priority aims were recommended:

(i) that personal care should take priority over cleaning, although certain guidelines were established about cleaning tasks;
(ii) that consistency of practice should be established across the whole catchment area;
(iii) that generally persons under 75 years of age should only be provided with a service where there was also a handicapping condition which reduced their ability to carry out personal care or essential household tasks.

The researchers together with professionals in the department also formulated more specific aims to promote the client's well-being; these included ensuring personal cleanliness, contacts with other people, sufficient nourishment, warmth and appropriate surveillance. Co-ordination with other services was also considered an important aim, as was the encouragement of self-help. For example, clients should be encouraged to undertake simpler and lighter household tasks, leaving the home help service to perform those tasks which the clients were unable to manage. The needs of relatives, friends and neighbours were also given due recognition in the proposed guidelines. These aims and guidelines go far beyond a basic cleaning service and indicate a deliberate thrust towards a comprehensive home care service for very elderly and frail people and towards an equitable distribution of resources over the whole catchment area of the social services department.

Johnson and his colleagues in a different context (Johnson *et al* 1981) urge greater clarity about aims in the meals services, especially the balance between nutrition and social support. They argue that where the purpose is clearly nutritional it will be important to ensure an intensive level of provision for an adequate period. On the other hand, where the service is part of a general social support strategy or used for surveillance purposes then the contact and any necessary follow-up action will have to be purposeful. Within these general strategic aims they would like to see more specificity of aims and criteria for different forms of meals provision which can range from a ready cooked meal for a very disabled frail or depressed person to the provision of prepared raw food ingredients to be cooked by a more active recipient. They also suggest that there needs to be a clearer perception about the role meals might play in the overall constellation of help provided for particular individuals.

However much aims and priorities are clarified and criteria established for a specific service, these will still have to be translated into individual prescriptions tailored to the needs of an individual client or household. Not only that, but objectives will also have to be communicated to, and as far as possible agreed with, the client. As already mentioned, service providers and recipients may have different goals in mind, or the priority they attach to one of a number of goals may differ. In the case of meals delivery, for example, the elderly person may be thinking only of the receipt of a meal, whereas the service providers may also aim at relief of loneliness and an opportunity to check regularly whether the recipient is well. This kind of discrepancy will not necessarily affect the effectiveness of a service, from either the caregiver's or the user's viewpoint, but in some cases it may do so: the emphasis on social support as an undisclosed priority may leave a recipient of home help anxious about basic cleaning jobs undone. This highlights a problem emerging constantly in the course of evaluative research in social care: the care-givers' failure to share explicitly with potential clients the aims and content of the social care proposed and, wherever possible, to obtain agreement to these plans.

An important question is whether aims are reassessed from time to time in accordance with recipients' current needs and capacities. There is substantial evidence in the studies that domiciliary services, once allocated, have a way of continuing indefinitely although the original crisis occasioning the service may long have passed and other types of social support may be more appropriate. For example, the crisis of bereavement and its attendant depression and apathy may subside and a luncheon club rather than a delivered meal may be more conducive to stimulating renewed social contact and activity. An aid may have long outlived its usefulness. Some social services departments have therefore adopted initial allocation of service for a specific number of weeks, and encouraged more regular reassessment of long-term clients.

Need for domiciliary care

The evidence both nationally and locally suggests that domiciliary care by and large goes to those most in need of it – that is to say to the frailest and most disabled and to the very elderly. Hunt (1978) showed that the great majority of bedfast and housebound old people, whether living alone or with others, had received visits from the social services within the last six months; only seven per cent of these respondents said that they had received no such visits. Four-fifths of those aged 85 and over said they had received visits from the social services, and these figures are possibly underestimates as no check was carried out to verify – even on a small sample – their validity. Bebbington (1979) showed, as discussed in the last chapter, that the extra services created during the 1960s and 1970s went mainly to those over 80 and to those in the severe incapacity grade.

However, when we come down to individual cases the studies raise considerable problems in defining and assessing the nature and intensity of needs. How to develop effective ways of assessing an elderly person's needs in the round, rather than more narrowly for a specific service, has proved particularly challenging. It has been found difficult to move on from the question 'how many hours of home help does this person need?' to a consideration of what range of possibilities are likely to be of use in helping this particular person in her social situation, taking into account not only statutory services but also the possible help which could be given by voluntary agencies or by informal networks already in contact with the applicant. Keeble (1979) has noted that 'a request for a bath aid is commonly believed to be the most frequent way in which disabled clients make their first approach to the Personal Social Services': are they then assessed for a bath aid, or is their situation looked at more generally? Vickery (1981) has referred to the change in attitude that is required as one in which the service provider sees himself less as a 'guardian of scarce resources' and more as a 'discoverer and creator of resources'.

Such broader and more imaginative assessments of need are being attempted in some social services departments and in a variety of research and demonstration projects, but most studies in domiciliary care have been more concerned with assessing need with a specific service in mind. Some of these studies have sought to judge levels of need for forward planning purposes (for example, Thompson 1974). Others have attempted to judge the variations in levels of need in different areas of a local authority in order to arrive at an equitable allocation of home help capacity (for example, Howell *et al* 1979), or to discover where need for newly-available home help hours is greatest (Plociennick and Harrison 1977), or to rationalise meals delivery arrangements. Still others have been carried out because of concern about methods of assessment and reassessment – or, rather, lack of systematic assessment and lack of any reassessment at all.

Researchers have used a wide variety of indicators of need for domiciliary services, including age, sex, marital status, living circumstances, ability to perform certain personal care and household tasks, mental state, help received from relatives and friends, and support from other agencies. Such information has been obtained by interviewing users directly, or more often from existing records or from those organising or providing the service. The investigators have then studied the relationship between their chosen indicators of need and the service offered; in general, they found little relationship between need as indicated by the clients' personal capacity and circumstances of living and service received (Gwynne and Fean 1978, Howell *et al* 1979, Hurley and Wolstenholme 1979).

Although suspected discrepancies between levels of service in various districts of a local authority were normally the reason for the research being undertaken, results were often startling: clients in one area might receive over twice as many hours of home help as clients in an adjacent area, even though their social characteristics, disabilities and living arrangements seemed quite comparable (Gwynne and Fean 1978). In two of the studies the only highly significant correlation that could be found was between the number of hours allocated and the number of tasks to be performed by the home help (Gwynne and Fean 1978; May and Whitbread 1977). But it did not prove possible to complete the chain by linking the number of tasks to be performed to the client's circumstances, nor was it possible to find the link between the hours allocated and circumstances of living. Several authors suggest that these connections do exist but that the complex nature of needs and of the assessment process makes them difficult to pinpoint. May and Whitbread note that 'it is perfectly possible for two households to appear identical with the crude measuring instruments used and yet to have radically different needs, with the result that their allocation will appear to be inconsistent'. Another study points to the more intangible factors that home help organisers take into account: for instance the client's customary standards of cleanliness, the state and quality of furniture, and the need not to undermine motivation for self-help (Avon SSD 1976).

More general factors may also play a part in the discrepancies found in resource allocation, for example in localities where the local government reorganisation of 1974 has brought together an urban area with high levels of service provision and adjacent rural areas with different philosophies and levels of service. Another contributory factor could be the existence of deliberate but different rationing devices, so that in one area the home help organiser might prefer to give all those above a minimum level of disability a standard two hours of service a week, whereas in another district the preferred policy might be to provide home help on a more flexible and intensive basis to a smaller number of cases.

Whatever the reasons, the mismatch between apparent need and actual service delivery seemed clear to those researchers who interviewed users directly. They were surprised at the numbers in each area who seemed to be in little current need of the service received. For example, in a study in Wales almost a third of a random sample of home help clients interviewed were capable of leaving their homes unaided (Gwynedd SSD 1977). As already indicated, the Bradford study (Hurley and Wolstenholme 1979) and an earlier study by Marks (1975) showed that home helps frequently carried out tasks such as dusting which the clients were capable of doing themselves. In the field of aids one follow-up study (Thornely *et al* 1977) found that only about two-thirds of the bath aids supplied were in use.

Similar situations are described in meals studies. For example, in a Kent study 40 per cent of recipients were found to be cooking for themselves on days when meals were not delivered (Brotherton 1975). Johnson and his colleagues, in their study of 150 meals recipients in Leeds (1981), concluded that difficulties experienced in shopping rather than extreme infirmity and immobility within the home constituted the greatest need, and that very few of those who were receiving meals on wheels were either in need of a nutritional supplement or were properly identified as being at nutritional risk. These conclusions are supported by a number of earlier studies in various parts of the country which show that while the majority of meals recipients (varying between 50 per cent and 75 per cent) were said to be housebound, a considerable proportion seemed reasonably mobile within their homes and able to do some simple cooking. However, several researchers expressed concern about how to assess the nutritional adequacy of food intake and how to judge the psychological element of lack of motivation to cook or eat which can be part of a depressive syndrome. Johnson and other investigators also throw considerable doubt on the often quoted need for social support and contact, since the majority of meals recipients – most of whom live alone – have a good deal of other formal and informal help flowing into their households. Thus over four-fifths of his sample received a home help visit once a week (similar figures are quoted in other studies) and 94 per cent of Johnson's sample had other forms of help.

These discrepancies between apparent needs and provision may be due in part to too great reliance on referral agents, or inadequate initial assessment, but lack of *reassessment* may be of greater significance. The home help studies revealed an appreciable number of recipients who had not been visited by an organiser or reassessed for years, and reassessment seldom occurs in the meals service. The meals studies often made plain a disinclination to take any steps which might lead to withdrawing the service once it had been allocated; this was particularly marked when a voluntary organisation was involved. In the case of aids, researchers were especially concerned to find cases where, in the absence of follow-up visits of any kind, an aid continued to be used after the condition for which it had been allocated had improved, and the continuing use of the aid was thought to have added to the handicap, perhaps hastening the seizing up of muscles from disuse. Some authorities rely on home helps and those delivering meals for up-to-date information about the recipient's condition and changing needs, but, as will be seen later, feedback mechanisms are often poorly developed.

Home help organisers often argue that no systematic assessment/review schedule can be as sensitive or accurate as the exercise of their 'intuition'. By this they seem to mean their understanding of the complex total situation of the potential client, based on experience and knowledge of elderly people and their circumstances. However, those concerned with more rational and equitable distribution of scarce resources point to the advantages of more systematic assessment procedures: as an *aide-mémoire* to experienced home help organisers; to newly-fledged home help organisers; to referral agents; to social services departments for planning, resource allocation and record keeping purposes; and to the community at large in the sense that clear procedures unrelated to the idiosyncracies (or priorities) of particular service allocators or recipients are seen to be fairer when resources must be rationed on some basis other than first come, first served.

Some researchers have tried to increase the number, type and sensitivity of the indicators of need to be used in schedules or checklists, for example by taking greater account of the client's psychological state, or of current and potential help from neighbours and relatives; others have made use of well-tried incapacity scales. In a London authority, as part of a planning exercise, a flow chart was devised, with yes/no questions asked about the client's social circumstances, mobility and disability, and the help already available; the answers determined the number of hours to be allocated in such cases (Thompson 1974).

Researchers at Exeter University, in studies carried out with the Devon and Cornwall social services departments, developed three models of allocating hours to areas, taking into account current or 'ideal' levels of provision in relation to disability, payment by clients, other support provided, mental state, and housing condition (Howell *et al* 1979). These models were developed as resource allocation techniques for areas, but the authors suggested that the five criteria (found through surveys to be most relevant) could also be used as a checklist for organisers in assessment of individual clients.

Investigators of meals services have in general shown less interest in the question of systematic assessment, although DHSS Circular 5/70 offers clear and workable criteria on the circumstances in which meals on wheels delivery may be applicable. The Circular suggests that people needing such help will most often be found among (i) those living alone (or alone during the day), who are sick or mentally confused or so physically infirm that they have difficulty in preparing or cooking a main meal; (ii) those in temporary difficulty (for example, the convalescent or bereaved); and (iii) those who have inadequate cooking facilities or have not the will to make proper use of their facilities but cannot get meals from other sources (for example, clubs). In addition this Circular stresses the need for regular review which would also give opportunities for regular assessment of other welfare needs.

Despite such explicit guidance, Means (1981) in his case studies of meals on wheels deliveries in a London borough, a mixed rural/urban authority and a rural authority, shows the enormous differences in practice, organisation and philosophy among the three authorities, ranging from a virtual 'open-door' policy where any referral from a professional will be accepted, to systematic assessment and reassessment procedures based on the guidelines outlined in the Circular just quoted. The move towards assessment for meals by home help organisers, even where the service continues to be provided by voluntary agencies, may indicate that common assessment for domiciliary services generally is increasing.

If a common assessment form were devised, and were related not merely to a specific resource but to a range of self-care, rehabilitative and caring options, who would be the most appropriate person to carry out such an assessment – the home help organiser, the social worker, or social work assistant? We will be returning to this question in Chapter 6. A particular problem might arise in relation to aids and adaptations, where, ideally, skills ranging from medical knowledge to practical engineering experience seem to be involved. Realistically, these are unlikely to be available. Researchers have concluded that the most appropriate person to assess is an occupational therapist, and that the role of the social worker should be confined to helping the user to come to terms with the disability and the dependence on an aid (Barrow and Derbyshire 1975, Melotte 1976, Keeble 1979).

Input

We now explore the ways in which the services set about meeting individual needs of clients as well as the overall aims of the services. Inputs include the quantity and quality of direct service provision, which are influenced by organisational features such as links between the domiciliary services and other activities within the social services departments, as well as relationships with other local authority departments, the health service, and voluntary organisations. For example, the provision of aids often demonstrates the overlap and confusion arising between the health and social services as to 'who should be providing what and which service should be paying for it' (Keeble 1979). The meals service illustrates the difficulties of combining statutory and voluntary elements in the complex process of purchasing, cooking and delivering hot meals to people's homes at specified times. Input is also made more or less effective by channels of communication that exist between the direct service deliverers and decision-making personnel within the service.

After raising some general questions about the appropriateness of routinely delivered services in relation to people's specific needs, input is discussed separately for the three services. We then take up organisational issues, including the vexed question of service charges.

Appropriateness of help

The simplest way of describing the inputs of domiciliary social care is in quantitative terms: number of hours of home help received per week, number of meals provided per week, type and number of aids delivered. These provide important indicators of 'coverage' and 'intensity'. But are they the 'right' number of hours or meals or the most appropriate aid? Are the home help visits and the meals provided on the most suitable days, meshing in with each other and with other services received, such as day care? What exactly does a home help do in the hours she spends in the client's home; what companionship and support does she offer? Are the tasks she performs the most appropriate from the recipient's point of view? Beyond this are questions of quality of performance: does the home help complete household tasks to an adequate standard, does she perform personal care tasks with sensitivity and skill?

Questions about alternatives also arise: are tasks such as fetching pensions, doing shopping or even escorting people to hospital appointments best done by a home help, or could they be done by a neighbour, a volunteer or on a semi-voluntary basis? Could some household tasks be accomplished by the elderly person, following furniture rearrangement, use of aids for cleaning and cooking, or teaching of methods of coping with new or increasing disabilities?

Similar questions arise in the meals services. Is the current provision of a ready-cooked meal the most appropriate, or could the elderly person be encouraged to go out to a lunch club, with arrangements for transport if necessary? Could a home help give more flexible assistance in preparation or cooking? Would meals prepared by paid 'good neighbours' be preferable in some situations? Would frozen meals to be heated by the recipient, or fresh food prepared for cooking, be nutritionally and psychologically more helpful for those capable of doing some cooking? (Very few of meals recipients – about five per cent – are bedfast or chairbound.) Would encouragement and instruction stimulate the desire to cook and eat when, for example in the case of recent bereavement, this is lacking, or improve cooking skills among widowers and the partially sighted? Similar considerations apply to the provision of aids which need to be closely integrated with the whole self care and support programme of a domiciliary care plan.

Such individual approaches take time and resources – at any rate initially – and may require not only different skills and greater knowledge of ageing processes and availability of resources on the part of service providers, but different, less stoic and protective attitudes towards elderly people.

What home helps do

The tasks which home helps do cover a very wide range indeed, and often include personal care and basic nursing as well as cleaning (which the studies show takes the largest share of time), laundry work, shopping and food preparation. Regularly the investigators note that certain jobs such as spring-cleaning, washing paintwork, outside window cleaning, interior decorating, gardening and small house repairs are not among the tasks home helps are expected to undertake and therefore such jobs generally do not get done – a matter of considerable concern to many home helps and clients. Apart from references to more voluntary effort and the occasional heavy work squad organised by the home help service, solutions are rarely contemplated. Innovative efforts such as the 'Link Scheme' promoted by Age Concern in which old (and younger) people exchange mutual skills rather than money has not been as successful as was hoped, as most needs of old people were similar – gardening, repairs, heavy cleaning – and exchange did not seem possible. The increasing momentum towards a 'home care' service, which considers household cleaning a low priority, gives some cause for concern. It is exactly because the very old cannot perform certain essential household and personal tasks that they need a home help.

Home helps themselves seem to see their jobs as 'more than simply housecleaning', but with the caring elements as a natural and integral part of the (indispensible) practical duties.

Home help organisers often indicate how home helps should divide their time as between certain tasks, such as cleaning, laundry work, cooking, shopping, personal care and so on. The question arises: do home helps follow these prescriptions, or do they have their own ways of arriving at a working arrangement with their clients? One study which explored these questions found that three-quarters of the clients did not receive the help which the organisers thought they needed (Gwynne and Fean 1978). Usually these differences arose because home helps did not undertake tasks assigned by organisers, but the reverse also occurred: home helps did jobs which the organiser did not assess as necessary. A variety of reasons may account for these discrepancies: the original assessment may not have identified the clients' actual needs or home helps may not have been adequately briefed initially; needs change over time and home helps may have responded to new situations of which the organisers were unaware; communication between home help organisers and home helps, and supervision on the job, may have been inadequate, especially given the possibility of underlying differences between organisers' and home helps' perceptions of the balance between cleaning and caring and of what ought to be done in any particular situation.

There are some advantages in an unstructured system, which allows for a flexible response to the changing needs and situation of the elderly person, and provides more job satisfaction to the home help because of the autonomy of her role. However, inefficient use of resources seems at least as likely a result, and some authorities are devising more efficient feedback and control mechanisms, which need not be in the rigid form of checklists of assigned tasks with assigned times. One possibility is a 'contract' agreed between client, home help and home help organiser, detailing what work is to be done. In such a system regular review and reassessment would be critical.

Another intriguing finding of the studies was the amount of work done for clients by home helps in their own time (Avon SSD 1976, Merton SSD 1976, Gwynedd SSD 1977, Howell *et al* 1979). A considerable percentage of home helps, ranging from a quarter to over half, said that they occasionally or regularly in their own time did extra shopping, collected prescriptions, took washing home, stopped in to see if the client was all right at the weekend: an input not to be overlooked, either from the point of view of actual tasks accomplished, or what it reveals about the relationship built up between client and home help.

The Coventry project, as well as other demonstration projects, for example in Hammersmith, and in West Sussex (Dunnachie 1979) and Cambridgeshire (Simons and Warburton 1980) have extended the range of services provided by home helps. In Coventry, home helps were especially recruited to undertake more varied tasks than usual, to work more unsocial hours and to respond readily to emergencies. They were encouraged and trained to deal with individual problems of clients, ranging from contact with the DHSS to negotiating with hire purchase companies over debts and with other local authority departments about housing and environmental health difficulties. In any emergencies, and particularly following hospital discharge, the home help team was able to provide very intensive care, usually for short periods. Home helps at times assisted in the rehabilitation of stroke victims or of those who had fractured a limb. A number of specialist home helps were recruited: a male domiciliary help who provided personal care to a number of male clients and who also acted as a handyman; a mobile emergency home help, whose service was provided free of charge for a period of up to four weeks; and finally a hairdressing service which was available to housebound clients.

Hand in hand with this widening of the role of the home help went an extension of the role of the home care organiser. As a fully integrated member of the district social work team the organiser gradually undertook certain tasks previously performed by other members of the team. Latto (1982) has summed up these developments thus: 'while the growth of the organiser's role was mainly in the interface with the social work team, extensions in the home help role tended to be in the boundary area shared with the council nursing service'.

Satisfactions and dissatisfactions of home helps

A number of studies asked about reasons for entering the service. A desire to help, especially the elderly, and the convenience of the hours which blend well with family responsibilities, were mentioned frequently by the home helps. Other reasons included the pay and the independence of the job; some said that they had become home helps because they liked housework, or because it was the only work they knew. When home helps in a rural area were asked how they viewed their work some 85 per cent 'simply stated it was good steady employment' (Gwynedd SSD 1977).

The extension of home help roles in the Coventry project often resulted in greater work satisfaction but also in strains, which the home helps expressed in their group discussion during the project. But they also said that the satisfaction of being more involved and more important to their clients and of having more comprehensive roles outweighed the stresses.

Dissatisfactions expressed by home helps in other studies concerned lack of sufficient initial information about the circumstances of the clients they were supposed to help, working conditions (for example, travelling, inadequate cleaning equipment), and the occasional complaint about difficult clients. One study suggests that more information is required about home helps' reaction to 'difficult' clients, and that more support is needed for dealing with such clients (Hillingdon SSD 1974).

Researchers in one area (Howell *et al* 1979) were so impressed by the wealth of home helps' comments and insights that they suggested home helps be given the opportunity to contribute more actively to the social care of the elderly, with more use being made of their perceptions and assessments of clients' needs. But at present few feedback channels seem to exist, for home helps rarely meet each other or have the chance to discuss their clients with home help organisers or social workers, although sometimes in-service training provides such an opportunity. In the Gwynedd study contact with social workers was, for example, described as 'almost non-existent'. In Merton, only 31 per cent of the home helps had had contact with social workers; some felt that they needed the help of social workers in dealing with difficult clients, while others thought that they had knowledge of the client which would help the social worker (Merton SSD 1976). When the researchers in Gwynedd asked home helps 'to indicate just one thing that they would like to change, improve or implement within the existing organisational framework', the answers most frequently given were 'more confidential communication with the area organiser and regular meetings within the area'.

Training

The majority of home helps questioned saw no need for any special training: 'they looked upon their jobs as similar to that of a housewife and considered that all that was required of them was to do in their clients' homes the same things they did in their own homes' (Merton SSD 1976). When pressed, most home helps referred to the need for practical nursing skills such as first aid, how to lift people, more knowledge about diet and so on. With increasing numbers of very frail old people remaining in the community, such training may well become a necessity, as may training in dealing with confused elderly persons. The surveillance role of home helps may also increase in importance, particularly if social workers give up their occasional surveillance visiting and instead act as enablers and advisers to other care-givers, including home helps. Training would then aim to increase home helps' sensitivity to problems and their awareness of available sources of help (Goldberg *et al* 1977).

Meals delivery

A major issue in considering the effectiveness of the meals service concerns the number of meals delivered weekly. This varies from two a week in most parts of the country to a much more intensive service of five or seven a week in London and some other urban areas. There is disagreement about the implications of such differences for individual elderly recipients, and general policy. Some researchers have argued that elderly people prefer to remain independent as long as possible (especially in relation to something as personal as food), and the provision of two or three meals a week may be sufficient to keep them going and can relieve what might otherwise prove to be too great a strain (Davies 1981). Others have suggested that provision at this level may create or encourage dependency; they therefore argue that the service should provide only an intensive five or seven day service for those most in need (Booth 1977, Bedfordshire SSD 1978).

But the number of meals delivered is of relevance only if the meals are actually eaten, and if their nutritive value reaches a certain minimum standard. Some studies asked about satisfaction with types of food, size of portions, and whether any food was 'wasted'. (When this word was actually used in an interview schedule, recipients insisted that no food was 'wasted' as it was, for example, given to neighbours or to the birds.) Some waste is inevitable, but Stanton (1971), in a study of meals on wheels and lunch clubs in north London, found that 'Eighty per cent wasted some part of the meal regularly and a few wasted almost the entire meal every day'; nutritive value differed markedly from kitchen to kitchen, with the highest protein, iron value and vitamin C levels twice those of the lowest. Variation was due to types of food provided, but also to portion size and cooking methods. Nutritionists in a Portsmouth study of meals on wheels found that over one-third of the meals provided less protein than recommended by the British Dietetic Association. Here the wide range found was considered to be in large part due to poor portion control (Davies 1981). Finally, the studies carried out for the DHSS by the Catering Research Unit in Leeds (Armstrong *et al* 1980) showed wide variation in nutrients which was associated with the supply sources, and appreciable deficiencies in vitamin C mainly because of losses between cooking and delivery.

Given the possible dangers in reheating food, recipients were usually asked whether meals were hot when delivered, and whether they were eaten immediately. Where inadequate heating methods were used, or delivery routes were longer than the DHSS's recommended 2–2½ hours 'pot-to-plate' time, reheating on a considerable scale seemed to be taking place (Croydon was an extreme case, with only 10 per cent eating the meal right away, and these were 'blind, chairbound, or afraid of using ovens' – Croydon SSD 1976). In any case, there is evidence to show that the nutritive value of many foods decreases over much shorter periods than 2–2½ hours when kept hot; the hotter the food is kept the better it may be from the bacteriologist's point of view but the worse from the nutritionist's. The large numbers of those who apparently regularly reheat meals has encouraged researchers to think about providing frozen meals to recipients, as well as long life food in pouches and raw ingredient packs, thus reducing the number of mid-day, and of total, deliveries necessary. Developments in Northamptonshire, for example, are described by Marston and Blunt (1981).

These ways of ensuring a higher nutritive standard of meals at the point of eating tend to involve less contact between provider and recipient. Since this social contact is usually very short and according to Johnson and his colleagues 'not widely valued by clients', its curtailment may not matter very much. But what about the monitoring functions of regular meals deliveries? All the authorities studied by Means (1981) encouraged written comments on delivery sheets, but there was considerable variation in the extent to which this monitoring element was incorporated as a central feature of service provision. Even where careful guidelines were worked out about how to observe the recipients' state of physical and emotional health and how to report on situations that cause concern, cumbersome bureaucratic channels of communication and individual differences between drivers 'militate against reliable feedback and above all against prompt response to emergencies'. Thus, as all studies indicate, the monitoring/social support feature of the meals service, so well described and intentioned in the Parliamentary debate of 1962, as noted in Chapter 4, needs urgent re-examination.

Aids and adaptations
In the case of aids and adaptations, evaluation must be very much concerned with relevance, timing and teaching; not only what aid is supplied, but whether it is the most appropriate one, whether it is supplied quickly enough to meet the current need assessed, whether any necessary instruction is carried out (and carried out adequately), whether the condition of the aid or adaptation is checked regularly for continuing safety and relevance to the user's possibly changed condition.

The complexities of input in this field are well demonstrated by a Lancashire study (Barrow and Derbyshire 1975). Researchers classified aids as 'fully useful' or 'less than fully useful'; for those in their study who were 65 years and older numbers were almost equally divided between the two categories. The 'less than fully useful' category was further divided into those aids which had been partially useful, and those which were 'completely useless'. Usefulness of aids was found to have been impaired by incorrect dimensions, instability, lack of functional relevance ('for example, if a bath rail gives leverage in one direction while the client's condition demands leverage in another direction'), inadequate preparation (aid assembled improperly, delivered too late, inadequate instruction given), plus a miscellaneous category including discomfort in use due to the materials of which the aid was made.

Organisation and co-ordination of services

The formal structure and organisation of the department providing the services is an essential input feature and hence important in any evaluation of the effectiveness of domiciliary care services. How does a home help service which is run rather separately, having formal links with the social services department only at headquarters level, compare with a structure in which organisers and home helps are integrated into area office teams? How do different degrees of collaboration with voluntary agencies influence the effectiveness of meals on wheels services? What are the most expeditious ways of collaboration between health and social services in the provision of aids? Are there any solutions to the long delays in completing adaptations to housing which are partly due to very cumbersome procedures involving a number of local authority departments?

Prior to 1971 the home help service was the responsibility of the health department, and it has been observed that managers of the new social services departments, who frequently came from the child care field, were only too happy initially to leave the home help service independent while they attempted to cope with a myriad of other problems; emphasis within the departments has in any case been strongly focused on children, with a peripheral social work role in the care of the elderly, which is mainly left to the domiciliary services. The integration of the home help service into the departments has therefore been gradual and uneven, and has been affected by the many new strands in domiciliary service provision: the development of more intensive and flexible caring arrangements; the taking over of meals delivery arrangements from voluntary bodies; the adoption of 'patch' systems of working aiming at greater responsiveness to local needs and in which home helps sometimes become part of the patch team as ancillary patchworkers (McGrath and Hadley 1981); and so on. A few studies have discussed closer co-ordination with or integration into area teams. One report (Payne 1977) described the movement from better communication through interlocking services, including common record systems, to shared decision-making. A particularly interesting aspect of the Coventry Home Help Project was that the organiser came to be seen as a full member of the area team: 'She attended the regular allocation meetings and gradually began to carry out tasks previously performed by social work staff. Her assessment of clients took into account the need for services other than home help and she initiated applications for these services or for social security grants or benefits to a far greater extent than other organisers. However, referrals for holidays, telephones and aids . . ., for day care, for sheltered accommodation, and for long or short term residential care were all dealt with by the organiser herself. This became the usual practice when home help clients were involved, and happened occasionally in other cases' (Latto 1980a and b). A monitoring study of fieldwork in an area office also pointed to the possible advantages of closer integration of the home help service into area offices, using home helps more deliberately as monitors working in closer contact with social workers than is customary (Goldberg and Warburton 1979).

Whatever the pattern of co-ordination or integration of service, the role of the home help organiser emerges as critical. The studies highlight two major organisational problems: the multiplicity of roles the home help organiser has to carry out; and the enormous variation in work loads even within one authority.

The home help organiser has at least three distinct functions:

(i)   the assessment and reassessment of clients' needs for home help (sometimes also for other services) and, where charges are made, financial position;
(ii) the recruitment and supervision of a work force – often largely or wholly part-time;
(iii) the organisation and administration of some thousands of hours of service, including programming, processing of time sheets, and so on.

A careful investigation into the home help organisers' roles in Cumbria (Gwynne and Fean 1978) came to the conclusion that the job was too big, and suggested that the administrative aspects should be separated from the management, supervision and assessment roles. Lack of adequate administrative and clerical support is a major factor in this overloading of organisers, but they are often reluctant to relinquish any of these roles. An instructive example is contained in Gwynne's continuing study of Cumbria's home help service (1980). It was found that timetabling and other aspects of programming took up a large amount of the organisers' time. This is a job which many of them feel requires their particular skills both in relation to personal and geographical matching factors. Close investigation showed that personal mismatching did not present a problem of any dimension and that the travelling patterns of home helps were 'hopelessly inefficient and wasteful'. The researchers suggested simple and efficient solutions: to transfer the bulk of programming to clerks and to reduce the home help's travelling time by a well-designed zoning system. However, in some areas there was resistance to these suggestions, and no progress was made, although in one town agreement resulted in a significant reduction of home helps' travelling time and the freeing of home help organisers for more assessment and supervision visits, while all the programming was being done satisfactorily by clerks.

These findings are particularly pertinent as a number of studies suggest that home help organisers are unable because of pressure of work to exercise their review functions adequately. Little systematic reassessment takes place and visiting of any sort is 'despite its importance . . . the activity most liable to reduction when organiser time is short' (Hillingdon SSD 1975). We have already seen that the discrepancy between what a home help organiser prescribes and what a home help does is probably due in part to lack of communication and adequate supervision of home helps, and the gaps and inaccuracies in essential information in records (frequently alluded to in the studies) also point to work overload.

The variations in home help organisers' workloads and caseloads shown in the studies are staggering, whether they are measured in terms of numbers of clients per home help organiser, number of hours to be programmed or number of home helps to be supervised. Even within one authority a home help organiser in one district was said to have 56 home helps to supervise while an organiser in a neighbouring district had 100; there were 275 clients per organiser in one area of the county and 530 in another (Gwynne and Fean 1978). Among London boroughs in 1976 an organiser in one borough had four times as many home helps to supervise as an organiser in another part of London (Stapenhurst 1978). Clearly caution is indicated in looking at such ratios. In addition to the amount of clerical help available and whether financial assessment and collection of charges are involved, turnover of home helps and of clients affects workloads. Two hundred part-time home helps representing 70 full time equivalents will cause far more work than 70 full time helps. The home help organiser's responsibility may be confined to the home help service, or may include assessment for (or even responsibility for provision of) meals on wheels or other domiciliary services. Many aspects of an organiser's workload will be affected by whether the area is urban or rural. But even bearing these cautions in mind the evidence produced by the studies and by the national statistics shows such gross variations that this poses a vital problem to be tackled.

From an organisational point of view, an important difference between the home help and meals services, and a limitation on their integration, is the continuing importance of the voluntary sector in meals preparation and delivery. Most of the available in-house studies did not question the value of the well-established voluntary contribution, and their terms of reference did not involve consideration of possible alternative ways of deploying such voluntary initiatives, despite the constraints on maintenance or expansion of service felt by the voluntary bodies themselves. Studies by independent researchers highlight the pros and cons of the voluntary contribution to the meals service. Means (1981) points to the greater cost of voluntary food-buying which is rarely done in bulk, and the shortage of volunteers which in some areas restricts the coverage and intensity of the service; he also highlights the *ad hoc* nature of some of the arrangements in rural areas. On the other hand he shows the flexibility and informality of a localised and less rule-ridden service, and demonstrates in a telling example how imaginative recruitment strategies can produce sufficient volunteers.

In many ways it seems that a complex undertaking such as the production and distribution of meals on a large scale, with its technological and administrative requirements, is not ideally suited to the more personal nature of voluntary work. Until recently the tendency has been for meals services gradually to be taken over by the statutory sector. However, the cuts in statutory services and the renewed emphasis on voluntary work may alter this. Whichever type of body is providing the services, however, there are technical and organisational problems to be solved: of the balance between meals delivered and meals available in lunch clubs, of the various options now developing which may well influence use of equipment and means of production, of kitchen design and siting, of route planning, of special diets for ethnic minority clients and those suffering from particular illnesses.

In the case of aids and adaptations, many studies have been specifically concerned with the organisation and administration of the service. Aids may be supplied by health authorities, social services departments, or voluntary organisations, and the boundaries of responsibility may be quite unclear. Within social services departments there may be complicated chains of decision-making, depending in part on whose job it is to assess and whether charges are involved. In the case of adaptations, the great variety of arrangements in force may involve dealing with a number of other departments within the local authority as well as outside contractors, which can cause delays of months if not years. Those leaving hospital after in-patient care may have an aid prescribed and issued at the hospital, or the assessment may be made at the hospital but with the aid issued by the social services department after return home. Aids may be decided on by doctors, social workers, occupational therapists, social work assistants, or others, and judgements sometimes differ both as to the type of aid required and whether an aid is required at all. This situation, not surprisingly, leads to difficulties, despite some advantages of flexibility. Few constructive suggestions about organisational solutions to these problems have emerged from the studies seen. In the field of major adaptations it is doubtful whether marginal improvements in procedure would lead to appreciably less delay and cost. More radical solutions, such as that proposed by Stockport, may be preferable: to include some units designed for use of elderly or disabled tenants in all future council housing development.

Service charges
One of the most hotly debated current issues which so far has produced little dispassionate research is the one of service charges, which clearly has a profound influence on 'who gets what' and whether the neediest stand to lose most.

Although authorities were empowered to charge for domiciliary services, Circular 53/71 in 1971 expressly restricted this in the case of those who were on supplementary benefit or who would have to seek such help as a result of charges. Until the reversal in policy in 1980 clients receiving home help who were on supplementary benefit could reclaim any charges as Exceptional Circumstances Additions. Judge and Matthews in their study *Charging for Social Care* (1980) show that consumer charges as a proportion of the cost of home help services steadily declined from the early 1960s (when they amounted to 12.5 per cent) to the mid-1970s (when the figure was only 4.3 per cent). However, the present cuts in social service expenditure and the change to selective policies in a Conservative welfare state have led to a considerable increase in charges as a source of revenue. A seminar in 1981 (Judge *et al* 1982) tried to evaluate the consequences of different approaches to charging policies in the home help service – free services, flat rate charges, and charges assessed in relation to income. While a number of contradictory hypotheses emerged, based partly on moral principles and partly on practical experience, objective research evidence based on adequate samples of clients of the consequences of different charging policies was seen to be woefully inadequate.

The arguments advanced for a flat rate charge are that most recipients seem to be able to afford a modest sum; that a flat rate scheme is administratively less costly than assessed charges; that it enables services to be allocated in accordance with need, as charges do not increase with the amount of help given; and finally that it gives recipients a feeling of independence, of contributing something to the service.

The main argument in favour of assessed charges is that people should as far as possible pay for services received according to their means. The argument applies particularly in areas where there is a substantial well-to-do elderly population who can afford to pay full cost but who should not be denied the opportunity of using a public service. There is also a fear among politicians that comfortably-off people who have employed domestic help all their lives would switch to council home help on retirement if this were a free service or a very cheap one (Archer 1981).

The arguments advanced for a free service, in addition to the moral and political ones, apply with some force where the vast majority of recipients are receiving supplementary benefit and where the cost of the administrative work of raising charges for a very small minority of better off clients would exceed the income to be derived from them.

As far as research evidence is concerned, Howell and his colleagues in Devon (1979) and Gwynne and Fean in Cumbria (1978) found that those who paid full rates received fewer hours of home help time than others of apparently equal disability who did not pay, but it was by no means clear that they were adversely affected by this. On the contrary, some researchers have argued that the tasks carried out for such clients may well be more directly related to their 'real' needs with less time spent on doing jobs which clients might manage themselves.

Judge and Mathews (1980) explored the possible deterrent effects of the imposition of a flat rate charge as evidenced in Bradford, Essex and Cheshire and came to no firm conclusions. The only more extensive study is that by Hyman (1981) who investigated the impact of a new flat rate charge of £1.50 per week on a stratified sample of 130 elderly clients receiving home help in an outer London borough. The sample was divided into four groups: those who cancelled the service (the majority of whom were on supplementary benefit), those who cancelled and re-applied, those who did not cancel and those who had not paid their bills. The researcher concluded that serious hardship resulted, particularly for those on supplementary benefit who 'absorbed the charges'. On the other hand she found (in accordance with experience elsewhere) that those who cancelled tended to be less needy in terms of handicap, social isolation and need for emotional support. She also claimed that although there was a procedure for consideration of reduction of the charge, this was hardly ever used and 'Innumerable cases came to light from the group that cancelled, from those who had not paid their bills and from those who reapplied for the service and even from those who had not interrupted the service that they could not afford the charges'. There was also evidence that informal and voluntary support was not providing a substitute for the home help service.

Clearly this study raises many questions which need to be explored further. What are the characteristics of clients who give up service after flat rate charges are introduced? How are costs absorbed by the other users? Are there any subgroups (for example those put at health risk) who give rise to special concern? How viable are alternative sources of help? How adequately are abatement procedures operating?

Judge *et al* (1982) conclude that in considering the costs and benefits of imposing minimum home help charges:

> on the benefits front it seems clear that the extra revenue made available from charges has helped to maintain the level of home help provision. It is also possible that the use of the price mechanism may have contributed to an improvement in economic efficiency by discouraging marginal demands for home help and releasing additional help for more needy clients. On the costs side, however, there has been a definite increase in the administrative workload in both local authorties and supplementary benefit offices. Also on the debit side is the hardship caused to clients. This reduction in client welfare is manifested in one of two ways: either, because of the loss of badly needed home help for some of the clients who terminated; or, through the increase in relative poverty of those paying the charge, or part of the charge, themselves.

These authors also urge that it is time to clarify which public agency is responsible for the payment of income maintenance subsidies.

In the meals service it is customary to charge a standard price for a meal, reflecting the cost of the food itself, with the local authority making up the difference between that and the cost of providing the meals. In some studies a few recipients said that they could not afford more meals, or made some comment about value in relation to cost, but the general impression gained from the studies was that the question of charges was not as vexed as in the home help service. Although in none of the studies examined was the fact or level of subsidy questioned, this situation may now have changed, given new financial constraints.

Outcome

Finally, evaluation means asking questions about outcome. What characterises success and achievement in the domiciliary services? (Interestingly, a question hardly ever addressed in any of the many evaluative studies examined.) How shall we judge it, from whose point of view – the point of view of the users: how satisfied were they? Or by the relief it brings to relatives and other carers? Should we judge it through the assessments made by the service providers and their satisfaction? Or is it possible to measure results more objectively, by assessing the extent to which previously identified needs have been met: for example the floors are washed, the place is dusted, the shopping gets done, the client now has a nutritious meal each day. Can we also try and measure the subjective elements: does the client feel more comfortable, more hopeful, more cared for, although the surroundings may still be fairly dusty and untidy? Does it signify success if we can show that the service reaches those most in need? And what about cost-effectiveness in relation to both the severity of the problems and the degree of improvement achieved?

As already indicated, most in-house surveys were concerned with suspected shortcomings of services and also raised questions about their appropriateness, such as the home delivery of cooked meals in varying circumstances or the balance between charring and caring in the home help service, or the uneven struggle to achieve adaptations in the home which the old person may never live to use. A considerable number of surveys were concerned with the satisfaction of users, and some tried to establish cost-effectiveness. A few researchers were able with support from outside funding agencies to carry out action projects in which the relative effectiveness of different types of service and methods of delivery could be assessed.

Meeting needs

One of the most important service aims, especially at times of economic stringency, is to ensure that resources and services should be deployed to best advantage and go to those who need them most. We saw that several studies detected gross disparities in service levels between similar, often adjacent areas which argued for resource shifts from one part of the local authority to another. But the studies also demonstrated that a redeployment of resources is often difficult to achieve. No-one wants to deprive elderly clients of help they have come to expect in order to give more to those in neighbouring areas; the alternative of topping up deprived areas to the level of the more affluent may be difficult or impossible in a period of retrenchment. In the case of individual clients, improved methods of assessment and allocation of services for new clients (for example, an initial six week trial allocation for home help or meals delivery) may appear inequitable. Even the gradual procedures of shifting resources suggested by some of the investigators may arouse resistance among referral agents, service deliverers, council members and others.

Similar potential difficulties in bringing about a closer match between needs and resources can be seen in the meals services, where some people receiving only two or three meals a week were found to be in need of a much more frequent service and others who received home delivered meals either seemed capable of attending lunch clubs or mainly needed help with shopping and preparing food (Bedfordshire SSD 1978, Johnson *et al* 1981).

Were any of the studies able to define more exactly the extent of unmet need for domiciliary services and to demonstrate what additional resources might be required to meet it? It will be remembered that in the Coventry project resources equivalent to doubling the number of home help hours (which in Coventry were already well above the national average) were made available in one district of the city. Although the client case load increased by 50 per cent during the three years of the project's life it did so only slowly despite carefully planned publicity exercises, and the total number of additional home help hours available was never fully taken up, even at the end of three years. The researchers believe that this slow increase would have continued, but there is also the suggestion that the 'bottomless pit' of undetected need does not in fact exist and that this extended service managed to saturate the area. Unfortunately, resources were not forthcoming to test this hypothesis by conducting a 'needs survey' towards the end of the project among a random sample of households in the target district. A unique opportunity was thus missed to document whether this extended service had identified all those who were in need and prepared to accept home help, or whether there still existed undetected needs despite the great efforts to make the service known and easily accessible to the residents of the district. Another suggestive finding has emerged from this study: those in most acute need were likely to be receiving home help already, but among people experiencing a moderate degree of disability and difficulty in coping there were unmet and presumably unexpressed needs for home help. A considerable proportion of the additional resources went to this group. Similar findings emerged in a small group of clients who were receiving intensive home help in Cambridgeshire (Simons and Warburton 1980). These observations corroborate tentative research findings in other fields, namely that it is the middle group – neither those whose difficulties are minimal or transient nor those whose difficulties are very severe and chronic – for whom a timely input of help may pay most dividends, possibly preventing or delaying chronic dependency.

Satisfaction with services
A considerable number of the researchers carried out surveys of users, but frequently the questions were concerned with specific aspects of the service, such as charges or different forms of organising home helps' time. Only rarely did they ask relatives or other carers for their views about how the services affected the elderly person's well-being, and little information is available about the views of service providers. The questions addressed to home help organisers, for example, usually invited their views about shortfalls between existing care and 'ideal' levels of care for individual clients, rather than about any outcomes of current care. Little is seen in the studies about behavioural and environmental changes.

Researchers who sought user views were cautious about accepting them at face value, noting that this generation of old people are likely to have low expectations and lack of knowledge of alternatives; they would not want to appear ungrateful, especially if they thought the service was being provided by a voluntary organisation. This was particularly noticeable in the meals studies in Leeds where all the meals were delivered by volunteers. Recipients would also be anxious about being critical in case services were then withdrawn.

The three home help studies which involved large scale client surveys (and smaller studies, too) found a high degree of expressed satisfaction. In Hillingdon (Hillingdon SSD 1977), clients were said to be 'very satisfied with the quality of the service provided' but a considerable proportion thought they did not get enough time and clients also expressed concern that certain tasks, such as repairs, decorating and heavy cleaning never got done. Similar results emerged in a study of home help clients and home helps in Newcastle on Tyne (1979). (These and other studies also reveal differences of view as to what kind of 'heavy' jobs are within the remit of a home help service and which are not.) Gwynedd clients were said to have 'a very protective attitude towards their domestic helps and for the most part simply wished to praise the work they carried out'. Nearly half said that they would not be able to cope without such assistance and a further 17 per cent said they might be able to manage, but only with difficulty (Gwynedd SSD 1977).

In the Coventry project detailed interviews were carried out with clients in the demonstration area and with clients in a comparison area. In this project the home helps were encouraged to form closer links with their clients than is usual and great efforts were made to keep the same home help with the same client for as long as possible. Although numbers are unfortunately very small – as Table 5.1 shows – the project clients attached more significance to their relationship with the home help than clients elsewhere in the city. They were more likely to regard her as a friend or even a family member and to confide in her. The researcher suggests that it was the combination of formal, consistent and practical assistance with very personal help and the time to listen and to talk that resulted in this satisfying support. Researchers in the Thanet Community Care Project reached similar conclusions.

Recipients of meals on wheels too expressed a high degree of general satisfaction in the studies surveyed, although there were substantial minorities in some areas who commented unfavourably about the size of portions, the ways in which meals were cooked or served and their temperature on arrival. Caution is indicated in accepting findings at face value, for the reasons already indicated and on methodological grounds: in some studies structured questions were asked on the quality of food, size of portions, temperature and in others opinions were invited on what recipients liked or disliked about the meals they received. As the Leeds study (Johnson *et al* 1981) notes:

Table 5.1 The relationship of clients with home helps

Home help described as	Project area	Elsewhere in the city
Member of the family	4	—
Friend	17	11
Friendly	—	10
Nice/good	4	6
Domestic help	—	9
Total responding	25	36

Source: Latto, S. (1982) *The Coventry Home Help Project — Short Report*, Coventry Social Services Department

When directly questioned about the quality of the food 72 per cent claimed that the meals were good or very good, while only 4 per cent thought the meals were below average or very poor. However, when these same recipients (a few minutes after the direct question on quality) were asked to comment on the meals in general, a different result emerged. Only 52 per cent commented that the meals were good or very good, while 16.9 per cent commented that the food was not very good or very poor.

While in several studies between one quarter and one half of the recipients interviewed would have liked more meals per week they usually had a very modest expansion in mind: for example 21 per cent of those receiving two meals per week would have liked three (Davies 1981) and those receiving four or five meals a week (presumably a very disabled and dependent group) would have liked a weekend service. Some studies report that recipients expressed a wish to persevere with their own cooking or with the help of friends and relatives on the days on which meals were not delivered. They gave two reasons: they wanted to keep their independence as long as possible, and they did not wish to lose the contact, goodwill and support of relatives, neighbours or friends. This is good confirmation of the thesis so often advanced that the statutory domiciliary services should find a balance of support which does not undermine the recipient's remaining capacity for self care nor inadvertantly cut out family and neighbourly support.

Hardly anybody commented on any benefit derived from the social contact with the people who deliver the meals. This is not surprising considering the very short time of contact (in Leeds 56 per cent of the volunteers stayed a few seconds and 41 per cent a few minutes) and the evidence already quoted that the majority of recipients have home help and that many receive a good deal of support and help from relatives, friends or neighbours.

What do recipients feel about alternatives to the delivery of a ready cooked meal? This topic was not explored systematically in the one-off surveys. It seemed that only a small proportion – no more than 20 per cent – of the recipients who were asked would prefer to go to a lunch club if transport were provided. Although home helps assisted in preparing meals in a small proportion of cases (no more than ten per cent) on non-delivery days, there was hardly any indication in the studies that the old people would have preferred home helps to give more help with preparation of meals. Should one conclude from this preference for the delivery of a ready cooked meal that most of us – but especially very old people – prefer what we are used to and do not want to explore innovative alternatives? The Leeds experiment delivering frozen meals heated en route in the delivery van on micro ovens found that these hot and attractive meals were acceptable to recipients.

Other options tried out in the Leeds experiments such as a frozen pack to be heated by the recipient in the oven, a long life food pouch which needed heating in boiling water, and prepared raw ingredients ready for cooking also found a favourable response, especially among those recipients who had no previous experience of the traditional meals on wheels. The frozen food pack was preferred over the pouch and the pouch over the raw ingredients. The acceptability of the various options largely depended on the level of disability and ability to heat or cook a meal. The Leeds experiments carried out for only six weeks on a very small number of recipients point to many possibilities of adapting domiciliary support sensitively to the particular difficulties and needs of individual clients, keeping alive as much self help and mutual help as the situation warrants. More extensive experimentation is clearly indicated.

Keeping old people 'active and independent' in their own homes
So far we have only discussed subjective indicators of outcome. What about more objective criteria of benefit to users? Such criteria are measurable: for example a cleaner and more comfortable environment can be observed, if this was the main aim of providing home help. A study of the provision of aids to over 750 adults, of whom 71 per cent were over 65, by a team from the University of Exeter Institute of Biometry and Community Medicine (Ward *et al* 1979) included 'a functional assessment of ability with and without the aid, a discussion with the patient of the process of supply of the aid, including any training and follow-up, and an assessment of the use and usefulness of the aid. This latter aspect included a demonstration of the aid where this was still available.' There are reliable measures for personal and household capacity and social activities, if one of the aims of providing domiciliary services is stimulation of greater self care and more social contacts. Simple instruments have been developed to measure with a

good degree of reliability loneliness, depression and morale, which could be used in studies or demonstration projects where a more comprehensive home care service sets out to affect the psychological well-being of a client in addition to providing practical support. Sadly, only the Coventry study – and even this one to only a very moderate degree – has undertaken such assessments. Yet there is no reason why some of these assessments should not be attempted, either in everyday practice or as part of a monitoring exercise, provided that base line assessments are made initially.

The Coventry project has not as yet reported any findings which compare the functioning or the environmental circumstances of clients at the beginning of the project with their situation at the end, and what is equally important comparing any improvements in the project group with the state of affairs in the comparison group which received ordinary home help services.

However results are available on the impact the enriched home help service had on the use of other community and residential services. The project clients used on average significantly more related services (3.5 other services each) and used them for longer periods than clients in the comparison area of the city who averaged less than one other service per person (0.75). The two main services used were medical out-patient clinics (35 per cent of the project clients and 22 per cent of clients elsewhere in the city) and other domiciliary services such as mobile meals (26 per cent and 17 per cent) and aids to daily living (34 per cent and 16 per cent). These results suggest that the more comprehensive assessment by the home care organiser, the closer contacts between clients and home helps, and the home helps' greater knowledge of community resources, together with close supervision by the organiser, led to the discovery of multiple needs and more widespread use of related community resources. The picture was reversed in the area of community nursing, which is not surprising in view of the personal care and nursing tasks the home helps were carrying out. While the project clients received on average 1.4 hours of community nursing per month the clients in the comparison area received 4.8 hours. This finding throws an interesting light on the extent to which services can be substituted for each other.

Did the enlarged home help service in conjunction with a more intensive use of other domiciliary services decrease the demand for residential places? The numbers involved in the demonstration project were too small to compare admission rates to residential homes or chronic hospital beds with the rest of the city over the three-year period but a simulation exercise suggested that the project had been able to avert demands for residential places. In this exercise, test cases consisting of all those elderly clients who had received home help on five or more days or more than ten hours service per week were put up to the panel which makes decisions on priorities for admission to residential homes. Of the 38 test cases submitted two were rejected but the remainder were either given a high priority classification or were considered suitable for placement in special units or geriatric wards. While it is unlikely that all those given a high priority rating would have wanted, or been offered, a residential place, the researchers claimed that in a sub-sample of 65 clients who were the subject of a cost-benefit exercise five clients had been kept out of an elderly persons' home, one had been kept out of a home for physically handicapped people and five had been kept out of hospital. Additionally in the case of five clients relatives had been enabled to go out to work. These cost-benefit calculations suggested that the extra expenditure on home help and on other related domiciliary services was easily outweighed by savings associated with the prevention of admission to residential or hospital care. The savings on hospital costs were particularly striking and raised important questions about how any major future expansion of domiciliary care should be financed.

Clearly these propositions based mainly on a hypothetical situation would need to be tested in real life. One such test will be discussed in Chapter 6 when we examine the results of the Thanet Community Care Project where the number of actual admissions to residential and hospital care occurring in the experimental group of vulnerable old people was compared with the number of admissions of similar people in the comparison group. In this study cost comparisons were based on empirical results.

Issues arising

Perhaps one of the most important general issues implicit in a number of studies is how to arrive at the 'right' balance between meeting the more general needs of the elderly population for domiciliary support and giving intensive service to those most 'at risk' who wish to stay in their own homes.

Developing criteria of need which are of practical use in determining resource allocation in individual cases and which take into account a whole range of domiciliary options is another critical issue. Since it is unlikely that highly skilled workers will generally be available at the assessment stage, guidelines based on research and on wisdom, gained from practice reinforced by imaginative in-service training, will need to be developed. More will be said about this in the following chapter.

The next issue which arises from this broader approach to needs and the potential use of related resources is the co-ordination of services. Since the problems of how to co-ordinate the various services so as to provide appropriate packages of help adjustable to changing needs will arise in subsequent chapters, we will deal with it in our conclusions. We shall also consider the possible changes needed in the role of the home help organiser in this broader context.

While the mainly descriptive research pointing to the complexities of the services and the existing disparities in provision has provided a useful backcloth, we now need to proceed to research aimed at monitoring input and evaluating outcome in different client situations and within a variety of organisational arrangements. As was already indicated in Chapter 2, and as we shall discover in the following chapters, some of the monitoring and evaluative tools are being fashioned now and hence these evaluative exercises need not be as complex and long drawn out as the pioneering efforts in Seatown, Kent and Coventry have been.

Finally, the problem of implementing even apparently straightforward conclusions emerging from research findings has raised its head, for instance in the home help organisers' disinclination to give up their programming functions. It is essential to explore systematically to what extent researchers' suggestions have been implemented and how effective any changes that have been introduced have proved in practice. For example, have more rational methods of allocating hours to areas actually resulted in more equitable help to individual clients? Does more help with shopping or the delivery of prepared food ingredients help people to maintain greater ability for self care than the provision of ready-to-eat meals? Does more careful instruction lead to more effective use of aids? Does a contractual agreement between client and service provider lead to more appropriate use of resources and more client autonomy than the usual more casual ways?

References

Archer, C. (1982) Charges by assessment, in K. Judge and others, *Charging for the Home Help Service* Report of a conference, June 1981, London, Policy Studies Institute.

Armstrong, J., O'Sullivan, K. and Turner, M. (1980). *The Housebound Elderly: Technical innovations in food service*, University of Leeds Catering Research Unit.

Avon Social Services Department (1976) Home help assessments: an examination of ideal and actual allocations, Summary published in *Clearing House for Local Authority Social Services Research* 1977: 4.

Barrow, S. and Derbyshire, M.E. (1975) *Survey on the usefulness of aids*, Lancashire Social Services Department, Unpublished.

Bebbington, A.C. (1979) Changes in the provision of social services to the elderly in the community over fourteen years, *Social Policy and Administration 13*, 111–123.

Bedfordshire Social Services Department (1978) The meals service of Bedfordshire, *Clearing House for Local Authority Social Services Research* 1978: 2.

Booth, T. (1977) Nutrition survey strikes a warning note for elderly, *Health and Social Service Journal*, 15 July.

Brotherton, J. (1975) *The Need for Meals-on-Wheels and Luncheon Clubs in the Dover District of Kent: Final report*, Kent County Secretary's Department, Research and Intelligence Unit.

Connelly, N. and Goldberg, E.M. (1979) Looking at meals on wheels, *Community Care*, 14 June.

Croydon Social Services Department (1976) *Meals on Wheels Service: An interim report*.

Davies, L. (1981) *Three Score Years . . . and Then?* London, William Heinemann Medical Books.

Department of Health and Social Security (1970) *Organisation of Meals on Wheels*, Circular 5/70.

Department of Health and Social Security (1971) *Help in the Home: Section 13 of the Health Services and Public Health Act 1968*, Circular 53/71.

Department of Health and Social Security (1978) *A Happier Old Age*, London, HMSO.

Department of Health and Social Security (1981) *Growing Older*, London, HMSO.

Dunnachie, N. (1979) Intensive domiciliary care of the elderly in Hove, *Social Work Service 21*, 1–3.

Goldberg, E.M. and Connelly, N. (1978) Reviewing services for the old, *Community Care*, 6 December.

Goldberg, E.M. and Warburton, R.W. (1979) *Ends and Means in Social Work: The development and outcome of a case review system for social workers*, London, George Allen and Unwin.

Goldberg, E.M., Warburton, R.W., McGuinness, B. and Rowlands, J.H. (1977) Towards accountability in social work: one year's intake to an area office, *British Journal of Social Work 7*, 257–283.

Gwynne, D. (1980) *Home Help Service in Cumbria*, Social Services Research Group, Report of a Conference on *Research and Policy-making in the Home Help Service*.

Gwynne, D. and Fean, L. (1978) *The Home Help Service in Cumbria*, Cumbria Social Services Department.

Gwynedd Social Services Department (1977) *A Research Review of the Operation of the Home Help Service in Gwynedd*.

Hillingdon Social Services Department (1974) Recruitment and retention of home helps: a further study, *Clearing House for Local Authority Social Services Research* 1974: 9.

Hillingdon Social Services Department (1975) *Organisation of the Home Help Service in Hillingdon*.

Hillingdon Social Services Department (1977) *Domiciliary Services Evaluation Part III: The Home Help Service*.

Howell, N., Boldy, D. and Smith, B. (1979) *Allocating the Home Help Service*, London, Bedford Square Press.

Hunt, A. (1978) *The Elderly at Home*, London, HMSO.

Hurley, B. and Wolstenholme, L. (1979) The home help study: A summary of the findings and implications of the (Bradford) social services research project, Published in *Clearing House for Local Authority Social Services Research* 1980:1.

Hyman, M. (1981) *The Home Help Service: A case history study in the London*

Borough of Redbridge, Redbridge Social Services Department.

Johnson, M.L., di Gregorio, S. and Harrison, B. (1981) *Ageing, Needs and Nutrition*, PSI Research Paper 81/8, London, Policy Studies Institute.

Judge, K., Ferlie, E. and Smith, J. (1982) Home Help charges, in K. Judge and others, *Charging for the Home Help Service*, Report of a conference, June 1981, London, Policy Studies Institute.

Judge, K. and Matthews, J. (1980) *Charging for Social Care*, London, George Allen and Unwin.

Keeble, U. (1979) *Aids and Adaptations*, London, Bedford Square Press.

Latto, S. (1980a) Help begins at home, *Community Care*, 24 April 1980.

Latto, S. (1980b) Help begins at home, *Community Care*, 12 June 1980.

Latto, S. (1982) *The Coventry Home Help Project – Short Report*, Coventry Social Services Department, In press.

Marks, J. (1975) *Home Help*, Occasional Papers in Social Administration No. 58, London, Bell and Co.

Marston, N. and Blunt, D. (1981) Frozen foods in the service of the elderly, *Social Work Service 27*, 18–22.

May, J.S. and Whitbread, A.W. (1977) Equal help for equal need? A study of the home help service in Warwickshire, *Clearing House for Local Authority Social Services Research* 1977: 2.

McGrath, M. and Hadley, R. (1981) Evaluating patch-based social services teams: a pilot study, in E.M. Goldberg and N. Connelly (eds.) *Evaluative Research in Social Care*, London, Heinemann Educational Books Ltd.

Means, R. (1981) *Community Care and Meals on Wheels: A study in the politics of service development at the national and local level*, Working Paper 21, University of Bristol School for Advanced Urban Studies.

Melotte, C.J. (1976) The supply of aids and adaptations, *Clearing House for Local Authority Social Services Research* 1976:5.

Merton SSD (1976) The home help service in the London Borough of Merton, *Clearing House for Local Authority Social Services Research* 1976: 6.

Newcastle upon Tyne Management Services Division (1979) *Home Help Service: Report of Acting Head of Management Services for Social Services Committee*.

Payne, M. (1977) Integrating domiciliary care into an area team, *Social Work Service 14*, 54–58.

Plociennick, J. and Harrison, K. (1977) Home help survey, Barnet Social Services Department. Published in *Clearing House for Local Authority Social Services Research* 1978: 6.

Simons, K. and Warburton, R.W. (1980) *The clients of three social work teams and the help they receive*, Report to DHSS. Unpublished.

Stanton, B.R. (1971) *Meals for the Elderly: A report on meals on wheels and luncheon clubs in two North London boroughs*, London, King Edward's Hospital Fund.

Stapenhurst, P. (1978) *Report on the Home Help Service and the Meals Service in Greater London*, London, Greater London Association for the Disabled.

Thompson, Q. (1974) Assessing the need for domiciliary services for the elderly, *Greater London Intelligence Quarterly 28*, 35–39.

Thornely, G., Chamberlain, M.A. and Wright, V. (1977) Evaluation of aids and equipment for the bath and toilet, *Occupational Therapy*, October 1977, 243–246.

Vickery, A. (1981) Consultation on 64 cases of elderly people living alone referred for social work help, Draft report, London, National Institute for Social Work.

Ward, P.R., Numeiry, M.A. and Williams, P. (1979) *The Supply of Aids to Physically Handicapped People*, University of Exeter Institute of Biometry and Community Medicine.

6 Social Work

In this chapter we want to consider studies which evaluate the contribution of social work to the care of the elderly. This is not as easy as it sounds, as social workers can be involved in many activities: in assessment, in mobilising resources which range from domiciliary services to admission to residential facilities, in advocacy on their clients' behalf, in counselling and casework with both the elderly and their carers, in co-ordinating services, and in community work. Potentially, then, social work has an important contribution to make to the social care of the elderly, but this contribution is dwarfed at present by the scale of the domiciliary and residential services, and social workers appear somewhat uncertain about their aims and their roles – which often are unco-ordinated with other health and social support services.

Problems of evaluating social work
How does one evaluate such ill-defined and multi-faceted functions as those subsumed under the name of social work?

From the 1930s to the middle 1960s evaluative studies of social work were mainly concerned with the interpersonal or relationship aspects of one-to-one casework. Social workers were apt to write in somewhat pompous language about the transactions between themselves and their clients, emphasising the complexities and subtleties of the casework process. They were relatively silent about the vast amount of down-to-earth practical help and advice they also gave to their clients, as if ashamed of this side of social work. Nor was much said about the social workers' functions of linking clients with a host of voluntary and statutory agencies in the community, and of interpreting their needs to these agencies. Hence descriptions of social work activities were often partial and misleading, and many people still believe that the majority of social workers are immersed in long-term intensive casework, discussing their clients' past experiences.

But even in the 1960s studies suggested that the reality was very different and more oriented towards the present interaction of the client with his surroundings and with practical help than these notions would suggest. For example, these studies showed that only one to two per cent of the caseworkers' responses in interviews with clients who were experiencing difficulties in family relationships dealt with intra-psychic causes of behaviour or with childhood origins of current difficulties (Reid 1967, Hollis 1968, Mullen 1968).

A factor which is not always stressed or understood when trying to evaluate social work activities is that social workers have traditionally been concerned with the 'outcasts' in society, those whose handicaps are longstanding or irreversible or who fail to make 'appropriate' use of community facilities. The movement away from institutional towards community care has confronted social workers with even more intractable problems now being contained in the community – tough adolescents, chronically mentally ill and severely subnormal people and their families, and last but not least very frail, disabled and often confused elderly people and their carers. As we shall see, 'results', 'success', 'effectiveness' are very difficult to establish in such situations unless one is content with rather modest and specific short term goals that social work may be able to achieve.

Doubts about the usefulness of social work

While the demand for social work and the number of social workers (both trained and untrained) have grown enormously during the last 30 years, vigorous doubts have been expressed throughout this period about their effectiveness, spearheaded by Wooton (1959). She suggested that the modern social worker (like her Victorian predecessor) was confusing economic difficulties with personal failure and misconduct, and that undue attention to the casework process and the casework relationship was deflecting attention from problems created by bad environments. And since the modern social worker saw her concern to be with psychological maladjustment rather than material need, she found it harder to say what she was driving at. Some of these arguments, more extravagantly formulated – such as 'privatising public ills' (Corrigan and Leonard 1978) – are now advanced by the Marxist school of social work in this country.

A more friendly but equally critical voice was that of Huws Jones in his address to the Annual General Meeting of the Institute of Almoners in 1959 entitled: 'Is our Social Worker Really Necessary?' He suggested that very little scientifically based research had been addressed to the questions: How effective is our social worker? How much difference does she make? What precisely does she achieve? He even boldly proposed visible and hence measurable criteria for evaluating the success of the almoner's job (culled from almoners' own writings): less delay in accepting treatment, helping patients to persevere with treatment, helping them to cope with stress which might impede recovery, and preparing them for return home. 'In short they get better sooner, they stay well longer, and they get back to their former place in society more speedily', compared with similar patients in hospitals with no adequate medical social work (Huws Jones 1959).

The next major critic was Briar (1968), who took social workers to

task for retreating from an array of functions as 'social brokers, advocates, reformers and participants in social policy' to the one exclusive
function of therapist, adopting a 'psychiatric disease' model as their
frame of reference. He argued that casework methods based on
explanatory theories did not provide knowledge of how to change
conditions.

Meyer and his colleagues in their seminal field experiment in social
work with adolescent girls criticised the almost exclusive concentration
of the caseworkers dealing with these girls on self-understanding and
attitudes (Meyer *et al* 1965). They suggested that social work might
achieve better results if it was directed towards helping clients to
change their situations and their goals. Sinfield (1969) picked out
another facet: he thought that the narrow interpretation of the modern
social worker's role and the profession's tendency to look into its own
processes led to the neglect of the clients' views and of the goals to be
achieved. Some of these notions were partially confirmed by Mayer and
Timms in *The Client Speaks* (1970): not infrequently clients seemed
bewildered by the so-called casework process and did not understand
what the social workers were talking about or driving at.

Even as recently as 1980 Sainsbury found in his study of long-term
casework with families in various settings that secondary purposes of
the casework were not always disclosed to the clients who complained
that they did not know what was going on, that the work seemed
aimless and endless; the researchers observed a loss in client morale
after initial hopefulness. These findings closely resemble those of Reid
and Shyne (1968), where deterioration indicating a law of diminishing
returns was more evident among the long-term clients than among the
short-term clients, and where clients expressed a preference for the
goal-directed and more explicit form of short-term casework. Sainsbury concludes: 'the casework we studied started with some kind of
agreed (or at least compatible) task orientation, but then sometimes
drifted into a travesty of the diagnostic model, in which service continues indefinitely and on the assumption that warm relationships are
all that are required to bring about improved social functioning' (Sainsbury 1980).

More recent work by Sainsbury and his colleagues (Fisher *et al* 1981)
monitoring long-term social work with people – some of them elderly –
who are mentally ill, and by Glendinning (1981) evaluating the outcome
of long-term social support to families caring for severely handicapped
children, has again highlighted the social worker's role as supporter and
confidante rather than change agent. In both these studies she appears
as someone who fulfils a kind of maintenance function by recognising
and understanding the clients' chronic dilemmas and burdens and in a
way sharing them. The social workers were not primarily regarded as

people who helped to solve problems or brought about a change in circumstances. Indeed, curiously the lack of improvement in clients' psychological and material conditions did not seem to detract from their feelings of satisfaction with the support they had received from the social workers. These findings are similar to those in respect of carers of seriously confused elderly relatives in a recent consumer study in Cambridgeshire (Littlechild and Warburton 1981). The studies raise important issues which will be taken up later.

The most outspoken critics of the effectiveness of social work are Brewer and Lait (1980) who, having pointed to the large degree of overlap between social work and other caring professions, come to the conclusion that there is no need for a 'free-standing' social work profession.

It is true that most of the evaluative studies of social work carried out in the late 1960s and early 1970s were disappointing. They showed very small if any gains in outcome among groups which had received skilled casework or other special social help when compared with groups of clients who received other forms of help, or none. But, as already mentioned in the methodological chapters, these poor results may in part be attributable to the fact that goals were too global or vague and hence not measurable, and inputs largely unspecified.

However, some positive pointers are gradually emerging, starting with the unexpected results in Reid and Shyne's study that more explicit goal-oriented short-term social work appeared to be more effective than long-term help among families experiencing relationship problems. Recent evaluative studies (Gibbons 1981, Reid and Hanrahan 1981, Goldberg *et al* 1983) suggest that the task-centred model of casework which has evolved from this brief method has a positive morale-building effect on the clients, who as a result feel more able to cope with their social difficulties. Concentration is on helping them achieve specific and limited goals in relation to problems they consider to be important – within brief periods.

Translated into work with the elderly, such a limited goal might be to help an old person accept any kind of assistance at all; once this is achieved appropriate help can be introduced while the social worker may withdraw. Or the social worker may help an old person through a period of mourning and towards re-establishment of social contacts. A short-term aim may be to enable an old person and her carers to come to a decision about radical changes in living arrangements; the objective may be to work out with the client how to cope more successfully with self or home care; or the aim may be to enable carers to limit their involvement with a very frail or disturbed old person and to allow other helpers to share the caring tasks. Achievement of such specific goals is measurable both objectively and subjectively from the point of view of how the clients and their carers regard the effects of such intervention.

The second positive indications are that consumer studies (McKay *et al* 1973, Glampson and Goldberg 1976, Glendinning 1981, Littlechild and Warburton 1981, Levin 1982) indicate that practical services, establishing links with other agencies, and advocacy are experienced as very helpful by different kinds of clients and in particular by the elderly.

Hence it is probably the social worker's gatekeeper function, skilled short-term intervention, and above all her role as mobiliser and co-ordinator of support services, that are of crucial importance and need evaluating.

Possible functions and aims of social work

In the preceding chapter we have frequently alluded to the need for more specific and at the same time more comprehensive assessments of the needs of clients in the context of their life situation and in relation to a variety of resources – both practical and social – that could be mobilized. The first important function of the social worker is thus as an assessor of problems or needs who takes into account not only the client's physical, material and emotional state and her social circumstances but also the contributions – actual and potential – made by her informal supporters and others and the physical and emotional stresses they may experience. Above all the social work assessor will try to detect what the client herself perceives to be her most pressing problems and her primary needs, and what possible solutions she would envisage or find acceptable.

The second function will be the mobilising of resources. The aim will be to devise a plan of help which is tailored to the client's needs and which is, wherever possible, agreed with her and her informal and formal carers. The implementation of such plans will often involve the mobilising and allocation of diverse resources.

Thirdly, the social worker may assume her more traditional role as a direct caseworker, which will usually be short-term until crises are sorted out, decisions made or more long-term support arranged. The social worker may have to re-enter a case from time to time as a direct helper.

Fourthly, the social worker will have co-ordinating and monitoring functions in order to ensure that the different support services function adequately and in an integrated fashion and are continually adjusted to the changing needs of clients. (Such functions may also in some circumstances be delegated to other key workers such as home help organisers, health visitors or occupational therapists.)

Fifthly, closely related to the above role, the social worker can act as a resource person/consultant to other helpers in direct contact with the elderly person in her own home, in day care or in residential situations.

Finally, social workers can act as community workers, helping to stimulate and support neighbourhood groups, social clubs and other forms of community action.

Some of these social work roles have not yet been systematically developed and implemented, let alone evaluated, while the casework role (insofar as it has existed in relation to the elderly) can be said to have atrophied in the current concentration of trained social work manpower on children and their families. But the role of case co-ordinator and resource person is coming more to the fore, as various combinations of statutory, voluntary and informal supports are being developed or strengthened and as it is being recognised that these support networks can make their optimal impact only if they are co-ordinated and reviewed regularly.

What are the needs of elderly people for social work?

It is as difficult to establish general criteria of need for social work among elderly people as for any other group, since they vary greatly in the way they cope with problems, hardships of various kinds or disability. At the extremes it is comparatively easy to establish the extent of potential need; for example we can extrapolate from the Hunt (1978) and Abrams (1980) surveys the number of old people who were found to be very disabled, had few if any support services, had very few contacts with other people and complained about loneliness/depression. We can assume that some form of social work assessment is desirable in such situations. Or again we can assume that the problems of almost any household which supports a seriously confused elderly person needs at the very least some exploration. Indeed a current survey into the needs of a randomly selected sample of 150 households containing a mentally infirm old person reveals a clear need for a skilled all-round assessment in a majority of cases (Levin 1982). We may also postulate that wherever the possibility of residential care is being considered the opportunity for a discussion with a social worker should be available. Cooper describes a project in Essex where special attention was paid to the quality of post-referral assessment, with a shift from 'resource-led' to 'resource-constrained, problem-oriented' assessments; he stresses the necessity of ensuring that social workers carrying out such assessments have a substantial understanding of the potential role of domiciliary and other services (Cooper 1981 a and b).

However, many material, social and psychological needs are less visible. They may also be difficult to identify while area offices cover large districts often containing over 50,000 inhabitants, home help services still function rather separately from area teams, and relationships with primary health care and psychiatric services are often tenuous. The less obvious pre-crisis needs of old people are more likely to be spotted where area teams serve small 'patches' and can become familiar figures within a small neighbourhood, or where social workers are attached to primary health care teams.

Several monitoring studies (Goldberg and Warburton 1979, Crosbie 1983, Grant 1981 a and b, Warburton and Simons 1981) indicate that between one-third and a half of referrals to social work teams in social services departments are elderly people, the majority of whom are over the age of 75, live alone or with an elderly spouse and experience problems in self or home care arising from their physical or mental frailty. It does not seem feasible and is probably unnecessary for trained social workers to attempt the screening of this vast and growing number of people needing social support services of various kinds. Yet these studies have shown that in some departments much of the social workers' time is taken up with screening relatively straightforward requests for practical help, while weighty decisions about admission to residential care may be made by social work assistants. In other authorities the requests are channelled to various assessment points: clients with mobility problems are referred to the occupational therapist, those recommended by a doctor or health visitor for domiciliary services to home help organisers, while serious crisis situations involving decisions about possible admission to residential care are referred to social workers or social work assistants. In areas organised into small patch teams, patchworkers (usually not trained social workers) pick up many referrals in informal ways through neighbours, warden schemes and close contact with other social and medical agencies operating in the patch. An important issue is how to ensure that the wide variety of social service personnel or volunteers who may be the first contact point can be alerted and taught how to spot those elderly people who may need more specific social work assessment and planning. Most front line personnel will recognise those *in extremis*, but studies such as *Helping the Aged* (Goldberg *et al* 1970) have shown that welfare officers often missed the less obvious sign of depression (which can present as apathy, sleeplessness, loss of appetite or self neglect). They were also not sensitised to hidden though pervasive family stress, nor was it easy for them to spot those apparently well supported situations in which informal carers shoulder excessive burdens which if unrelieved are likely to lead to breakdown. Knowledge derived from both research and practice now seems sufficiently advanced for guidelines to be produced which could help those who first come into touch with elderly people and their carers to spot those situations which need more searching assessments by skilled personnel.

The other area of need which surveys and monitoring studies regularly uncover is that for information and advice on a wide variety of financial, social and legal topics. It is becoming ever more difficult for social service providers to absorb and keep up to date with the information people may require in relation to welfare rights, housing, family law or other kinds of services. It would seem that specialised information and advice sections within the social services departments or in conjunction with citizens advice bureaux could serve these needs better than the uneven struggle of individual social workers to keep up to date with the details of changing developments and regulations.

Before considering what social workers actually do for and with elderly clients, it is important to discuss their attitudes to social work with elderly people as documented in a variety of studies.

Social workers' attitudes to work with old people

Neill was the first investigator to show that in the mid-1970s the elderly, along with the mentally handicapped, were the least popular client group, especially among trained social workers whose case loads were weighted towards family and child care problems, while the case loads of unqualified social workers and social work assistants were weighted towards the elderly and the physically disabled (Neill *et al*. 1973 and 1976). These findings, based on one social services department only, have been confirmed by several other more extensive studies (Holme and Maizels 1978, Stevenson and Parsloe 1978, Howe 1980, Simons and Warburton 1980). For example, Holme and Maizels showed that the majority of social workers in the more senior positions and those with the smallest case loads were not working with elderly clients, while the majority of social work assistants and those with larger case loads did not work with children. Howe, examining case loads in 12 area terms in one county and six area teams in two metropolitan boroughs, showed that 43 per cent of all fieldworkers had case loads which were markedly biased towards working with children and their families; this increased to 63 per cent in the metropolitan boroughs. Only 22 per cent of the case loads were biased towards the elderly and physically handicapped, and this figure was even lower in the metropolitan boroughs – 15 per cent (see Table 6.1).

Furthermore social workers who held professional qualifications were more likely to have a marked bias towards working with child care and family cases than social workers who were not qualified. In their turn unqualified social workers were more likely than social work assistants to have a greater bias in the direction of child care cases. Howe concludes: 'the answers to the question of "who does what" can be seen to be a function of the characteristics of the client group on the one hand and the characteristics of the fieldworker on the other'.

Both Neill and Howe produce similar figures for work preferences. Between 50 and 60 per cent of social workers had a preference for working with children and their families. The elderly and physically

Table 6.1 Extent of biased caseloads: proportion of all fieldworkers with biased caseloads(a)

| Category | Type of authority | | |
| | County | Metro-politan | Total |
	%	%	%
Children and their families	29	63	43
Mentally ill and mentally handicapped	9	0	5
Elderly and physically handicapped	27	15	22
Proportion with no marked caseload bias	35	23	30
Total	100	101	100
Proportion with a caseload bias, whatever the category	65	78	70
N =	156	129	285

(a) Caseloads which have one client category comprising more than 70 per cent of the total number of that fieldworker's cases.

Source: Howe 1980

handicapped were preferred by about 30 per cent of social workers in Neill's study and by 17 per cent in Howe's study, while the mentally ill and mentally handicapped were the least preferred in both studies. There are indications that developments such as the introduction of specialist teams for work with the elderly or the community approach in patch-based systems of social care which gives social workers new opportunities of working with and through other helpers on behalf of the elderly are infusing new enthusiasm into social work with old people. The imaginative public relations work and political pressure exerted by vigorous voluntary organisations like Age Concern, Help the Aged and the Centre for Policy on Ageing also contribute to interest in helping the elderly. Some of the most innovative current social work demonstration and experimental research projects are concerned with the social care of old people. Finally, when blaming social workers for not showing sufficient enthusiasm for work with old people one might remember that the majority of qualified fieldworkers are young married people who find it easier to identify with problems encountered by young families that with difficulties experienced by the generation of their grandparents.

Social work input
Monitoring studies in a southern English town 'Seatown' (Goldberg

and Warburton 1979), in a London borough (Crosbie 1983), in Cambridgeshire (Warburton and Simons 1981), and in two rural areas in North Wales (Grant 1981 a and b) show that most elderly clients who come to the attention of social workers in area offices will be assessed, receive some advice and information, and be put in touch with appropriate forms of practical help. Their cases will then be closed from the point of view of active social work though domiciliary services and aids to daily living may continue for long periods. This short-term social work involves contacts with other agencies – mainly general practitioners, health visitors, district nurses and hospitals. A small proportion of very frail or very confused clients, comprising about ten per cent of old people referred to the Seatown area office, received more active and intensive social work support over an extended period. This also seemed to be the case in the other study areas. In addition to a great variety of practical services, regular surveillance, some form of counselling and emotional support were also part of the social work in this small proportion of cases.

Despite the preponderance of short-term work in the referral phase elderly clients whose cases may be open for several years can constitute half the long-term population in a social services department. This is mainly because of the gradual build-up of chronic case loads consisting of people with intractable physical, social or emotional disabilities; their problems do not seem capable of resolution, and thus do not allow social workers to 'close' them with a clear conscience. Such clients will receive occasional review visits, often with the aim of ensuring that domiciliary services are still functioning appropriately, that clients are in touch with medical services if need be, and that they are still able to 'carry on'. There is little indication of social workers or assistants involving volunteers or 'good neighbours' or of using domiciliary helpers as channels of information or early warning systems in this long-term surveillance effort. Even in rural North Wales, contacts with voluntary agencies and key agents of voluntary care, such as the clergy, were few and far between. It comes as a surprise that the general pattern of short-term help and long-term surveillance has been found to be very similar in rural and urban areas, and that there also appears to be very little difference in the way 'generic' and 'specialist' teams provide services and supports to elderly clients (Grant 1981 a and b).

This rather stereotyped broad-brush picture does not do justice to the small proportion of cases – some ten per cent of the referrals and some long-term clients – who receive more intensive support. Vickery, acting as a social work consultant to two area teams participating in the monitoring study in the London borough (Crosbie 1983) has conveyed a more detailed picture of social work with a sample of 64 such elderly people living alone (Vickery 1981). Her aim was to find out what kind of clients and situations the workers were selecting for this intensive work, how they were assessing the clients and their circumstances, what patterns of intervention the social workers were typically adopting and if necessary to open up new lines of inquiry or action and specifically to encourage the workers to pay attention to the functioning, needs and adequacy of the clients' caring networks. This exploratory study brings out both the possibilities of social work with elderly people and their carers and the limitations inherent in organisational aspects and in social workers' attitudes and skills. Vickery quotes impressive examples of imaginative social work carried out with very confused people on task-centred lines, of bringing about changes in the environment, of sensitive clarification of conflicts and misconceptions between carers and clients, and of purposeful negotiations with other agencies. The author also highlights positive and negative aspects of current deployment of available resources. For example, she stresses the flexibility with which places in old people's homes were used in one area. On the other hand, the central allocation of home help hours, which was calculated on the previous year's allocation, did not allow for flexible allocation of hours suited to individual needs.

There were also the usual problems of delays in the delivery of aids, scarcity of telephones for sick clients who lived alone, and shortage of transport (rather than vacancies) preventing clients from attending day centres. Shortage of geriatric and psycho-geriatric facilities and of district nurses, and difficulties in collaboration with general practitioners also limited the help that could be given. It seemed that volunteers were not deployed to best advantage: the Old People's Welfare Committee used volunteers for three-monthly check-up visits on all known elderly people rather than for more intensive work with a small number of people who were lonely, bereaved or at risk.

Although Vickery tried to encourage the social workers to transcend some of the organisational and resource limitations by searching for alternative possibilities – for example new sources of volunteers, informal day care, formation of mutual help groups – the resource restraints just enumerated clearly impeded the social workers' activities. But Vickery also observed that the social workers often restricted their roles further by their limited assessment and definition of problems and needs. There was first of all the service rather than problem oriented definition of need, which we have already noted in discussing assessment for domiciliary care. Another observed phenomenon has been termed by a director of social services as the 'budgerigar response': the offer of a resource that is easily obtainable but not appropriate to the client's need, or the misuse of a scarce resource such as extending home help hours solely for purposes of surveillance. Some social workers had very little knowledge of the neighbourhood networks in which their clients lived, which might have been tapped for informal help. Vickery also noted the limited range and nature of contacts that some social workers had with staff to whom they did not have easy access such as home helps, since the channel to them was supposed to be through the home help organiser.

Links with relatives, though numerous, seemed to depend largely on the relatives' initiative. Vickery contrasts the reluctance by social workers to become involved with relatives of elderly people with their very different practices when dealing with children or mentally ill people. She suggests that a possible reason for this could be the fear that relatives might become far more demanding of the workers' time and skill than the client. Related to this may be the social worker's noticeable avoidance of dealing with conflicts evident in many families concerning the care of their elderly relative. Finally the author suggests that the teams themselves seemed to reinforce the view that for old clients area teams existed mainly to provide services. 'They were not only refraining from canvassing their skills as counsellors, resource finders, advocates, they were actively discouraging referrals for which their concrete services did not seem relevant.'

The social work carried out in *Helping the Aged*, the experimental study 15 years ago (Goldberg *et al* 1970), suggests that some of the aspects stressed by Vickery can become part and parcel of social work with elderly people. The aims which informed the social work input in the earlier study were to ensure the old people's well-being and physical comfort, to reinforce and possibly even to add to the roles which, however small, they could still perform. The skill in social work with the elderly was seen to consist in being sensitive to both the possibilities and the limits of the client and his or her supporters. This meant that the social worker had to find the 'right' balance between accepting the legitimate 'closing of accounts' (a process that has been called disengagement) on the one hand and encouraging social contacts and other enriching influences that are still possible on the other.

It will be remembered from Chapter 3 that in this experiment the social work with old people carried out by trained social workers was compared with that of untrained but often experienced welfare officers in a Welfare Department in a London borough during the late 1960s. The characteristics which distinguished the work of the trained social workers from that of the welfare officers are particularly instructive if considered in the light of Vickery's observations: first, the social workers recognised more problems, particularly in the psycho-social sphere, such as hidden depression and subtle but disturbing family situations. Second, while the departments' welfare officers most commonly considered that their clients needed domiciliary services and supervisory visits (as seems to be the view still within social services departments), the project social workers more often saw a need for practical services in combination with casework with the old person or their relatives, or with both. This difference was very great and highly significant statistically – 58 per cent of cases in the special group as against 23 per cent in the comparison group. In other words the trained workers laid as much emphasis as their welfare colleagues on practical help and the provision of services but at the same time they paid attention to their clients' subjective experiences, to re-activating skills (like knitting), to drawing in relatives by imaginative suggestions and encouragement, or by gently discouraging over-protective dependency-inducing behaviour on the part of informal carers.

Third, Table 6.2 conveys that mobilising practical support for old people is anything but a straightforward matter, a point also stressed in the London borough study (Crosbie 1983). The table contains a formidable list of practical services which the social workers attempted to provide but which did not come to fruition for various reasons. Part of the explanation appeared to be that this generation of old people born before the turn of the century tend to be resigned to their decreasing mobility, growing isolation and restriction of their life space, and may prefer to leave things as they are. Skill and sensitivity is needed to know when to desist and respect old people's choice to be left alone. This extends to the serious dilemma facing social workers occasionally whether to take the risk of letting people live in hazardous situations or to resort to protective and control functions. Vickery's as well as Goldberg's study contain telling case examples on this topic. Table 6.2 also shows that the social workers in the special group, despite their casework activities, rendered substantially more practical help to the old people than their colleagues in the group served by welfare officers.

One of the most striking differences relates to links with community facilities, such as day centres, clubs, holidays and outings. Another noticeable difference was the amount of voluntary help used or sought in the special group – for over half the cases – in contrast to 14 per cent in the comparison group. The endeavour to enlist the help of volunteers was mirrored in the far more numerous contacts the experimental social workers had with a large variety of voluntary agencies in the area. Similarly the project workers mobilised or tried to mobilise significantly more health care for their clients than did their colleagues in the comparison group. In other words the social workers' repertoire of intervention techniques and the formal and informal resources they tapped were generally richer and broader than those of the welfare officers and approached in some important respects the kinds of activities Vickery was advocating some 15 years later.

Finally, when relating the social workers' input to the independent assessor's estimate of the clients' needs for social work, it appeared that

Table 6.2   Practical help received and attempted

| | Received | | Attempted but not received | |
| | Percentages | | | |
Type of help	Special group	Comparison group	Special group	Comparison group
Housing:				
Rehousing	6	5	14	6
Admission to residential home	1*	1*	7	12
Domiciliary services:				
Home help	22	6	8	7
Meals on wheels	15	2	5	5
Adaptations	14	2	6	2
Aids	30	23	3	2
Voluntary visiting/ Voluntary help	32	8	25	6
Personal assistance	14	10	2	0
Decoration of home	8	2	7	2
Occupational therapy	5	4	6	1
Health services:				
Chiropody	16	13	3	2
District nurse/bath attendant	6	6	2	2
Medical attention/ hospital admission	31	10	5	3
Community facilities:				
Club/day centre	35	13	35	27
Holidays	23	14	31	13
Outings	21	10	8	4
Transport/escort (e.g. to club)	25	7	3	2
Material aid:				
Christmas parcel	34	21	3	0
Financial help	17	9	5	1
Provision of material goods	5	7	0	0
Extra nourishment	16	2	4	2
Other	4	1	0	1
Average No. of items of help received	3.9	1.8		
	N = 110	N = 104	N = 110	N = 104

* One client in each group was temporarily admitted to a private home.

Source: Goldberg, Mortimer and Williams 1970, p. 115

the trained social workers (who were unaware of these estimates) varied the amount of help they gave people more sharply in accordance with their needs than did the welfare officers in the comparison group. These results resemble those emerging in the Thanet Community Care Project where social service input (and hence cost) is more closely correlated with level of disability in the experimental than in the control group.

The social worker as a co-ordinator of services

Next we want to consider the social work input that is associated with the role of case manager/co-ordinator/monitor. Although this role is generally recognised as increasingly important in the complex social services network, it is as yet underdeveloped, often not explicitly acknowledged, and poorly documented.

The study which has developed and is evaluating this role is the Thanet Community Care Project (whose methodology was outlined in Chapter 3) and its replication studies in Gateshead (Challis *et al* 1981), Gwynedd (Tarran 1981) and Sheppey. The researchers set out to remedy what they considered failures in the current system of community care for frail elderly people:

(i) The frequent inability of the home help service to match resources to a variety of needs of clients which may require specific forms of help at unsocial hours.

(ii) The comparative failure of social workers to tap a wide range of potential sources of care, such as neighbours, other volunteers or paid casual helpers.

(iii) The inadequacy in quantity and quality of social work input.

(iv) The comparative absence of ways of organising and monitoring work which increase accountability without reducing social workers' creativity.

(v) The arbitrary way in which social workers take costs into account – if they do at all.

In order to increase both the range of methods at the social workers' disposal and their accountability, the experiment gave them the control of a budget and encouraged them to introduce new procedures. All expenditures on a case had to be met from this budget which as a rule was not to exceed two-thirds of the cost of a residential place. The social workers were given the unit costs of existing departmental services to aid them in their resource decisions. The budget could be used for statutory services as well as for new extra-departmental resources to maintain clients in the community and improve the quality of their lives. In order to enhance accountability the social workers were asked to record their activities as well as the resources used on a case review form which was adapted for the care of the elderly from the generic instrument developed by Goldberg and Fruin (1976). The social workers' main role became one of case manager, co-ordinator and monitor of various sources of help. To perform these roles successfully the social workers had to employ a wide range of social work techniques, including casework.

Apart from the conventional domiciliary services the main new resource these workers developed was the recruitment of local people, often neighbours, to perform certain tasks for small payments. These tasks, in the main, complement those carried out by domiciliary services and by the principal carers: helping to get the old person up in the morning or back to bed at night, 'filling in' on a variety of tasks at weekends, sitting while the carer has a respite, providing companionship, ensuring that a very depressed or confused person actually eats her meal, helping confused people to shop and organise their household tasks in a more rational manner. For very vulnerable old people who live far from their families, this practical and emotional support seeks to provide a substitute for the relatives' care. For those living with or near their families, the emphasis will be on complementing or supplementing their care. In Thanet, where many old people had moved to the area on retirement, substitute care was needed; in Gateshead, where close-knit family networks abound, relieving the burden on supporters was a frequent aim. Another distinction in operating techniques partly related to the social context and partly to the social workers' background is that in Thanet, where most clients lived alone and were fairly isolated, more emphasis was placed on matching of client need and interests with those of the helper, and the growth of a mutually satisfying relationship, than on geographical proximity. In the replication study in rural North Wales the social worker, who has an orientation towards community work, started from the premise that most people get on with most people, and hence proximity (in any case essential in the widely dispersed rural settlements) was the main principle of helper selection. The community approach is also evident in the way in which this social worker got several people in a village – who knew each other anyway – to form a flexible rota system for those cases which needed very frequent visits and attention.

The social workers in all three schemes have also experimented with informal day care and group discussions in helpers' homes and occasional short-term placements with helpers. The researchers suggest that the social workers' responsibility for a budget encourages the imaginative use of new resources and their co-ordination and flexible adjustment to the client's needs, and seems to be more satisfying to practitioners than the usual routine procedures for elderly clients (Challis and Davies 1980 and 1983).

The social worker as a resource person
Next we want to consider the input of the social worker in her role as a

resource person or consultant to other paid or voluntary and ancillary workers (also a feature of the community care projects). Two current studies will elucidate the social worker's role as a community-oriented resource person to a wide variety of ancillary workers and neighbourhood networks. One is the evaluative pilot study taking place in Normanton in North Yorkshire, which is seeking to compare patch-based social services teams with the more conventional social services delivery in a demographically similar neighbouring area office (McGrath and Hadley 1981). The other is the Neighbourhood Services Project in Dinnington, South Yorkshire. This action research aims to integrate all health and welfare services – statutory, voluntary and informal – at a neighbourhood level, and to evaluate whether this new approach meets the needs of the users of the services more effectively than the strictly departmentalised delivery of services (Bayley *et al* 1981).

Hadley and other proponents of the patch-based system of social services, like Davies and his colleagues, start from a critique of the present mode of service delivery and the social worker's role in it. They question the premise that the delivery of social services is 'mainly a technical matter to be tackled by the managers and professionals working in them' and that it can best be achieved by 'increasingly rigorous application of rational systems of planning and management'. They suggest that the emphasis on professional expertise in large bureaucratic structures such as social services departments increases the gap between service providers and users. This managerial emphasis also implies a hierarchical structure of services in which, for example, the qualified social worker is usually at the top of the fieldwork hierarchy 'typically primarily involved in one-to-one transactions with clients and likely to see emotional or relationship difficulties as the appropriate focus for professional intervention'. The home help is at the bottom responsible to a home help organiser working in isolation from the rest of the area team. Hence – Hadley and McGrath (1980) argue – their knowledge of clients is rarely used (as we have already noted in several contexts) and 'their potential to offer clients far more than a practical cleaning service is often ignored'. Since, so it is argued, social workers usually work with their own caseloads in isolation from others they do not gain an overview of the area as team members and are less likely to collaborate in developing new initiatives. The community-oriented patch system of service delivery, which has been emerging in the late 1970s, emphasises decentralisation and community involvement and a more flexible and open definition of professionalism which recognises and supports the potential of lay workers, ancillaries and voluntary action. The patch system seeks to strengthen informally and formally organised voluntary support and to increase the effectiveness of statutory intervention by early identification of those at risk and by deploying a larger proportion of so-called ancillary workers with the ability to provide help in frontline positions. These ancillaries, it is argued, can provide this immediate help effectively, provided they are adequately backed up by experienced social workers 'who can advise them on any aspects of their work and assume full responsibility for the minority of cases which require substantial professional involvement'. Although the study is concerned with all client groups, the researchers suggest that 'the community-centred methods would appear to be well suited to help elderly clients living at home'.

The area officer in Normanton who originated the patch scheme under study postulates that the method enables patch teams to mobilise more resources, to be in touch with a higher proportion of those at risk and to provide help earlier than conventionally-organised area teams. He argues that since the teams are more integrated into the area they serve they also derive more job satisfaction. The researchers who are testing these hypotheses by comparing various components of input and outcome with those of a neighbouring conventionally-organised area team find some confirmation for these hypotheses in their early provisional findings (personal communication). How much the organisational features contribute to these apparently favourable results and how far any positive outcomes are associated with the back-up and resource role of the trained social worker as patch leader will be difficult to tease out. As usual, one also needs to take account of the enthusiasm engendered by innovative experiments.

The Dinnington Neighbourhood Services Project, directed by Michael Bayley of the University of Sheffield, is arguably the most ambitious and exciting neighbourhood venture yet attempted, since it is making a serious attempt at inter-service collaboration.

The project, which is situated in a mining village comprising some 7,000 inhabitants, is based on:

(i) The awareness of the rapidly increasing numbers of the very old, combined with the likelihood that there will be few additional resources to meet additional demand.

(ii) The awareness of the importance of informal help and the potential benefits if it were possible to interweave statutory services with the informal help already given by family, friends and neighbours. Thus the overall purpose is to develop a pattern of service which will use all available resources, statutory, voluntary and informal.

The study contains an action component in which two specially appointed workers – one attached to housing, the other to the personal social services – are helping service personnel and volunteers in the social, health, housing and education services to work with natural helping networks, using methods developed in the United States by

Collins and Pancoast (1976). The fieldwork is organised on a neighbourhood or patch basis and extends to all client groups, although there
is a heavy concentration on the elderly. The project embodies features
of both the community care projects and the Normanton evaluation;
like the former, the Neighbourhood Services Project seeks to increase
the versatility of approaches used by social workers and to strengthen
their co-ordinating and consultative roles, including greater autonomy
at field level. Like the patch system it concentrates on a small neighbourhood and seeks to strengthen the roles of ancillaries, particularly
those of home helps and wardens who in a pilot survey were shown to
occupy a special position through working and living in the village and
putting in most hours with clients, 'bestriding the boundary between
statutory services and informal care'.

Its 'action goals' also have much in common with the other two
projects:

(i) To meet consumer needs better and to meet the needs of more
     people at the same cost as the present services.
(ii) To increase contact and co-operation between the statutory
     carers, the informal carers and the voluntary bodies.
(iii) To reduce crisis referrals.
(iv) To provide job satisfaction for workers.
(v) To reduce demand for residential care.

Although this study's principal function is to examine the success of the
project's innovations and to test the above propositions, a quasi-
experimental design – comparing the outcomes of the Dinnington
project with a conventional service in a similar district – was rejected as
inappropriate. The researchers argue that such a design would have
assumed knowledge about the nature of the control area's community,
its services and informal networks that could not have been available.
The research methodology consists of a series of monitoring studies at
certain intervals of users, their informal carers, non-users of services, of
statutory and voluntary workers and their activities. It also includes
process studies by observation. Thus it may be possible to show
changes in user attitudes and satisfactions, in worker activities and
attitudes, and particularly in their inter-professional collaboration and
in ways of working with informal caring networks in the community.

The social worker's role as a resource person has also been stressed in
relation to day care and some assisted lodgings schemes. In Chapter 7
we refer to the support given by professionals to the volunteers running
a small club for elderly confused people which was considered an
essential feature of this scheme's viability. Similarly Thornton and
Moore (1980) and Penfold (1980) suggest that social work support to
families offering lodgings to frail elderly people is an important ingredient in its success. A more controversial issue, which as far as we know

has not as yet been investigated, is the role of the field social worker with specialist knowledge in the social care of the elderly as a resource person to residential staff whose background is often in nursing or domestic science rather than in the social and behavioural sciences.

The social worker as community worker

Lastly, we come to the input of social workers in their roles as community workers. Clearly many of the functions in the evaluative projects just discussed have strong associations with community work – recruiting and organising volunteers or semi-volunteers, creating informal neighbourhood care networks, improvising informal day care. Indeed, Hadley (1981) makes the point that in the patch-based system 'community work . . . is part of the job of every member of the patch teams. For example, it might be decided to support a tenants' association, set up a luncheon club for the elderly on the patch, or encourage the establishment of a local advice centre'. He also includes support of informal caring networks as part of community work in this service delivery model.

However, there have been few systematic evaluative studies of community work in social care since the somewhat diffuse attempts in the Home Office-sponsored Community Development Projects of the 1970s. Recently Hatch and his colleagues (1981) carried out a systematic exploration of how social services departments attempt to incorporate a community dimension into their activities. They discovered three different strategies of involving the community: subsidising and working mainly through formal voluntary organisations, incorporating a community dimension in all social work roles, and creating specialist posts. Hatch and his colleagues suggest that even in community-oriented patch-based social work there could be a useful role for a specialist community worker.

At field level the three relevant functions of a specialist would be: organising volunteers, liaising with voluntary organisations, and community development. How these different functions can be most usefully related to each other, what part should remain the domain of the specialist and what part could be incorporated into the fieldworker's role, requires evaluative action studies in different social services structures. One point seems clear: unless the community dimension becomes firmly embedded into statutory social care practices, there seems little chance of relieving loneliness, stimulating feelings of belonging and usefulness, particularly among old people in urban areas, and of creating a sense of reciprocity in actual and potential carers.

Organisational features

Both the community care model of autonomous and responsible case management, in which social workers are encouraged to use statutory and other resources flexibly and cost-effectively, and the more loosely structured community-based functions of the social worker as a resource person and back-up to a variety of statutory and voluntary workers in a neighbourhood or patch, have features in common: both aim at more decentralised forms of organisation and at greater closeness to the clients' everyday life and their customary networks, and increased responsiveness to their needs before a crisis point is reached. Both aim to support the clients themselves as well as the informal networks which bear the tending burdens. Both systems involve volunteers and paid unskilled helpers, as well as skilled social workers. But there are some basic differences: the patch system gives considerable latitude of assessment and action to the frontline worker, who is usually not a trained social worker, in an endeavour to respond quickly and informally to expressed community needs. The community care projects, which so far have only dealt with a specially selected, highly vulnerable group of clients, presuppose expert assessment by qualified senior social workers resulting in a carefully structured plan and package of services. This approach, which includes the social worker's responsibility for a budget, demands detailed accounting of costs and careful monitoring involving more formality in organisational control than the patch system. It also more or less presupposes specialisation, whereas the experienced patch leader is required to have a broadly-based generic approach to social problems. We will pursue the implications of these different approaches in the concluding chapter.

In conclusion, the monitoring and experimental studies demonstrate the continuing importance of the direct assessment, advisory and casework roles of social workers in the social care of an important minority of physically and mentally vulnerable old people. Developments in brief task-centred methods suggest that social workers' expertise in assessment and in joint problem solving may be required only for short spells while the long-term practical service and supporting roles for both the clients and their informal carers are shouldered by others – home helps, good neighbours, volunteers and so on. Since the social and medical care of growing numbers of very old and vulnerable people will be mainly provided by informal care networks, primary health care teams, volunteers, ancillary workers and a variety of day and short-term residential services, it is certain that the indirect roles of social workers as case managers, co-ordinators of services and resource persons will develop and assume central importance. It is also possible that other professionals, such as health visitors or occupational therapists, will move into such co-ordinating roles as is happening in the United States (Caro 1981). Finally it is likely that more appropriate training will be needed for these newly developing social work roles.

Outcome

What are the outcomes of the various social work endeavours discussed in the last section? And what conclusions can we draw for future practice, policy and research?

Consumer views

As discussed in Chapter 3, seeking the views of social work clients on the help they have received and the impact it has made on their lives is a comparatively recent phenomenon. At the time of writing the results of three consumer studies which included elderly people are available, although several others are in progress. The first reports the opinions of the clients in the experimental study *Helping the Aged* (Goldberg *et al* 1970), the second took place in 'Seatown' (Glampson and Goldberg 1976) and the third in Cambridgeshire (Littlechild and Warburton 1981). The common thread running through these three studies is the old people's appreciation of practical help sensitively provided and the feeling of security derived from knowing that there is a caring department in the background.

In all three studies about four-fifths of the clients felt satisfied with the services or help they received, although the term used in *Helping the Aged* was 'helpful'. In this study nearly twice as many clients in the experimental group as in the comparison group had found their contact with the social workers helpful, and twice as many clients referred to practical help. Aids and appliances such as wheelchairs, bath seats and special gadgets were mentioned more than three times as often, and it seemed clear that these aids had made a great deal of difference to their lives. What permeated their positive comments was the pleasure about needs being met, both material and psychological (there were many comments about the personal attributes of the social workers and the relationships they had with them), a feeling of being cared for and the sense of security arising from knowledge of where to turn in time of need. Similarly, in the Seatown study two-thirds of the old clients said that the help they had received made a difference to them personally: aids, services, practical help had made their lives more comfortable and easier. They too valued the feeling of security and support in the background on which they felt they could rely. Both these studies were concerned with clients who received medium or long-term help, while the Cambridgeshire study consisted of a consecutive series of clients who had been referred three months previously, of whom about half had only one or two contacts with the social worker. Again four-fifths expressed satisfaction. Although most of them referred to the benefits accruing from the aids and services they had received, they implied that this had not changed anything in their circumstances. Possibly 'change' was interpreted in more fundamental ways than one could expect from a fairly short-term contact in which mainly practical help was proffered. For example, the carers of the elderly mentally disordered clients did not perceive any change, since the basic problems and the burden of caring still remained. Interestingly in this study, as in other studies (Glendinning 1981, Fisher *et al* 1981) where circumstances had not changed through the intervention of social workers, clients still expressed a high degree of appreciation and satisfaction: the social workers were seen as sympathetic listeners and advisers rather than as change agents. In contrast to the Seatown studies, where social workers grossly underestimated what they had achieved and the degree to which their clients were satisfied with the help they had received, the social workers in Cambridgeshire overestimated the amount of change that had taken place.

An important finding emerging from the Cambridgeshire study was that in about three-fifths of the cases clients and social workers disagreed about the help received from other sources. While social workers were more likely to mention general practitioners (GPs) and other health personnel, the clients talked about the amount of help they got from relatives, friends and neighbours of which the social workers seemed to be unaware. The other discrepancy evident in both the Seatown and Cambridgeshire studies related to closing procedures. A substantial minority of clients thought that their cases were open and they seemed to expect continuing contact with social workers when the social workers considered their cases closed. In a much smaller proportion the reverse was the case and clients thought their cases were closed when in fact they were still open. It seems that while a good deal of expertise is directed towards initial contacts and assessment, comparatively little attention is paid to closing procedures which are of equal importance, particularly among elderly, often lonely and frail people for whom a visit may be an important event.

The high degree of satisfaction expressed by elderly people is often ascribed to low expectations or unwillingness to be seen to criticise. However, in Seatown, where consumer studies were carried out in 1973 and 1975, the satisfaction among elderly clients – probably as a result of a substantial expansion of services – had risen withing this period; also the elderly clients who had come into contact with the department more recently had more specific expectations of the services. These trends suggest that old people react appropriately to current changes.

Outcomes of monitoring studies

The main aim of the monitoring studies using the case review system (Crosbie 1981, Goldberg and Warburton 1979, Grant 1981 a and b, Simons and Warburton 1980) was to ascertain 'who gets what' in an area office – who the clients are, what problems are being tackled, by what means, and with what objectives in mind. The 'outcomes' recorded on a case review form usually reflect the practitioners' judgements on the closure of their cases. As neither the clients' views nor independent observations were available it was considered safer and more reliable to restrict the outcome categories to the main reasons for closure. A case can be closed because *aims have been achieved*; because nothing more can be done, or the case has been deemed 'of low priority' and thus *the department withdraws*; because the client was *referred to another more appropriate agency*; or finally because he *removed* himself from the scene either in this world or on to the next.

Within this limited framework, outcomes in Seatown showed a rather different profile according to whether the elderly client was a recent referral dealt with by the intake team over a short period of time (no longer than three months for about 75 per cent of the elderly cases) or a long-term case. Among the referrals where aims were mainly directed towards bringing about small changes in the personal/social environment by providing a service or practical aid (four-fifths received such help), over half the cases were closed because the aims had been achieved, which represented the highest success rate of any client group. These assessments corresponded well with the independent consumer study in the same area in which the elderly and physically disabled who had received most practical help emerged as the most satisfied of all client groups.

Outcomes appeared to be judged differently among the long-term elderly clients, of whom only two-fifths of cases were closed during the study year in contrast to 90 per cent of the referrals. In only 14 per cent of the long-term closures did the social workers consider that their aims had been achieved, even though the main aim was usually the preservation of the status quo. On the other hand in over half of these cases the reason for closure was 'department withdraws' – the social workers had done all that was possible, although certain problems remained; often domiciliary services were still being delivered and could act as an early warning system if need be. Two-thirds of the long-term elderly clients were expected to continue on the books of the department almost indefinitely. Similar estimates emerged in the monitoring studies in Cambridgeshire (Warburton and Simons 1981) and North Wales (Grant 1981b).

When comparing social work plans with aims achieved, it appeared that in over two-thirds of the cases for whom the continuance of domiciliary services and surveillance were prescribed, unanticipated events outside the control of social workers intervened before the next review. Such events could be illness necessitating admission to hospital, increasing frailty leading to a crisis and sometimes admission to a welfare home or death. These observations suggest that the occasional social work type of surveillance of very frail old people is not particularly useful and that much closer neighbourhood contact and support, either along the lines of the Community Care model or on a patch basis, is needed, and that much better lines of communication need to be established between domiciliary helpers and social workers.

Outcomes of experimental studies

While the purpose of monitoring studies is mainly ongoing review, accountability in deployment of resources, and adjustment of objectives in accordance with clients' needs and circumstances, the question posed by experimental field studies is usually: is treatment A more effective than treatment B? Thus the emphasis shifts markedly towards outcome, although – as was discussed in Chapter 3 – adequate specification and description of input is vital if we want to show why and in what ways treatment A was more or less effective than treatment B, and if we want to replicate the experiments or eventually implement the more effective practices.

The outcome question posed in *Helping the Aged* was: are trained social workers more effective in promoting the well-being of elderly clients than welfare officers without formal training? The methodology and the findings of this study have already been discussed in Chapter 3; we observed earlier in this chapter that the amount and quality of the social work input differed markedly in the experimental and comparison group; this resulted in a significantly greater reduction in practical needs in the experimental group, and in significant improvement in a number of crucial areas of social and psychological functioning. The reduction in practical needs was significantly related to input, as measured in number of contacts and items of practical help given, but the researchers were not able to identify with any precision the elements in the casework process which were responsible for changes in attitudes and feelings, which could only be gleaned from studying individual case examples.

As already indicated, this study has raised crucial methodological issues which might have been partially resolved by replication studies. For example, it has been suggested that the uneven case loads in the two groups were responsible for the different outcomes: the welfare officers had a bigger case load – among them many inactive cases – but much smaller patches, while the experimental workers only carried active cases, were unfamiliar with the area and had a much larger district to cover. It is clear that future experiments should seek to control workload and caseload factors. Such studies could be designed in two ways. If relative effects of different treatments are to be investigated then it would be desirable to keep the caseloads in the control and experimental groups as similar as possible. If on the other hand it is the intention to explore the effect of size of caseload on outcome then one would seek to vary the size of caseload experimentally, while keeping the type of treatment essentially the same for both groups. In order to test the hypothesis that the two workers' personalities, their natural gifts and their enhanced motivation rather than their skills were responsible for the better outcome, one could control numbers of workers in experimental and comparison groups and ensure that both groups of workers are equally well informed about the nature of the experiment.

The study also raises resource issues, since no social services department can afford the luxury of trained social workers providing skilled assessment and concentrated casework for the majority of referrals of elderly people over the age of 70 as was the case in this study. As has already been discussed, if front line workers without formal training make initial assessments, it will be vital that they should be able to spot those people and their carers who need more skilled attention. But further questions arise: how far can the skills that trained social workers are said to possess be diffused by case discussions, supervision and in-service training? Would an expansion of the indirect co-ordinating and back-up roles of social workers in combination with their brief task-centred interventions enable ancillary workers to support fairly complex situations? Some of these questions will be partially answered by the results from the Thanet Community Care Project and its replications, and by other projects in progress. But it is equally important to carry out experimental studies which seek to assess the outcomes of specific intervention techniques carried out by workers with different types and levels of training.

The study of the elderly welfare clients has also highlighted as yet unresolved problems of collaboration with volunteers and other professionals. The social workers encountered difficulties in keeping young volunteers interested and in locating suitable older voluntary visitors. Despite the intensive help the experimental workers were able to give these old people during the course of a year, they felt that the rather restricted lives of many of their clients could have been enriched by volunteers from the neighbourhood. But both recruitment and collaboration posed problems, as often the young volunteers worked to the volunteer organisers rather than to the social workers. The other difficulty experienced was the collaboration with the clients' doctors and the health services generally. The social workers repeatedly noted the reluctance of some general practitioners to intervene actively with the very old, and how little the general practitioners knew about the mental condition of their patients. The minor miseries of old age, such as foot discomforts, neglect of eye examination, wax in the ears, dizziness, urinary symptoms, constipation and poor sleep had increased in both groups at the end of the experiment, despite the attention the clients had received from the social workers. It became clear that the workers had not been able to spot most of these disabilities, nor had they been brought to the notice of the doctors by the clients themselves since they usually would only produce one particular complaint that was worrying them when they saw their doctor. It seemed to the researchers that closer team work between social worker and doctor was essential, which might be achieved by part-time attachments of social workers to general practice or by regular consultations and reviews of elderly clients on the general practitioners' lists. The question of regular screening by community nurses was also considered. Finally, the question was thrown up whether geriatricians should be available for consultation to social service workers concerned with the community care of old people. Little progress seems to have been made in these directions since these questions were first raised in 1970.

Outcomes of quasi-experiments
The final results of the pilot evaluation of the patch-based social service delivery in Normanton are not yet available. Interim findings from the Thanet Community Care Project were published in 1980 (Challis and Davies 1980), and some final results which show considerable benefits accruing to the experimental group have become available as this book is going to press (Challis and Davies 1983). It was possible to match 74 clients in the experimental group on six crucial variables (sex, age, living group, disability, confusion and attitude to help) with 74 clients in the comparison group who had received what the authors call 'conventional care'. Both groups of clients were followed up at the end of a year, and their well-being and location compared with the findings at the first evaluation interviews. As Table 6.3 shows there were striking differences. Sixty eight per cent of the experimental clients remained in their own homes compared with 34 per cent of the clients in the control group; they were less likely to enter residential care (12 per cent compared with 27 per cent), and thirdly there was a marked difference in the death rate (14 per cent compared with 32 per cent). These differences in outcome were highly significant statistically; that is to say the probability of them arising by chance is less than one in a thousand.

Even when cases were not matched and the two samples of 92 experimental and 116 control clients were compared regardless of level of disability etc., the differences were still considerable and statistically significant.

The next question is whether these outcomes were achieved at the cost of clients' or their carers' quality of life. This was not so: the experimental clients had improved significantly in morale and they were significantly less lonely, depressed and anxious compared with

Table 6.3 Location of matched cases after twelve months

| | Experimental group | | Control group | |
| | Very disabled | Moderately disabled | Very disabled | Moderately disabled |
Outcome				
Own home	18	33	10	15
Local authority care	3	—	5	11
Private residential care	1	5	—	4
Moved away	—	1	—	1
Geriatric hospital	2	1	3	1
Psychiatric hospital	—	—	—	—
Died	7	3	13	11
TOTAL	31	43	31	43

Source: Challis and Davies (forthcoming)

clients in the control sample. Similarly the experimental clients' need for various forms of practical help with personal care and household jobs had decreased significantly in contrast to the control group, where levels of need hardly changed.

At what financial cost were these results achieved? Although significantly more clients in the control area received residential care, the average cost borne by the social services department per case per month was less in the experimental group (£51.62) than in the control group (£58.66). However, the researchers stress that the principal research question was not so much 'what difference does this particular scheme make to clients as a group?' as 'to which clients in what kinds of circumstances is this scheme more beneficial and cost-effective compared with the existing provision?'. In order to answer this question the researchers developed what they call 'normative propositions' about the allocation of resources and cost in relation to outcome. They postulated that:

(i) Costs involved in achieving positive outcomes (as measured on morale indicators and survival) would be inversely related to the informal support available. (Scales were developed indicating low, medium and high levels of informal support.)

(ii) Costs involved in achieving positive outcomes would increase with the level of dependency – the more disabled, the greater the input and the higher the cost. (Four levels of disability were distinguished according to the Isaacs/Neville categories – Isaacs and Neville 1976.)

(iii) Costs involved in achieving positive outcomes would be independent of either understatement or overstatement of needs in the form of unjustified demand pressure. In other words, allocation of resources would not be curtailed because people initially rejected help or minimised their difficulties, nor would they be excessive because of vociferous pressure from clients or their families. (The attitudes to help were rated by the evaluator.)

So far the results bear out some of these 'normative' relationships between potential for informal support, level of disability, consumer pressure and resource allocation, cost and outcome. Not only were resources allocated more rationally in the experimental group than in the control group – that is to say the amount and intensity of input took account of the amount of informal support available, was positively correlated with the level of dependency, and was relatively unaffected by 'under' or 'over' demand – but the resource distributions also proved more cost-effective in relation to outcome in most situations.

There have been some interesting exceptions, however. The normative proposition about the relationship between cost and informal support did not hold in either experimental or conventional provision. In the case of the latter, informal support tended to increase costs: supporters, if unassisted (which was frequently the case), became a pressure group demanding expensive residential care. It appeared that in the experimental provision there was no relationship between informal support and increased costs because the carers, given support earlier, were enabled to continue their caring activities.

The conventional provision proved to be more cost-effective for old people with the highest dependency ratings largely because they were an 'unmet need' group who received very little from the conventional services; often the provision available was unsuitable and therefore rejected by a family caring for a very frail old person.

Caution is indicated in interpreting these interim results, as the researchers have yet to relate cost to other outcome variables such as reduction in practical needs. They also have not yet been able to include costs borne by the health services. Further work may be required to tease out the important but subtle relationships between service input and potential for informal support. These relationships may become clearer in the analysis of the Gateshead project where the support of informal carers is a more prominent feature. The comparative analysis of community care project data in various other areas will further elucidate these relations. However, there is little doubt that the ability to relate costs and outcomes to three such crucial interacting variables as levels of dependency, potential for informal support and consumer pressure represents an important step forward in evaluative research methodology. The practical outcomes in themselves – undoubtedly enriched by innovative enthusiasm – are also remarkable. They indicate that packages of service, imaginatively tailored to individual needs and carefully monitored, not only 'keep very vulnerable old people out of institutional care' but significantly improve the quality of their lives and apparently serve to prolong life as well.

Clearly the general implications of this experiment are considerable: they point towards greater autonomy of social workers not only as mobilisers of resources but also as resource holders, monitors and co-ordinators of care services. The experiment also opens up possibilities towards developing purchase of service by statutory authorities. Finally the project seems to indicate the need for greater specialisation in social work with old people. Community care projects in other areas, including very rural ones in Kent and North Wales, and a northern metropolitan district with a densely populated inner city area and outlying villages, may produce variations of the model in accordance with socio-demographic and cultural features. It is also evident that the model holds out promise of applying similar methods to other chronically disabled client groups needing long-term practical and emotional support and care.

Conclusions and issues arising

Although orthodox social work seems to play such a peripheral role in the social care of old people at present, both past and current evaluative studies suggest that social workers may have a more central contribution to make in the future. Their assessment or diagnostic skills will need to be used more extensively, particularly among very vulnerable old people and among those whose problems transcend the need for straightforward practical assistance. The social workers' casework roles may have to take on new directions – away from long-term intermittent 'support' towards more specific short-term therapeutic interventions. Their roles as mobilisers of resources, co-ordinators of services and resource persons to a variety of other carers or caring schemes may have to expand considerably.

Finally we are left with three questions:

(i) Do these functions demand post-qualification specialisation in gerontology?
(ii) Do these functions demand a major shift in the training of social workers and others towards preparation for indirect roles as case managers and co-ordinators? Could such roles be shared by personnel with different professional backgrounds, such as health visitors or occupational therapists, so that the back-up services would become multi-disciplinary?
(iii) How can collaboration between health and personal social services be brought about that is not dependent solely on the good will or insight of individual workers but is based on firm organisational arrangements and structural mechanisms designed to enhance collaboration?

References

Abrams, M. (1980) *Beyond Three-score and Ten: A second report on a survey of the elderly*, Mitcham, Age Concern.

Bayley, M., Parker, P., Seyd, R. and Tennant, A. (1981) *Origins, Strategy and Proposed Evaluation*, Neighbourhood Services Project – Dinnington, Paper No. 1, University of Sheffield Department of Sociological Studies.

Brewer, C. and Lait, J. (1980) *Can Social Work Survive?* London, Temple Smith.

Briar, S. (1968) The casework predicament, *Social Work 13*, 5–11.

Caro, F.G. (1981) Demonstrating community-based long-term care in the United States, in E.M. Goldberg and N. Connelly (eds) *Evaluative Research in Social Care*. London, Heinemann Educational Books Ltd.

Challis, D., Chessum, R. and Luckett, R. (1981) *Gateshead Community Care Scheme*, Report No. 1, Gateshead Social Services Department.

Challis, D. and Davies, B. (1980) A new approach to community care for the elderly, *British Journal of Social Work 10*, 1–18.

Challis, D. and Davies, B. (forthcoming) *Matching Resources to Needs in Community Care: An evaluation of the experiment in the social care of the frail elderly*.

Collins, A. and Pancoast, D. (1976) *Natural Helping Networks: A strategy for prevention*, Washington DC, National Association of Social Workers.

Cooper, M. (1981b) *Needs assessment of elderly clients: new operational procedures briefing*, Essex Social Services Department Research Section.

Corrigan, P. and Leonard, P. (1978) *Social Work Practice under Capitalism: A Marxist approach*, London, Macmillan.

Crosbie, D. (forthcoming) A Role for Anyone? A description of social work with the elderly in two area offices, *British Journal of Social Work*.

Fisher, M., Newton, C. and Sainsbury, E. (1981) Social work support to people suffering mental ill-health and to their families, University of Sheffield Department of Sociological Studies. Unpublished report to DHSS.

Gibbons, J. (1981) An evaluation of the effectiveness of social work intervention using task-centred methods after deliberate self-poisoning in E.M. Goldberg and N. Connelly (eds), *Evaluative Research in Social Care*. London, Heinemann Educational Books Ltd.

Glampson, A. and Goldberg, E.M. (1976) Post Seebohm social services: the consumer's viewpoint, *Social Work Today* 9 November.

Glendinning, C. (1981) *Resource Worker Project Final Report*, University of York Department of Social Administration and Social Work, Social Policy Research Unit. Unpublished report to DHSS.

Goldberg, E.M., Mortimer, A. and Williams, B.T. (1970) *Helping the Aged: A field experiment in social work*, London, George Allen and Unwin.

Goldberg, E.M. and Fruin, D.J. (1976) Towards accountability in social work: a case review system for social workers, *British Journal of Social Work 6*, 3–22.

Goldberg, E.M. and Warburton, R.W. (1979) *Ends and Means in Social Work: The development and outcome of a case review system for social workers*, London, George Allen and Unwin.

Goldberg, E.M., Gibbons, J. and Sinclair, I.A.C. (1983) *Problems, Tasks and Outcomes: The evaluation of task centred casework in three settings*, London, George Allen and Unwin.

Grant, G. (1981a) *Monitoring Social Services Delivery in Rural Areas: Intake cases in two contrasting teams*, Social Services in Rural Areas Research Project Working Paper 14, University College of North Wales, Bangor, Department of Social Theory and Institutions.

Grant, G. (1981b) *Monitoring Social Services Delivery in Rural Areas: Long-term work in two contrasting area teams*, Social Services in Rural Areas Research Project Working Paper 15, University College of North Wales, Bangor, Department of Social Theory and Institutions.

Hadley, R. (1981) Social services departments and the community, in E.M. Goldberg and S. Hatch (eds.) *A New Look at the Personal Social Services*, PSI Discussion Paper no.4, London, Policy Studies Institute.

Hadley, R. and McGrath, M. (1980) *Going Local*, London, Bedford Square Press.

Hatch, S., Smolka, G. and Mocroft, I. (1981) Social services departments and the community. Unpublished report to DHSS, London, Policy Studies Institute.

Hollis, F. (1968) A profile of early interviews in marital counselling, *Social Casework, 49*, 35–43.

Holme, A. and Maizels, J. (1978) *Social Workers and Volunteers*, London, BASW/George Allen and Unwin.

Howe, D. (1980) Divisions of labour in the area teams of social services departments, *Social Policy and Administration 14*, 133–150.

Huws Jones, R. (1959) Is our social worker really necessary? *The Almoner 12*, 61–69.

Hunt, A. (1978) *The Elderly at Home*, London, HMSO.

Isaacs, B. and Neville, Y. (1976) The needs of old people: the 'interval' as a method of measurement, *British Journal of Preventive and Social Medicine 30*, 79–85.

Levin, E. (1982) The supporters of confused elderly persons in the community, Research report in preparation, London, National Institute for Social Work.

Littlechild, R.J. and Warburton, R.W. (1981) *Ah Yes, I Remember It Well. A research study of the perceptions of team members and clients referred to a Social Services team in Cambridgeshire between October and December 1980*, Cambridgeshire County Council Social Services Department and University of Birmingham.

Mayer, J. and Timms, N. (1970) *The Client Speaks*, London, Routledge and Kegan Paul.

McGrath, M. and Hadley, R. (1981) Evaluating patch-based social services teams: a pilot study, in E.M. Goldberg and N. Connelly (eds.) *Evaluative Research in Social Care*, London, Heinemann Educational Books Ltd.

McKay, A., Goldberg, E.M. and Fruin, D.J. (1973) Consumers and a social services department, *Social Work Today*, 15 November.

Meyer, H.J., Borgatta, E. and Jones, W. (1965) *Girls at Vocational High: An experimental study in social work intervention*, New York, Russell Sage.

Mullen, E.J. (1968) Differences in worker style in casework, *Social Casework, 49*, 546–551.

Neill, J.E., Fruin, D.J., Goldberg, E.M. and Warburton, R.W. (1973) Reactions to integration, *Social Work Today, 4*. 15.

Neill, J.E., Warburton, R.W. and McGuiness, B. (1976) Post Seebohm social services: the social worker's viewpoint, *Social Work Today*, 1 November.

Penfold, M.E. (1980) *Family Homes for the Handicapped Final Report*, North Yorkshire Social Services Department.

Reid, W.J. (1967) Characteristics of casework intervention, *Welfare in Review*, 5, no. 8, 11–19.

Reid, W.J. and Hanrahan, P. (1981) The effectiveness of social work: recent evidence, in E.M. Goldberg and N. Connelly (eds) *Evaluative Research in Social Care*, London, Heinemann Educational Books Ltd.

Reid, W.J. and Shyne, A.W. (1969) *Brief and Extended Casework*, New York, Columbia University Press.

Sainsbury, E. (1980) Client need, social work method and agency function: a research perspective, *Social Work Service 23*, 9–15.

Simons, K. and Warburton, R.W. (1980) The clients of three social work teams and the help they receive, Unpublished report to DHSS. Cambridgeshire Social Services Department.

Sinfield, A. (1969) *Which Way for Social Work?* Fabian Tract 393, London, Fabian Society.

Stevenson, O. and Parsloe, P. (Directors, DHSS Social Work Research Project) (1978) *Social Service Teams: The Practitioner's View*, London, HMSO.

Tarran, E. (1981) *Caring for dependent elderly people in rural areas by means of enhanced forms of community support. Interim Research Report of a community care project in Anglesey – "Gofal"*, Social Services in Rural Areas Research Project Working Paper 20, University College of North Wales (Bangor) Dept. of Social Theory and Institutions.

Thornton, P. and Moore, J. (1980) *The Placement of Elderly People in Private Households: An analysis of current provision*, Department of Social Policy and Administration Research Monograph, University of Leeds.

Vickery, A. (1981) Consultation on 64 cases of elderly people living alone referred for social work help. Draft report, London, National Institute for Social Work.

Warburton, R.W., and Simons, K. (1981) An overview of the results to emerge from the Case Review System deployed by three social services teams in Cambridgeshire to record who their clients were and what helped they received, Cambridgeshire Social Services Department.

Wootton, B. (1959) *Social Science and Social Pathology*, London, George Allen and Unwin.

7　Day Care Services

What is day care?
Day care is regarded as an important element within the community services; it can delay or avert residential care and at the same time enrich the lives of the able-bodied 'young olds' as well as the frail 'old olds'. For elderly people living alone, possibly supported by various forms of domiciliary services, day care can provide as a minimum a change of scene and the stimulation of contact with others. For the physically or mentally frail old person living with relatives – perhaps themselves elderly – it can provide the break for both which may ease difficulties and stresses in the relationship.

Day care spans a wide range of aims and activities. There are purpose-built centres provided by local authorities and voluntary organisations, offering many activities and services, including transport. There are day places in local authority old people's homes. There are day hospitals providing rehabilitative therapy or maintenance treatment for those who are arthritic, who have suffered strokes or trauma or organic brain damage or who have functional mental disorders. All these facilities aim at providing care or therapy. But there are also many other kinds of day services intended primarily or in part for elderly people, including lunch clubs, drop-in centres, social facilities attached to sheltered housing schemes or to housing estates generally; there are sheltered workshops, further education classes and so on. At one end of the spectrum a five or seven day a week full time service may provide a high degree of care for very disabled elderly people in a purpose-built centre or day hospital; at the other end may be a social club run by its members and meeting for a few hours each week in a church hall.

There is as yet no fully developed 'day care service' in the sense of a continuum from day hospitals for the treatment and rehabilitation of severely mentally and physically disabled people through day centres for the maintenance of frail and disabled elderly people to social centres serving as recreational facilities for the more able-bodied. Day care facilities are still somewhat patchy, provided under a variety of auspices, both statutory and voluntary. There can also be considerable overlap between the different facilities: in the characteristics of users, in auspices, type and level of activities, and so on. Thus a day care facility may serve at any one time varying proportions of the elderly and other groups (for example, younger physically handicapped), recently-retired active people and quite disabled or confused older people, those who have been referred by professionals and those who come of their own accord, those who participate actively and those who are passive recipients of care.

Given this wide variety of users and organisational frameworks, by what criteria can the developing day care services be assessed, how can we look at the effectiveness of current provision? As in the examination of other aspects of social care, our first question will be concerned with aims. Secondly, we will have to establish what needs this service is intended to meet, and how these are assessed initially and subsequently. For example, how can we distinguish need for day care in any given context from need for friendship, access to an interest group (not necessarily age-based), need for counselling after bereavement, or need for a more total environmental change, such as residential care? How are the needs of one person balanced against the needs of others in a situation of limited resources and enormous variation of provision in different areas? We then need to consider the content of day care, including organisational aspects and how their appropriateness can be assessed. Finally, as always, the question arises how to measure the impact of day care.

After a note on the sources of information available and the background of day care, we shall take up these questions in turn.

Sources of information

In the past few years a number of social services departments have carried out studies of one or more day centres within their authorities; descriptions of innovative schemes appear in social services journals from time to time. However, more complete and systematic information arising from major pieces of research has recently become available. The National Institute for Social Work (NISW) five year study of adult day care, sponsored by the Joseph Rowntree Memorial Trust (Carter 1981), examined day care facilities for all adult user groups, including the elderly, in a stratified random sample of 13 local authority areas in England and Wales. One hundred and nine day units for the elderly, including 16 situated in residential homes, were studied. Postal questionnaires were completed by the heads of all these units and interviews with staff and users were carried out in 35 of them. (The elderly were also found in substantial numbers in units for other groups, notably the physically handicapped.) A similar study was carried out in Scotland (Tibbitt and Tombs 1981). In addition, three studies of day care for the elderly were commissioned by the DHSS from the Universities of Birmingham, Bradford and East Anglia: these attempted to describe the complete range of facilities in their respective areas, with a more detailed look at a sample of these. (Bowl *et al* 1978; Clegg 1978; Fennell *et al* 1981).

In the field of day hospital care, more specialised authoritative background studies have also become available recently. Two comprehensive national surveys of day hospital provision and its development between 1970 and 1980 were carried out by Brocklehurst (Brocklehurst 1970, and Brocklehurst and Tucker 1980). Martin and Millard (1978), in a more intensive study of geriatric day hospitals in one region, tried to separate the therapeutic effectiveness of such hospitals from their social purposes. MIND sponsored a survey of 27 days hospitals for the elderly mentally infirm in England and Wales (Peace 1980).

Background

Most of the rapid growth in day care provision for the elderly has been quite recent. The National Institue for Social Work (NISW) study of day care showed that three-quarters of the day care units for the elderly had been established since 1970 (Carter 1981). The National Assistance Act 1948 had empowered local authorities to provide centres for the handicapped where care and social activities might take place; in 1960 this power became a duty. The National Assistance Amendment Act 1962 empowered local authorities to provide meals and recreation for the elderly; they could use voluntary bodies as their agents in this, or assist such bodies in cash or in kind.

It is not clear how widely local authorities have used these powers and how extensive the voluntary contribution is. This uncertainty stems from the comparative 'invisibility' of much voluntary provision, and the complexity of voluntary-statutory financial and other relationships; also the character of some voluntary centres may preclude administrative tidiness, such as the keeping of attendance registers. It is frequently noted, too, that many of the more ambulant users attend several clubs or centres, and even those requiring transport may well use more than one. DHSS guidelines recommend three to four places per 1,000 elderly (as compared, they estimate, with about two already existing), but this seems to refer to places in the more formally organised day centres provided directly by local authorities (DHSS 1976). Hunt, in her survey of those aged 65 and over living in the community, asked all except the bedfast and housebound whether they ever went to 'any social centres specially for elderly people' – 'social centre' was deliberately not defined. Seventy seven per cent said they never went at all, while 11.6 per cent said they went once a week or more (men: 6.8 per cent; women: 14.8 per cent) (Hunt 1978).

The fullest information available comes from the national day care studies. The NISW researchers describe as 'startling' the variations in provision among the 13 authorities studied, from a country with an estimated 0.8 places per 1,000 people aged 65 and over, to two London boroughs with an estimated 15.6 and 25.8 places for the elderly; these figures include voluntary, Area Health Authority and social services department provision, but exclude lunch clubs meeting for less than three or four hours a day, and centres for the elderly mentally infirm. In the two London boroughs just mentioned, the bulk of provision was voluntary: 12.4 places out of 15.6, and 24.4 out of 25.8. Overall, the studies indicate that the voluntary sector provides 57 per cent of the day care places for the elderly in England and Wales. In Scotland three out of four day centres are provided by voluntary organisations.

The aims of day care

The aims of day care vary in relation to the perceived needs and levels of functioning of elderly people involved.

(i) The most frequently mentioned aim is the opportunity for the elderly – especially those who live alone – to get out of the house, to socialise, and to enjoy a meal in company.

(ii) The second aim often mentioned is to relieve strain on relatives, especially on those caring for the very elderly, physically disabled or mentally confused who require almost constant attention.

(iii) Some day centres, but especially psychogeriatric day hospitals, aim at functional improvement – the re-awakening or awakening of latent capacities that are still usable. Such aims of functional and attitudinal improvement are particularly relevant to the needs of the very depressed and isolated who have 'given up', and also to the needs of those whose carers give them few opportunities for exercising the skills they still possess. Techniques such as social skills training and reality orientation bring the aim of functional improvement within the reach of even seriously confused day care users.

(iv) Geriatric day hospitals aim at rehabilitation and maintenance after a stroke, joint or bone disease, falls and so on, and they also may aim at containment and stabilisation in relation to relief of pain in chronic or terminal illness. Recently the aims of day hospitals have become more sharply focused on medical assessment, rehabilitation and maintenance treatment, rather than on social aims and long-term support (Brocklehurst and Tucker 1980). These developments are probably related to the rapid expansion of social day care centres in both the statutory and voluntary sectors.

(v) Finally, one of the aims of day care for the elderly (especially that taking place in residential homes) may be to offer a substitute for residential care, or to prepare the elderly for residential care.

Some researchers, after examining activities and objectives 'in action' as it were, have remarked on the 'modest' goals of day care providers. It has been suggested that they tend to settle for levels of activity and attendance lower than, in principle, seem attainable. It has also been questioned how much the aims of day care are designed to enrich everyday life *outside* the day care setting, rather than merely to fill in a day in the lives of lonely and disabled people by a pleasant outing. We will take up some of these questions later on in this chapter, but they clearly point to the need for more detailed user studies, both by interview and more informal observation in day care settings.

Needs for day care

Elderly people seen as appropriate users of day services at present seem to fall roughly into five categories:

(i) Those who are reasonably well and active, who choose to go – or are encouraged by family, friends or professionals to go – to lunch clubs, drop-in centres, the less formally-organised day centres. This may be partly seen as a pleasurable way of passing the time and meeting people, partly as a source of a meal, or as an incentive to develop new skills and interests or as a preventive activity.

(ii) Those who are physically fit but who, because of isolation, loneliness, or recent bereavement are thought by others (and may well feel themselves) to be in need of some kind of external stimulus to encourage or renew interest in living, and prevent a chronic state of depression. (Since at a conservative estimate at least one-fifth of the very elderly in the general population are often lonely and some ten per cent suffer from depression, the potential needs in this group are very great.)

(iii) Those who have completed hospital in-patient treatment, for example, after a fall or a stroke or for diseases of the joints, but who will benefit from further treatment at a day hospital; or who have some condition where pain may be kept in check and deterioration slowed down through regular therapy.

(iv) Those who are physically disabled to such an extent that they cannot leave their own homes without aid. Day care with transport may provide their only opportunity for a change of scene, for access to the company of others and some services. The need to provide respite for care-giving relatives is important here.

(v) The confused or mentally ill elderly, especially those who are living with relatives. (Perhaps, too, those living in residential homes not segregated by mental state, although this may not be practicable as the number of confused residents keeps rising.) Depending partly on the degree of confusion, but perhaps more frequently on availability of particular day facilities and their transport arrangements, attendance may be at geriatric or psychogeriatric day hospitals, or at integrated or segregated clubs or centres.

The extent to which individuals within these five groups have access to various types and amounts of day care may depend on many factors: whether they live in a rural or urban area and in the north or the south (Carter has pointed to a marked difference in the availability of physiotherapists in different parts of the country), the type and level of health service provision, the weight attached by social service providers to day care, the strength of the local voluntary contribution, and the availability of transport.

There are some indications that those in greatest apparent 'need' of day care may receive least (Edwards *et al* 1980): the NISW data suggest that the most disabled who are completely dependent on transport get substantially less day care than the fitter and more mobile elderly. Thus the average attendance of very disabled users who are dependent on transport was between one and two days per week compared with three to four days for the more mobile group. It is of course possible that the more disabled elderly can only summon up enough energy to turn out one or two days in a week.

It has also been suggested that among the mobile elderly it is the most gregarious who are likely to be users of day care facilities, possibly the very people who could be encouraged to run their own social and recreational facilities. On the other hand (as already mentioned) there may be relatively isolated, lonely and depressed elderly people who could benefit from spending some time outside their homes in a stimulating environment if they could be helped to overcome their resistance or apathy. Another group whose needs are possibly not being met at present are those very disabled, frail and isolated elderly people with pronounced intellectual and cultural interests. The studies also indicate that the preponderance of women in the centres shape their activities so that the interests and needs of men are often not catered for.

There may well be situations in which day care is an inappropriate way of meeting needs. The East Anglia researchers quote examples of almost intolerable stress on caring relatives, and possibly also on the elderly person. In such cases they considered day care served to 'prolong the agony' and residential care ought not to have been delayed or averted (Fennell *et al* 1981). Bergmann *et al* (1978), and more recently Mendel (1979b) have argued that the prognosis for some seriously confused elderly people who live alone is so bad that available resources should be kept for those living with supporting relatives; and Arie (1975) has suggested that places should be reserved for those who are aware and retain some consciousness of the change which day care provides. All these considerations point to the crucial importance of careful assessment of need, which takes into account the old person's state as well as the needs of his carer, followed by a realistic appraisal of the specific benefits to be derived from day care.

Referral and assessment

Assessment criteria will vary according to the aims pursued and the needs to be fulfilled. Attendance at a luncheon club or at a drop-in centre will be almost entirely at the discretion of the elderly person, while in the case of day centres catering for more disabled users access may depend on assessment and referral by a social worker or other professional. However, there are also examples of a deliberate policy to mix referred frail and disabled elderly with drop-in users in the hope that their complementary needs may be conducive to a more lively atmosphere and encourage mutual help. In general, the studies do not reveal how criteria of need for day care are defined and how the service providers weigh up the specific contribution of day care in relation to other help such as voluntary visiting, mutual help, neighbourhood care, etc. Nor do the studies or our own observations tell us how much day care is part of a *co-ordinated service plan* related to other domiciliary or health services in response to assessed needs in individual cases.

Assessment criteria are much clearer for referral to day hospital care, although problems of co-ordination can arise when the maximum therapeutic benefit has been derived from hospital attendance and other possibilities of maintenance and/or social care need to be explored.

Content of day care

How does one assess the essential inputs of day care and their appropriateness for various client needs? Inputs range from material resources such as buildings, equipment and transport, to the nature and extent of the activities taking place, the behaviour and attitudes of staff and users and their interactions.

Most of the researchers comment on the need, not necessarily for purpose-built *premises*, but for premises well adapted to the requirements of very frail/disabled elderly people, with adequate access space for wheel chairs, absence of stairs, suitable toilet arrangements and so on. On the other hand, shop premises or converted church halls may provide an adequate setting for a relatively mobile group. Since well adapted premises require a good deal of capital outlay, day care centres run by the voluntary sector are usually less well equipped and hence more restricted in what they can offer to the very disabled than the statutory sector.

Every writer on day care considers that *transport* is an essential factor in determining the success of the enterprise. It has been pointed out that unpredictability of transport gives rise to anxiety among relatives and the users and can undermine the benefits which the user may gain from attendance. Extended pick-up rounds may mean that some people only spend two or three hours at a centre while others have a very long day. Transport is a costly ingredient – the tables on cost in the East Anglian report show that it often constitutes about a quarter of the total costs or half the salary bill. Martin and Millard (1978) also estimate that transport costs to day hospitals in the South West Thames hospital region double the salary bill. The East Anglian researchers suggest that a centre of average size (having between 25 and 30 users), typically catering for the housebound, handicapped and frail, should have for its exclusive use in the mornings and evenings two local authority ambulances with tail lifts and a driver and an escort. The reports also vividly demonstrate the key roles of drivers and escorts in making the journey smooth and enjoyable. The ever rising cost of petrol may make the problem of transport even more difficult in the future, and may force planners to think more in terms of neighbourhood activities; some of the community care projects discussed in Chapter 6, and the Coventry Home Help Project, have experimented with informal day care in private houses. A mobile day centre which provides companionship and recreation in two localities around Sunderland for some 40 frail, mildly disabled elderly people has, according to Kaim-Caudle (1977), 'proved itself to be an economic and acceptable day care provision'. Another apparently promising development in psychiatric day care overcomes the transport problem in rural areas by bringing the day care team to the patients on a sessional basis in three small market towns in West Dorset (Shires 1977).

Another important input to day care is the cooked mid-day meal. Although the nutritional contribution can be critical among those unable or unwilling to cook – the confused, the very frail, the very depressed – it is the social aspect of having a meal in company that is stressed by staff and users alike. Some researchers see the extension of lunch clubs with flexible hours and informal activities catering for those who do not need specific rehabilitative or therapeutic activities as a potential relatively inexpensive development already taking place in housing estates and other urban centres. It might even prove possible to develop small informal lunch clubs in rural areas, now that frozen meals are easily available.

How does one evaluate what goes on in the day centres? Social activities may be confined to knitting and chatting and watching television, or may extend much beyond this to craftwork, singing, bingo, entertainments, outings and educational pursuits. Clearly activities are partly related to the functions and objectives of particular day facilities, the resources at their disposal, both material and in staff skills, and the philosophy which informs the regimes; activities will also depend on the capacities, the degree of homogeneity and involvement of the users, and so on. Researchers have raised a number of important issues about both the type and level of activities found in centres: 'there is a tendency for centres to settle to a lower level of attendance and activity than is in principle attainable' (Fennell *et al* 1981). The Birmingham researchers comment that activities in the voluntary sector tend to be routinised and unvaried (Bowl *et al* 1978). Carter (1981) too has deplored the dull routine found in many centres for the elderly. These researchers concede that some users may genuinely want nothing more than the opportunity to sit and chat, and those who are very frail and disabled may not have the energy to do anything else after making the effort to turn out. But it has also been shown that day care can play a more stimulating and positive role in the lives of elderly people. At the Miller Day Centre in Caterham, users help with the making of costumes, printing of tickets, folding programmes etc. for the attached amateur theatre endowed by the same charity (Anon. 1978); Cheeseman (1980) reports an autobiographical writing project she undertook in a Stoke-on-Trent day centre; Simes and his colleagues (1980) describe their exploratory project bringing library services to three day centres. Day centres can, also, be more related to everyday life than often seems the case at present: helping users with their mending and alteration of clothes; using the kitchen for relearning or discovering simple cookery skills which might make their meals more attractive and nutritious; or perhaps rekindling interests in politics or current news.

Imaginative experimenting and case studies are badly needed to explore such possibilities. One sociological case study of a day centre in North London describes how a social culture was created substituting social involvement, mutual help, orientation to and enjoyment of the present, and a certain amount of control over the environment for the helpless 'limbo' state in which many of the users were said to live outside (Hazan 1980). The author observed how people who could not be socialised into such a mutual help culture were 'frozen out'. This study – with its vignettes of users, care personnel, and their interaction within the structure of the setting – reminds us how little is known about the perceptions, expectations and processes of adaptation that elderly people experience in day care and how these experiences relate to their everyday lives.

Day care activities, especially in the well equipped local authority premises, also include much appreciated *services* – chiropody, hairdressing, laundry facilities and bathing equipment (this last not so much because the elderly have no baths in their homes, but because they may require special equipment or help). A sensitive line needs to be drawn between making these services easily accessible to the very disabled and frail, while not discouraging those who can still, for example, visit the hairdresser, from doing so.

Day hospitals, and some of the fully equipped day centres, offer *treatment* to the disabled users. However, the NISW study found that treatment was frequently a relatively minor part of attendance at day hospitals. Yet Brocklehurst and Tucker (1980) report that in over four-fifths of the cases rehabilitation, assessment and maintenance were the main reasons for patients' attendance at day hospitals and that only 17 per cent were thought to come for mainly social reasons. On the face of it, figures collected during a sample week in 1977 in 104 geriatric day hospitals in Britain suggest considerable treatment activity. For example, among an average daily attendance of 23, nurses gave attention to 18 patients per day, a physiotherapist treated 19 patients, and an occupational therapist 14 per day. Only a few patients were seen during the sample week by speech therapists, dieticians or social workers. These figures do not indicate how much time was actually spent with individual patients. Since there was on average only the equivalent of one full-time occupational and physiotherapist per day hospital, the amount of time spent with a patient per day could hardly have been more than ten minutes in many of the hospitals. Group activities clearly would extend the contact time. But these time budgets barely allow any time for discussing with relatives how to help patients. Martin and Millard, who called their study *Day Hospitals for the Elderly: Therapeutic or Social?*, have also explored how much treatment actually occurs in these facilities. In the South West Thames Region hospitals investigated, the amount of time available for occupational therapy was very low, and that for physiotherapy even less.

At a third of the units, less than ten minutes, and at two-thirds, less than twenty minutes of time was available per day. This hardly justified the claim made at all bar one of the geriatric day hospitals that physiotherapy is a major reason for attendance. One does not need to be present all day to see either a doctor, occupational therapist or physiotherapist for less than twenty minutes.

Martin and Millard come to the firm conclusion that the therapeutic and social activities of many of the day hospitals are incompatible, and that many of the units because of their size, staffing, and lack of new patients fulfil a social rather than a therapeutic role. Hence they suggest two types of day hospitals for elderly people, one a small therapeutic unit for about 20 day places, located in the centre of a catchment area at the acute hospital, which would be geared to intensive rehabilitation in association with a medical out-patient department for treatment and investigation, and the other a medium-sized club with 20 to 30 places for those people who are severely disabled and who would gain benefit from regular attendance at a social gathering which was also associated with some medical, nursing and rehabilitation supervision.

Brocklehurst, as early as 1970, suggested that the purpose of treatment and rehabilitation in day hospitals for the elderly would be defeated if at the completion of treatment there was no outlet to a day centre. During the 1970s the situation improved and by 1977 17 per cent of those discharged were referred to day centres. But many physicians in charge of day hospitals had encountered difficulties in referring their patients because of waiting lists or transport problems in day centres. Despite these efforts to step up the transfer from day hospital to day centre, the East Anglian researchers found that the organisers of day care in that region had never contemplated this kind of link-up!

What dosage of day care is appropriate in different situations? Patterns of attendance may not be related to individual need but to administrative constraints, such as transport and availability of places. We have already mentioned the NISW data which indicate that the very disabled and physically or mentally frail elderly who cannot leave their houses by themselves get less day care compared with their mobile contemporaries, because of their dependence on transport. The studies show that the majority of users attend two or three days a week. In the day hospitals twice weekly attendance was found to be the common pattern. The majority of the users declared themselves satisfied with this frequency of attendance, but between one-fifth and two-fifths would have liked to go more often.

The studies seem to suggest that, particularly in rural areas, day centres are not always full to capacity, which may indicate a need for regular monitoring. The NISW study reports only a 70 per cent occupancy rate in the community-based social services day centres for the elderly during their sample week. The mean occupancy during the sample week in Brocklehurst's national survey in 1977 was 75 per cent, and Martin and Millard report an occupancy rate of only 63 per cent in the South West Thames region. Yet, as we have seen, day hospitals experience difficulties in referring patients to day centres on account of waiting lists. A simple expedient used by providers of very scarce day care resources for severely demented patients is that of over-booking, since among this very frail group attendance will always be irregular.

Where the main aim of day care is to relieve the burden on relatives, all researchers have pointed out that the day needs to be long enough to enable the carer to go out for a few hours or even, more controversially, to go out to work full time.

Different researchers come to rather different conclusions about the optimal social composition of day care users. The summary report of the DHSS-sponsored locality studies goes for homogeneity: it suggests that new users should find in the centre sufficient numbers of others similar to themselves in terms of social class, area of residence, disability and sex (Fennell *et al* 1978). At Desborough Hall, a joint voluntary-statutory centre specifically intended to cater for both referred disabled and drop-in mobile elderly people, the fitter members help the less fit, and part of the success of the centre is seen to be the blurring of helper/helped roles (Fletcher and Robinson 1974). The evaluators found no underlying strain or evidence of ill-feeling or friction between younger and older clients, the more and less able, referred and drop-in clients or between any other groups. The researchers suggest that in this mixed milieu clients identify with participatory roles rather than with the traditional client role which tends to emphasise their relative inactivity and dependence.

Reed (1979) attempted a more sophisticated evaluative study of the pros and cons of mixing handicaps and age groups in a day centre. Although the elderly formed only a very small proportion of the population studied, which consisted of 130 mentally handicapped people, 25 mentally ill people and 15 physically handicapped people, his methods are worth noting: having defined what he means by an integrated centre (i.e. where different handicapped groups attend at the same time and have opportunities to interact during a significant part of the time spent at the centre), he postulated that in order to achieve integration, participants must be prepared to come to the centre and to continue coming, be willing to interact with each other, to help each other, and to accept each other.

Before testing these propositions he investigated systematically what opportunities for integration were provided by the organisation, layout, transport arrangements etc. of the centre. For example, in relation to the organisation of the centre he came to the conclusion that it provided three kinds of provision under one roof, rather than a generic approach to problems of handicapped people. He then showed how the various work and leisure activities tended to divide people up into certain ability and sociability groups. After analysing these structural constraints on integration he explored how much size of group, age of members, nature of activity and the formality of the situation were associated with integration, using sociometric, observational and interviewing techniques. Here he found, for example, that members integrated better in small informal groups where the work was more skilful rather than in big formally organised groups where occupations were unskilled. On the other hand, he discovered that disparity in age can favour integration: the very much older physically handicapped adopting quasi-parental attitudes towards the much younger mentally handicapped. Complementarity of handicaps led to helpful interaction: the mentally handicapped could help the physically disabled by pushing their wheelchairs or handing things down from shelves, and some of the physically disabled and the mentally ill were able to show the mentally handicapped how to do things.

One of the crucial tests of the success of any facility where attendance is voluntary is whether people are prepared to come and to keep coming. However, as Reed himself indicates, it is not easy to determine how many people are deterred from applying before even seeing the centre on hearing of its mixed clientele. First he investigated how many offers of places were not pursued because of the centre's predominant association with the mentally handicapped. He then monitored the attendance, which incidentally turned out to be very satisfactory (an average of 91 per cent of possible attendances for all members). Finally he followed up the drop-outs. The evidence seems to show that only a very small proportion of the people who left did so because they disliked the mixed nature of the centre.

Since this appears to be the first systematic approach to the evaluation of a mixed day centre, it may be worth summarising Reed's conclusions very shortly: the benefits of integration were seen, as at Desborough Hall, in people with different handicaps helping each other although the *number* of people prepared to do so appeared to be small. When an elderly or physically handicapped person can assist a mentally handicapped person it can raise his self-esteem and feeling of usefulness, and the mentally handicapped are helped by spending a considerable amount of time in a more adult atmosphere. Cost advantages may be derived from economies of scale, the enlarged scope also offering the different groups a wider range of facilities and learning situations than is possible in separate centres. Finally, an intangible benefit may be the awareness of other people's problems, which may lead one to view one's own disability from a different perspective. Adequate staffing levels embodying the expertise required for the different handicapped groups were seen as essential pre-conditions for the success of integrated or mixed day centres.

Clearly more such systematic, carefully designed studies of mixed and more homogenous centres are needed to inform the planning and organisation of day care.

How far the mentally confused elderly can intermingle with the alert elderly day care users is another burning problem. Researchers have provided some evidence to suggest that on the whole the ordinary users do not like to mix with the very confused and mentally deteriorated participants.

The general picture emerging in this and other countries is of two different types of day activities for the elderly. One is the 'senior citizen centre', offering at best not only a meal but many other social and educational opportunities to ordinary, fairly mobile elderly people. Such a centre could be part of a general community centre or be age-segregated. The second type is the day care centre which caters for referred, carefully-assessed elderly clients with particular physical or mental disabilities or needs. How feasible it is from the cost point alone to blend these two types of facilities is questionable, since the more robust mobile groups do not need specially adapted premises or treatment facilities.

Staff attitudes and regimes

The quality of the staff, the way they relate to users, and the manner in which the centre is run, may well be the critical factors determining the possibilities for rehabilitation and the enjoyment and enrichment users derive from their experience.

The NISW and the DHSS-sponsored studies as well as the Scottish study found that organisers of day centres (both voluntary and statutory) had little formal training and generally did not feel the need for it. Many had experience of elderly people in residential homes and hospitals, and their enthusiasm and commitment to the job is stressed in all the studies. Interestingly the majority of those heads of units and staff who had either some qualifications or who had participated in in-service training expressed interest in further training, while those with no training experiences did not. It seems that organisers are generally left to their own devices on appointment and that they work in comparative isolation from other centres or colleagues in the residential or community field. The spread of imaginative ideas is thus restricted. These findings on the association between past training experiences and attitudes towards further training, coupled with the desire expressed by some staff for more interchange with colleagues in similar institutions, raise important issues for future training policy.

In day hospitals the staffing position is of course very different. Nearly all employ state registered or state enrolled nurses, qualified physiotherapists, and occupational therapists; about two-thirds have speech therapists and chiropodists and 75 per cent have social workers attached, though most of them give only one to two sessions per week. While the consultant physician is held to be in overall charge, a nursing sister has the day-to-day responsibility in the majority of day hospitals, and a remedial therapist in a tiny minority of hospitals. Martin and Millard have deplored the 'nurse orientation' of most day hospitals and they suggest that the small therapeutic units they visualise for the future should be staffed predominantly by therapists although the staffing patterns in the bigger, more socially oriented, maintenance units might need to be different.

Voluntary helpers, who are the mainstay of most voluntary day centres, are often themselves elderly – for example a quarter of the voluntary staff interviewed in the NISW study were over the age of 70.

The researchers occasionally observed a 'them/us' attitude among volunteers who seemed to derive a great deal of satisfaction from their roles, which was not realised by the users, who did not dare to be critical as they felt that the volunteers gave their services entirely from the goodness of their hearts. However, there are other examples of closer user/volunteer relationships. Age Concern Peckham Pop-in Parlour encourages the participation of users and volunteers in the functioning of the centre (Manthorpe 1979). Osn of the most impressive examples is a small experimental day centre for confused elderly people in Buckinghamshire which is entirely staffed by middle-aged volunteers whose enthusiasm and involvement grew as time went on, but who also realised their need for more knowledge: about caring for old people, especially the semi-nursing care needed, and better understanding of confusion and senility (Chisholm and Fletcher 1979). These latter ideas are reinforced by a small experimental action project for confused elderly people initiated by MIND in Sheffield. This project had as one of its purposes to establish 'how and to what extent volunteers can offer a contribution to this special group of elderly people'. It took almost six months to build up a core of regular helpers who received ongoing support in fortnightly meetings with two professionals (Mendel 1979a).

A whole range of volunteer participation seems to be required in day care, from mutual help to devoted specialised help to the very frail and confused.

'Participation' is the watchword nowadays in all community and group efforts. How much can old people be expected to participate in the planning and running of centres, or at least to be consulted about their likes and dislikes, ideas for programmes and so on? And would such participation lead to greater enjoyment on the part of the users, and greater liveliness of the centres? There are examples of voluntary centres catering for the mobile elderly which are largely run by the users themselves. As for the rest, there seems to be a very low level of participation in decision-making or organising activities. The East Anglian researchers comment that while many old people thought that a users' committee would be a good idea, very few were ready to serve on such committees. A view often expressed was 'we have done our bit, now we'll enjoy being waited on a little'. Sensitive judgement will have to be exercised between encouraging latent possibilities and acknowledging the very old person's right to 'put their feet up'. Yet there is the recent experience in a day centre for the younger physically handicapped in Stockport. Those attending the centre were at first startled and dismayed by the suggestion that they should be responsible for the organisation and running of their own centre (with domestic and care staff), but after eighteen months they were making a remarkable success of things and enjoying the experience greatly. Stockport Social

Services Department has now extended this approach to day care centres catering for elderly people, with apparent success. No detailed evaluation has as yet been undertaken.

The observations of members' interactions and their lively participation in decision-making and in organising their activities, reported by Hazan (1980) in *The Limbo People*, also point to considerable possibilities in an enabling environment. Here again it seems that a measure of heterogeneity – there was a mixture of very elderly reasonably fit people, younger disabled, and some mentally disturbed participants – provides scope for mutual caring and helping which diminishes the passive recipient role of people who come to be 'entertained'.

It seems that there is ample scope for sensitive exploration and experimentation, with as few preconceived ideas as possible as to how elderly and very old people wish to interact and arrange their lives. The so-called experts may need to assume a learning role, remembering that the grouping together of old people in clubs, day centres, holiday centres and homes is a comparatively recent phenomenon which may be on the increase, considering the growing proportion of old people who live alone and whose access to their mobile families may become more difficult.

Organisation and administration

Finally, the organisation and administration of day care is an important input variable that affects outcome and effectiveness. As day care covers such a wide range of activities under different auspices (from social clubs with virtually no caring content to something approaching hospital care), it is bound to present a fragmented appearance. Some researchers consider that a coherent 'day care policy' has yet to emerge. We have already alluded to the lack of liaison and joint planning between day hospital and day centre care generally, though some promising developments are contemplated and taking place: several investigators advocate linked and possibly jointly financed day hospital and social day care facilities in order to achieve optimal deployment of resources as well as a maximum benefit for the users. Day care enterprises financed and run jointly by local authorities and health authorities have been pioneered; they also act as focal referral, consultative and assessment centres for community based workers, both social and medical.

The NISW study also comments on organisational discontinuities *within* social services departments. The impression was sometimes conveyed that decisions were taken without a detailed understanding of the nature or content of the day care task. The result was that many units were left to struggle with decisions with hardly any support and back-up. We have already mentioned the comparative isolation of the day care service, which means that the other services have little idea about the nature of day care and conversely day care staff have little knowledge of what other services or other day care centres have to offer. Associated with this comparative isolation the researchers observed a lack of accountability on the quality of service. In day hospitals admission and assessment procedures, record-keeping and progress reviews are much more common and systematic than in day centres. Case conferences were the favoured reviewing mechanism in day hospitals, which Brocklehurst commends as an excellent method. However, he questions the lack of participation of patients and their relatives in these reviews, in which important decisions are made which affect their lives.

There is little evidence of assessment and systematic reviews in day centres. The summary report of the DHSS-sponsored locality studies remarks 'Considering the resource investment, we think social services departments are surprisingly uninvolved in monitoring, supervising and supporting the staff in putting the resource to use'. Regular reviews in relation to aims and attendance patterns seem particularly necessary in view of the low occupancy rates combined with waiting lists and the difficulties day hospitals experience in transferring patients to social day centres. Clearly systematic monitoring is more difficult to achieve in the voluntary sector, although it may well be that small voluntary centres have a better idea about their attendance patterns, reasons for absences and so on than the large statutory centres.

The studies revealed unease on the part of statutory authorities about interfering in the work of voluntary bodies; hence they required only a limited financial accountability for grants received. Yet both the NISW and the Scottish studies showed that the voluntary sector provides the bulk of day care places for the elderly and that most of these centres receive substantial financial support from statutory sources. In Birmingham, 40 voluntary bodies were found to be receiving grants for day care, ranging from £25 to £80,000 per year. Despite this, the social services department are said to lack 'a proper analysis of existing services, from which to decide upon the nature and location of future developments'. The researchers considered that 'if that sector of contribution to the day care of the elderly is to be maximised, social services must be prepared to take stock of voluntary provision, relate it to complementary statutory provision (including that of the NHS) and provide guidance and encouragement in areas where it is most needed'. The East Anglia researchers argue that 'especially where (charitably run) centres substitute for local authority provision, the understandable inhibition policy-makers feel in offering advice to the voluntary organisation is misplaced'. Clearly here is a field for much exploration and policy development if we wish to make maximum use of the day care resources available.

Many of those attending day care centres also receive a number of domiciliary services: home help, meals-on-wheels, district nursing, chiropody and so on. To what extent is day care seen as an alternative to other services, or as part of a planned package of services, or as provision considered quite independently? This may depend on whether domiciliary and day services are organised by the same agency, at the same level, or even by the same person.

The co-ordination of services is possibly one of the most vital contributions to their effectiveness, and yet the studies leave an uneasy question mark on this score. There are comments on social workers withdrawing from cases once the client has been admitted to day care, of little or no contact with caring relatives in day hospitals and day care centres, and of lack of co-ordination with domicilary services. These deficiencies are particularly serious in the cases of brain damaged or very frail elderly people. Some investigators advocate more relatives' groups at the day care centres (Jeffreys 1979; Peace 1980). Others maintain that what relatives most want is relief from the pressure and worries of unrelenting care, and hence do not wish to be drawn into the day care orbit (Mendel 1979b). However, all researchers are agreed that the carers need more support in their own right. These supportive contacts – as the MIND survey indicates (Peace 1980) – are mainly established by community psychiatric nurses rather than by social workers as is often assumed; the important question arises whether their skills are interchangeable.

In general it is becoming clear from the manifold evidence of lack of co-ordination of services and of supportive contacts with informal carers that one of the roles the social services departments will need to develop more systematically is that of case co-ordinator, a function discussed in more detail in Chapter 6 on social work.

The relationship of day to residential care, especially where it takes place within residential homes, raises a different set of issues. The NISW study found that all social services departments in their sample provided *some* day care in residential homes; for a number of the departments all their statutory day care was of this type. As pressure for day care grows and funds for purpose-built centres may not be available, this arrangement may assume even greater importance.

Day care in residential homes can take a variety of forms. There may be only a very few day attenders, or as many as there are residents. There may be sharing of premises and activities with the residents, or sharing in part or virtually none at all. The NISW researchers have described the basic patterns as 'segregated' and 'integrated'. After analysis of some of the problems found, they suggest that it may be easier to run a 'segregated' service, but 'segregation' of itself does not guarantee success (Edwards and Sinclair 1980). However, if 'success' turns out to be closely linked with 'segregation', the supposed cost advantage of this type of provision may well disappear. In any case cost, however important, cannot be the only consideration. Researchers have in general concluded that day care in residential settings is an inferior form of day care at present. 'Less stimulation than at home' is one comment. On our visits to relatively progressive residential homes we have found an attitude of comparative indifference to the day care attenders who in one home were referred to as 'the day care'.

Evaluating outcome

Most of the studies that form the source material for this overview are descriptive case studies or surveys since little was known until comparatively recently about the number, distribution, service providers and types of activities offered in the name of 'day care'. Only two studies (Mendel 1979a and b and Macdonald *et al* 1982) aimed explicitly at the assessment of outcome, and a few others tried to assess progress after a period of attendance. Yet all the major studies go far beyond mere head counting and attempt some evaluation of day care from the point of view of client needs and satisfaction, the content and the organisation of day care. 'Outcome' in day care can mean many different things in accordance with the different aims pursued: rehabilitation after a traumatic event such as a stroke; improved social and physical functioning in a more chronic, insidiously deteriorating situation, or merely a holding operation with no expectation of change. Or the primary aim may be respite for relatives or other informal carers. Luncheon clubs and social centres may be there for the enjoyment and enrichment in general of the lives of elderly people and for the relief of loneliness. Hence criteria can range from fairly specific and objective measurable indcators to very general notions of well-being. We have already touched on impressionistic assessments of some of these outcomes in the previous sections. Here we shall discuss studies which attempt to measure outcome in more precise ways.

Relieving burdens on relatives

The most painstaking and revealing impact studies were carried out in two small projects offering day care to ten and fourteen confused old people respectively, with the intensive one-to-one help of volunteers who were guided by a paid organiser (Chisholm and Fletcher 1979, Mendel 1979a and b). The aims of both these centres were to relieve the burden on the principal carer and to bring some enrichment into the lives of the confused elderly person. The interviews with the relatives revealed the enormity of the burden they carried. Although the Park

Club only met once a week and the Woodhouse Project twice weekly, the relief the principal carers expressed after six and nine months attendance respectively was pronounced. The clients looked forward to coming to the centres and seemed happier and more cheerful according to both relatives and staff. Although they responded positively to the individual attention, affection and stimulation provided by the devoted volunteers, it is doubtful whether their self-care capacities or orientation in time and place 'improved'.

Both studies highlight the central importance of the role of the volunteers. The projects were able to attract steadfast helpers (out of 19 volunteers at the Park Club only two had left within one year), but point to the investment in their training and support which is needed in their demanding role. Both studies show clearly that the principal carers need more social work support, especially if and when the time approaches for the client to enter residential care, which seems to be the outcome in at least half of those confused elderly people who attend day centres. The investigators in both these projects think that an expansion of such small day care ventures for the confused elderly with the help of reliable volunteers guided by one paid organiser is desirable and feasible.

On a larger scale, a team from the University of London Institute of Psychiatry (Macdonald *et al* 1982) followed up, after nine months, over 100 elderly people in four settings: local authority day centres and residential homes, day hospitals and hospital wards. The groups were matched by 'level of dependency and the probability of dementia'. Preliminary findings, using a range of tests, were that type of care did not seem to affect mortality or changes in dementia scores, but that there was 'some indication that improvement in dependency measures is associated with day centre care'.

Consumer views

The point most often made by users in all the studies was that day care provided social contacts, friendship and company. How central this social function is can be deduced from the fact that well over one-third of those who were asked this question said that they were lonely. The NISW study also suggests that day care can improve the client's well-being and self-confidence. 'This place has made me feel happier, because otherwise I'd be at home all day – it stops me being scrappy'. Carter further points out that day care can provide a framework for daily living – something to get up for, what she calls 'markers to provide a timetable'. Such notions are confirmed and elaborated in interesting ways in Hazan's study.

Edwards and Carter (1981) also attempted some ratings on client improvements by classifying users' answers to a question about what coming to the day unit had done for them. The majority of the elderly people made comments which suggested to the researchers that day centre attendance had maintained their functioning. Interestingly a much larger proportion of elderly clients who attended day hospitals – one-fifth – gave answers which were classified as improvement. This finding fits in well with the opinions expressed by patients interviewed in Brocklehurst and Tucker's study where two-fifths felt that they had improved.

Edwards and her colleagues (1980), who took a closer look at the different types of day centres provided for the elderly and especially those at residential homes, showed that users who were very disabled and attended residentially-based and voluntary centres gave significantly less favourable replies than those who attended SSD community-based centres. The replies were particularly negative in the residential centres, where only 1 out of 17 clients said they had improved and four made negative comments, while in the community-based centres 7 out of 26 felt they had improved and only 1 made a negative comment.

As is usual with very elderly clients, only a small percentage in all the surveys voiced criticisms. These related either to boredom – having little to do – or to dislike of the characteristics of other users who, because of disability or senility, were found to be depressing or disturbing. However, it must be remembered that clients can vote with their feet – by not coming at all. For example, in one study (Bligh 1979) out of 166 clients offered a place 30 had either attended once and not returned or not been to the centre at all. It emerged from this and other studies that many clients experience shock when visiting a centre for the first time and encountering very disabled or confused elderly people, and that more thought needs to be given to careful introduction to day centres. It has been suggested that volunteers could play an important part in this. An observation which suggests that day care fills a great need – whatever its shortcomings – was a finding already mentioned, that between one-fifth and two-fifths of the users interviewed wished to attend the centres more often.

Most users expressed enthusiastic appreciation of the staff, who – Fennell suggests – are similar to users in class background and usually live in the locality. Only a very small percentage of users, less than five per cent in the NISW study, wanted to improve any aspect of the staff. The characteristics they valued most highly in them were an ability to be friendly, to like people and to have an ability to get on with them.

Relatives' views

Brocklehurst and Tucker interviewed a sample of 74 relatives, and over two-thirds said that the patients' attendance had made a difference to them – they could go shopping, do their housework in peace, had a chance to rest and felt a relief from worry. However, only 2 out of the 74 said that the patient required less care at home as a result of the day hospital treatment. There were some complaints by relatives that the treatment was not sufficient and that there did not appear to be enough remedial staff, although one of the main findings stressed by the authors was that the relatives seemed to know very little about the treatment patients were receiving, and few had actually visited the day hospital. Brocklehurst and Tucker consider that this lack of communication between day hospital and relatives may underly many of the patients' problems. To what extent are relatives expected to assist in the programme of rehabilitation which is carried out? They also question whether relatives are involved in any way in continuing rehabilitation and maintenance on discharge from hospital.

The researchers of the Universities of Birmingham and East Anglia also interviewed a sample of relatives about the effect of day care, and nearly three-quarters expressed positive or very positive views. Most of the relatives emphasised the old person's increased cheerfulness, alertness and interest in life, rather than the resuscitation of old skills of memory or mobility. No relative put forward a solely negative view of the effects of day care upon users. Many were grateful for the boost it gave to morale, but a substantial minority would have liked more day care time, including some who would have wished to take up work again or extend their working hours. Some of the criticisms concerned the unreliability of transport, lack of appropriate treatment such as physiotherapy, and the exhaustion that can ensue from the lengthy process of preparing a relative for the day care outing.

Cost effectiveness
Some of the investigators in the day hospital field are trying to address the problems of cost effectiveness of day hospital care. It has been pointed out that the cost of day care needs to include the total cost of resources used in the client's life support system, at the very least the social and health care services provided at home, even though the informal care given by relatives and friends is taken for granted. Since geriatric day hospital care is expensive, Martin and Millard ask the question whether other less costly forms of treatment would achieve the same results. All the day hospital studies point to the fact that a varying proportion of patients attend beyond the point at which further rehabilitation by means of intensive therapy can be achieved, and the day hospital then fulfils a predominantly social role. Martin and Millard ask 'would it be better if the health authority paid the cost of transport to a day club, restaurant or pub? These would provide the necessary social stimulation and might even perhaps be more therapeu-

tic.' They further point out that it has not yet been demonstrated that day hospital care reduces the amount of in-patient care.

Bennett (1980) is wrestling with exactly that problem. Having developed a fairly low cost model of day rehabilitation for the elderly by keeping staffing at a minimum and putting emphasis on family and voluntary help (since active participation by relatives and friends was seen as fundamental to success) he then searched for feasible methods of comparing costs with the alternative – long-stay hospital care. The hypothesis would be that the group treated in the day unit would have more years of life but fewer years of institutional life on average. He found this test 'extremely difficult if not impossible' to carry out since many uncontrolled variables can enter the picture in such a long-term comparative study.

In general, then, most evaluative studies of day care are still at a descriptive stage and few if any attempts have yet been made to compare outcomes of day care with those of other forms of social care in order to assess their relative effectiveness. However, since day care is usually only *one* ingredient in a package of services and since there are often waiting lists for day care places, it may prove feasible to mount a relatively short-term experimental study. Clients deemed suitable for day care (and who are not in a crisis situation) could be randomly assigned to day care or to appropriate social care services only and put on the waiting list for day care. It would then be possible to compare outcomes (say after six months), in relation to various self-care, social and psychological indicators, for those – and their informal carers if any – who only had domiciliary services and those who received day care as well.

Some issues arising

Possibly the most important issue is how to integrate day care into a continuum of community services. This would involve:

(i)   Updated, accurate knowledge of community resources, both statutory and voluntary, in an area.

(ii) A deliberate development of the concept and practice of a case co-ordinator.

(iii) Greater clarity and specificity in assessing needs for different kinds of day care. This would include the ability to assess whether certain physical or emotional needs could be alleviated by other community measures less expensive than formalised day care; for example, whether isolation and loneliness would respond to neighbourhood care schemes or neighbourly get-togethers, or whether depression calls for a clinical diagnosis and specific treatment, followed by ordinary day centre activities, and so on.

(iv) Greater emphasis on regular monitoring of progress which may necessitate transfer from one facility to another or to other community or residential services.

The second main issue concerns the effective organisation of day care. Here the following questions and issues arise:

(i) To what extent should a broad policy be adopted of distinguishing between community day centres open to all, offering meals and a range of diversionary activities, and day *care* for specific types of needs, both physical and mental?
(ii) Further experimentation is indicated in the segregation or mixing of various types of disability and age groups.
(iii) In day care, as in other aspects of the personal social services, how can we bring about better joint planning and meshing in of the statutory and voluntary sector, of the personal social services and the health services?

The third major issue relates to staffing:

(i) What kind of training and skill developments are appropriate for various types of day care personnel, including volunteers?
(ii) How does one ensure that new developments in, say, social skill training and reality orientation are made available to ordinary day care staff?
(iii) How can staff be best supported in the at times demanding and unrewarding tasks of long-term day care, and how can they be helped to guard against dull routines and institutionalism?

References

Anon. (1978) Drama down at the day centre, *New Age*, Spring, 25–27.

Arie, T. (1975) Day care in geriatric psychiatry, *Gerontologica Clinica 17*, 31–39.

Bennett, A.E. (1980) Cost-effectiveness of rehabilitation for the elderly: Preliminary results from the community hospital research programme, *Gerontologist 20*, 284–287.

Bergmann, K., Foster, E.M., Justice, A.W. and Matthews, V. (1978) Management of the demented elderly patient in the community, *British Journal of Psychiatry 132*, 441–449.

Bligh, J.H. (1979) Clients' views of day centres for the elderly and physically handicapped in Hammersmith, *Clearing House for Local Authority Social Services Research* 1979:1.

Bowl, R., Taylor, H., Taylor, M. and Thomas, N. (1978) *Day Care for the Elderly in Birmingham* (2 vols.), University of Birmingham Social Services Unit, Unpublished.

Brocklehurst, J.C. (1970) *The Geriatric Day Hospital*, London, King Edward's Hospital Fund.

Brocklehurst, J.C. and Tucker, J.S. (1980) *Progress in Geriatric Day Care*, London, King Edward's Hospital Fund.

Carter, J. (1981) *Day Services for Adults: Somewhere to go*, London, George Allen and Unwin.

142 *Social Care for the Elderly*

Cheeseman, J. (1980) The forgotten authors, *New Age*, Winter 1980/81, 21–23.

Chisholm, I. and Fletcher, P. '1979) *The Park Club: A study of a club run by voluntary effort to help support confused elderly people and their families*, Buckinghamshire Social Services Department.

Clegg, P.E. (1978) *Day Care for the Elderly in the Metropolitan Borough of Kirklees*, University of Bradford, Unpublished.

Department of Health and Social Security (1976) *Priorities for Health and Personal Social Services in England: A consultative document*, London, HMSO.

Edwards, C. and Carter, J. (1981) *The Data of Day Care*, London, National Institute for Social Work.

Edwards, C. and Sinclair, I. (1980) Debate: segregation versus integration, *Social Work Today*, 24 June.

Edwards, C., Sinclair, I. and Gorbach, P. (1980) Day centres for the elderly: variations in type, provision and user response, *British Journal of Social Work 10*, 419–430.

Fennell, G. *et al* (1978) Summary of recommendations from a study of day centres for the elderly in East Anglia, Birmingham and Bradford, Report to DHSS, Unpublished.

Fennell, G., Emerson, A.R., Sidell, M. and Hague, A. (1981) *Day Centres for the Elderly in East Anglia*, Norwich: University of East Anglia School of Economic and Social Studies.

Fletcher, P. and Robinson, J. (1974) *Desborough Hall: Study of a day centre*, Buckinghamshire Social Services Department.

Hazan, H. (1980) *The Limbo People*, London, Routledge and Kegan Paul.

Hunt, A. (1978) *The Elderly at Home*, London, HMSO.

Jefferys, P. and others (1979) The Herga Centre, In MIND, *Approaches to Day Care for Elderly People who are Mentally Infirm*. London, MIND.

Kaim-Caudle, P.R. (1977) *The Sunderland Mobile Day Centre*, University of Durham Department of Sociology and Social Administration.

Macdonald, A.J.D., Mann, A.H., Jenkins, R., Richard, L., Godlove, C. and Rodwell, G. (1982) An attempt to determine the impact of four types of care upon the elderly in London by the study of matched groups, *Psychological medicine 12*, 193–200.

Manthorpe, J. (1979) Pop into Peckham, *New Age*, Summer, 8–9.

Martin, A. and Millard, P.H. (1978) *Day Hospitals for the Elderly: Therapeutic or social?* Geriatric Teaching and Research Unit, St. George's Hospital, Blackshaw Road, London SW17.

Mendel, J. (1979a) Confusion unconfounded, *Community Care*, 16 August.

Mendel, J. (1979b) Report to Family and Community Services (Sheffield Social Services Department) on MIND's Woodhouse Project, Unpublished.

Peace, S.M. (1980) *Caring from Day to Day*, London, MIND.

Reed, C.A. (1979) *Integration of Handicaps at a Combined Day Centre*, Leicestershire Social Services Department, Reprinted in *Clearing House for Local Authority Social Services Research* 1980:8.

Shires, J. (1977) A travelling day hospital, *Social Work Today*, 22 March.

Simes, M., Anderson, B., Bowen, J. and Steel, R. (1980) *Do Books Still Matter? The library and information needs of the elderly in community day centres*, Leeds Polytechnic School of Librarianship (Public Libraries Management Research Unit) and Bradford College School of Business and Social Studies.

Tibbitt, J.E. and Tombs, J. (1981) *Day Services for the Elderly and Elderly with Mental Disability in Scotland*, Edinburgh: Scottish Office Central Research Unit.

8   Voluntary Action

We have already noted the substantial voluntary contributions to the social care of old people in the context of domiciliary services, especially the meals services, and of day care. We have also discussed (in Chapter 6) the difficulties social workers have encountered in recruiting and collaborating with volunteers. But there remain other aspects of voluntary social care which will be the main topics in this chapter. This still leaves out of our consideration the role of formal voluntary organisations as whole entities, although we discuss some of their activities which have been the subject of evaluative studies, for example in relation to Task Force.

The current role of the voluntary sector
In Chapter 4 we sketched out briefly how the state was gradually taking over functions for the social care of the elderly from the voluntary sector, although voluntary organisations still continued to play important, if changing, roles in the welfare services.

There was a growing realisation however that the state could never hope to care for people 'from the cradle to the grave'. Even if the resources were available there were increasing doubts about the wisdom and practicality of the 'one door policy' and current thinking converges more and more on a pluralistic conception of welfare functions seeking for the 'right' balance between informal, organised voluntary, and statutory social care. This notion comes very close to the philosophy of the last general review of the voluntary sector – the Wolfenden Report (1978). This report usefully distinguishes between four systems of social care: the informal, the commercial, the statutory and the voluntary. The 'informal system of social helping' by family, friends and neighbours is still the mainstay of social care for the sick, the handicapped and the old; it is still largely ignored by professionals as a system that needs support and strengthening, although 'caring for the carers' has become an often-heard slogan. Several studies examined in Chapter 6 have shown how unaware many social workers still are of the important roles informal carers, especially neighbours, play in the lives of their elderly clients.

The commercial system is most in evidence in relation to residential care. However, the growth of indexed earnings-related pension schemes and the increasing doubts about the effectiveness and efficiency of large bureaucratic monopolies of social care with their high overhead costs make it conceivable that the private sector will assume more importance in the community care field in the future. Purchase of service by local authorities in both the voluntary and private sectors, already customary in residential care, is being seriously discussed in relation to community care and practised on a small scale in the Kent community care projects and their derivatives.

The statutory system, in providing social services through national and local government agencies, is of course the main form of social provision, with the advantage of universal coverage, of planning and control by representatives of the electorate, and the ideal of equity of treatment. We have already discussed the difficulties of ensuring equity of provision taking into account variations in needs, in social environments and in political values, and the obstacles experienced by large-scale organisations in responding promptly and sensitively to individual needs or encouraging user participation.

The voluntary system, once the chief provider of organised social services, stagnated somewhat during the first decades following the big postwar push towards the welfare state. However, despite the rapid growth of the statutory personal social services in the 1960s and 1970s which, so some people thought, would eventually replace the uneven voluntary contributions, the voluntary sector has remained alive and kicking. Indeed, important voluntary organisations combining service and pressure group activities such as Age Concern, Shelter, the Child Poverty Action Group and others were born during the period and flourished, as did self-help groups such as the Royal Society for Mentally Handicapped Children and Adults, stroke clubs, and Gingerbread.

The 1970s also saw the birth of the Good Neighbour Campaign and what has become almost a movement of neighbourhood care which encourages locally based informal social care and is gradually replacing the traditional patterns of voluntary visiting organised by a centralised voluntary agency. It was not only the realisation that statutory care from the cradle to the grave was a Utopian dream which brought about these developments, nor the retrenchment in public expenditure, but a host of other political, social and demographic trends – not least the rapid increase of very old people in our midst. The Wolfenden Report saw the voluntary system as innovating, complementing, supplementing, extending and influencing both the informal and statutory systems. However, as the report pointed out, the very strengths of voluntary effort – informal, speedy and autonomous action – also constitute its weakness *vis-à-vis* a statutory service, since there is often little accountability and guarantee of maintenance of standards, and certainly no claim to universality. Hence much thinking and experimenting is directed nowadays towards collaboration between the statutory and voluntary efforts, ensuring an equitable distribution of basic services while at the same time encouraging supportive, innovative and gap-filling voluntary initiatives.

As to the relationship between the voluntary and informal system, Wolfenden suggested that 'ideally the voluntary and informal system should exist in a symbiotic relationship'. For example, when informal caring networks are no longer capable of supporting the very elderly in the community unaided, neighbourhood care groups may be able ho give some support to informal carers or substitute for some of their roles in the absence of any informal carers.

The Wolfenden Report, like the Beveridge report on voluntary action 30 years earlier (Beveridge 1948), stressed the contribution the voluntary system can make to the pluralistic conception of social welfare. The voluntary sector offers the possibility of direct involvement by ordinary people. Modern voluntarism has discarded the Lady Bountiful concept and is trying to create opportunities for greater reciprocity in voluntary effort as evidenced in mutual help groups, and neighbourhood care legitimising and to a certain extent formalising what used to be (and often still are) entirely unorganised and spontaneous neighbourly activities.

What can voluntary action contribute?

We have seen in the preceding chapters that the statutory sector can barely ensure a sufficient quantity and an equitable distribution of the most basic domiciliary services and day care opportunities, and the same applies to residential facilities. We have also argued in Chapter 4 that it is illusory to expect the voluntary and informal systems to bear unaided the growing tending and caring needs created by the steep increase in the number of very elderly people. The continuing cut-back in public expenditure and the evidence presented by evaluative social care studies point to the over-riding importance of deploying statutory professional resources as efficiently as possible. We identified some of the means of doing this: good information and advice facilities, accurate initial assessment, locally based easily accessible social service agencies which are well integrated into their surrounding community. We also saw the importance of responsiveness to changing needs and circumstances by good communication and co-ordination within and between service agencies, of exercising imagination and inventiveness in mobilising hitherto untapped resources, and last but not least awareness of cost achieved by more decentralised responsibility for budgetary control. But even if some or all of these conditions are met there is still an enormous gap to be filled by both organised voluntary effort and more loosely contrived informal networks of neighbourly care and by spontaneous neighbourliness. People are needed to 'keep an eye', relieve loneliness and depression, carry out a myriad of little tasks such as shopping, collecting prescriptions, taking people out – in general to help old people feel that they belong and matter and can still participate in the life of the community.

A substantial amount of voluntary work which is difficult to quantify – particularly the uncontrived good neighbourliness – goes into this kind of community concern for old people. Activities extend from traditional visiting services, lunch clubs and day centres run by large voluntary organisations such as Age Concern or small local groups, through thousands of small neighbourhood care schemes, to self-help groups such as food co-operatives, to assertive pressure groups like the British Pensioners and Trade Union Action Committee.

In this phase of renewed growth of voluntarism which seeks new forms of organisation and expression, research is still largely descriptive and exploratory and even less concerned with outcomes than the research we have discussed so far. Indeed, we shall consider later whether the concept of 'outcome' is an appropriate one in such a diffuse field where a more participatory style suggests the blurring of the boundaries between the helpers and the helped and where involvement and 'being' is stressed rather than quantifiable achievements. Hence we shall abandon our strict adherence to the analytic framework of aims, needs, input and outcomes in this chapter. After discussing some organisational issues, which include the relationship between social workers and volunteers, we shall consider evaluative studies dealing with three approaches to voluntary social community care which also represent a progression from old people seen largely as recipients of help – although they actually may give a good deal in return – to active participation of younger old people in mutual help and pressure group activities.

The three approaches are:

(i) Individual voluntary help to old people sponsored by voluntary or statutory organisations.
(ii) Neighbourhood care schemes.
(iii) Self-help and pressure groups.

Since the success of voluntary effort depends greatly on the recruitment and retention of sufficient volunteers, we shall also explore what research has to say about the rewards of volunteering. Finally, we shall wrestle with the question of what the limits of voluntary social care are.

Organisational framework

We have seen that social workers are potentially important mediators between statutory service delivery and voluntary supporters of old people and their carers. Yet all the monitoring studies so far available report on the small use social workers are making of volunteers and neighbourhood care networks.

A recent analytical description by means of case studies of the link between social services departments, volunteers and voluntary organisations confirms that there are few direct links between social workers and volunteers (Hatch *et al* 1981). It seems that where decentralisation in social services delivery is most strongly developed, social workers are more involved in mobilising and using volunteers and neighbourhood networks than they are in centralised social service delivery systems. However, this study also shows how hard it is to develop this direct approach in practice because of competing demands on social workers' time, interest and resources. Hence the more usual way of involving volunteers is either through the medium of voluntary organisations or through the establishment of specialist posts within the social services department. Working through voluntary organisations tends to separate the volunteer contribution from that of the statutory workers who may also be involved. Various mechanisms of collaboration between statutory and voluntary organisations have been created but, as recent research by Leat *et al* (1981) has shown, although such mechanisms may further better understanding they may not overcome the specific problem of collaboration at field level. The third and possibly most effective way of linking professional statutory and voluntary help is through specialist community workers within the social services department. These specialists usually organise volunteer help for the department and support and develop existing and new community resources, which can be used by field workers and residential staff.

Social workers and volunteers

Here we come up against the problem of social workers' attitudes towards volunteers and the delineation of volunteer and professional roles, a subject which has been discussed in very similar terms in the Aves Report published in 1969, in the study by Holme and Maizels in 1978, and by Hatch and his colleagues in 1981. Although the Aves Committee set up to enquire into the role of volunteers in the social services thought that the functions of social workers and volunteers needed to be more clearly defined, they were of the opinion that the boundary must remain flexible. The professional social work bodies giving evidence to the Committee were cautious and somewhat ambivalent in their attitudes towards volunteers, for example: 'the voluntary worker can only be expected to deal with particular situations, as they separately arise, in a practical manner, often through the medium of friendly contact', or again 'it is considered that voluntary workers should not be involved in situations where the focus of treatment is an emotional problem concerning family relationships'. The Aves Report suggested that these views were too cautious and that a partnership of a more positive and constructive kind should be possible between social workers and volunteers, that the social workers and the volunteer services were complementary, and that much still had to be learned about how to make the most effective use of their combined resources. And to quote again, 'it must also be remembered that the effectiveness of any service depends to a considerable extent on its acceptability to clients, and there may be a need to learn more about the feelings of clients of different kinds and in different circumstances towards being offered help by other professional people or voluntary workers.' As far as we know no investigations have aimed at exploring clients' views on paid professionals in comparison with volunteers as helpers, although this is a very important topic. For example, Levin (personal communication) has found that families supporting elderly relatives suffering from senile dementia often express negative attitudes towards volunteers because they feel ashamed to reveal the full extent of their relative's disturbed behaviour to a volunteer.

Holme and Maizels, who produced the first national study of the deployment of volunteers by social workers in social services departments, showed that in 1975 fewer than two out of five social workers carrying caseloads in social services departments were at any one time using volunteers. Most of these social workers only used the services of one or two volunteers for one or two of their clients, and had few if any contacts with these volunteers. (More recent studies have found a similar state of affairs.) Professional attitudes towards employing volunteers resembled those described in the Aves Report. Volunteers were largely used for befriending and practical tasks among elderly and disabled clients and far less, if at all, in family and child care work which might have involved them in casework type of activities.

> Casework, in the opinion of the profession, called either for a degree of skill, understanding and experience which most volunteers are felt not to have, or entails responsibility and accountability – often of a statutory kind – that should not or cannot be shared . . . Thus it seems that for most social workers casework marks the boundary between themselves and volunteers. (Holme and Maizels, 1978, p. 172)

Yet paradoxically, while the social work profession claimed casework as their unique professional skill, lay counselling movements concerned with social and emotional problems related to adolescence, marriage, bereavement, ageing and so on grew at an unprecedented rate. Finally, Hatch and his colleagues (1981) found similarly that 'the organisation of volunteers to transport people, dig gardens, visit the elderly or help in day centres was usually acceptable to social workers.

None of this reduces their scope for carrying out casework with individuals, but there is more difficulty in getting social workers to supervise volunteers and to become involved in team projects, voluntary organisations and local community groups generally. These require a shift in their work towards becoming mobilisers and supporters of community resources and away from being providers of a personal service on an individual level – in other words a reinterpretation of the professional role.'

Although Hatch and his colleagues along with others, including ourselves in Chapter 6 and elsewhere (Goldberg and Hatch 1981), stress the need for social workers to develop their roles as mobilisers and supporters of community resources, little progress has been made since the Aves Report in delineating the functions and roles of what Holme and Maizels have called two 'conflicting systems', namely the paid direct service by skilled professionals and friendly voluntary help.

However, useful attempts have been and are being made to describe and evaluate the effectiveness of volunteer input, both in relation to schemes sponsored by voluntary or statutory agencies and by independent local initiatives.

Domiciliary visiting schemes

Two evaluative studies – rather different in aims and scope – surveyed the needs of old people receiving social visits from volunteers, and described the organisational framework of the visiting service, the input of the volunteers and the old people's and the researchers' evaluation of these visits. One, carried out by PEP (Shenfield and Allen 1972), sought to explore the general organisation and effectiveness of voluntary visiting in England using a sample of 120 old people drawn from 20 local authority areas, receiving visits under varying auspices, ranging from large voluntary and statutory agencies to small warden or neighbourhood schemes. The volunteers ranged in age from school children to pensioners. The other study sought to evaluate domiciliary visiting by young volunteers attached to Task Force, a voluntary organisation established in 1964 to organise the work of young volunteers in the service of the old (Hadley *et al* 1975). At the time of the inquiry, Task Force operated in ten London boroughs, and the investigation took place in four of them. Shenfield and Allen were able to interview their sample of old people and volunteers only once. Hadley and his colleagues had an extensive sample of 261 old people who similarly were only interviewed on one occasion, but they also interviewed an intensive sample of 86 old people and their volunteers on three separate occasions during the course of one year. These researchers also had the advantage of being able to observe the work of this voluntary organisation systematically.

Despite the great difference in scope and intensity in these two studies, some findings of considerable importance are essentially similar, and in some respects reminiscent of difficulties already discussed in the professional services, such as inadequate assessment, review and support.

The age distribution, sex and marital state of the client samples in both studies were similar, and resembled elderly welfare clients under local authority care. Over four-fifths were women, two-fifths were 80 years and older, over two-fifths had no children alive. As far as it is possible to compare their social contacts, which were measured somewhat differently in the two studies, these also appeared of a similar range: about two-thirds had seen their children in the week preceding the interview and about half of the old people had only one or two other friends or neighbours whom they had seen during the previous week. Again, very similarly, this very old client population, mostly referred by welfare or health agencies, received far more domiciliary services than the average population in their age group: over half were in receipt of home help visits and about one-third received meals-on-wheels.

What can we learn about input and outcome of voluntary visiting in these two studies? As is usual, the large majority of the old people in both samples enjoyed or appreciated the visits. In both groups there seemed to be an association between liking the volunteers and the amount of practical help received. Both groups of researchers tried to establish 'need' for visiting, by taking isolation (the number of relatives, friends, neighbours who were in regular touch) and subjective feelings of loneliness as their criteria. Although they went about this in different ways, they came up with remarkably similar results: Hadley and his colleagues found that 37 per cent of their intensive sample had a 'low need' for visiting, while Shenfield and Allen concluded that 36.5 per cent were not in 'great need' of visiting. The researchers in both studies blame what they term haphazard assessment and random allocation respectively for this state of affairs.

Hadley and his colleagues also attempted to measure success or failure of volunteer visiting by assessing the quality of the relationship between the volunteer and the old person, using both subjective and objective criteria. They defined a successful relationship as one that became a valued part of the old person's network of social contacts. In 20 of the 86 cases the visits were judged to have substantially improved the quality of the old people's lives. The volunteer had become a significant member of the old person's network, and in several instances was the only 'significant other' the old person had. Thirty-one relationships were deemed to be partially successful, that is to say the old person recognised that the relationship helped in some way to meet her need for social contact. The largest group of 35 (41 per cent) were rated as unsuccessful: the volunteers had made little or no positive contribution to the lives of the old people, a substantial proportion of whom were rated as being most in need of visits. The authors attribute the comparatively large number of failures to the random allocation procedures, the lack of selection of volunteers and of review and support, and to the fact that some of the school volunteers may have been pushed into this activity since it was part of the school curriculum. However, if we look at the other side of the coin, the results show that two-thirds of the old people in the intensive sample said that they had never been let down by their volunteers when they had promised to come and three-fifths of the relationships had become an enjoyable part of the old persons' lives. Was the likelihood of the relationships blossoming into enjoyable experiences associated with any characteristics of volunteers and old people? Some interesting associations emerge, though caution is indicated as numbers in each category are very small. For example, the volunteers in the succesful relationships tended to visit their old people more often than other volunteers, to visit alone rather than in couples (which was quite usual among the school children), and to stay longer on each visit. They were also more likely to do jobs for the old people and to express concern over their health. The most successful relationships were formed with the 'young olds', and more of them belonged to the middle class and were classified as high need cases than in the unsuccessful ones. The volunteers achieving the most successful relationships also appeared to be more middle class than the volunteers who were less successful.

Shenfield and Allen based their judgement of success on somewhat different criteria – enjoyment of the visit by the old person and dependence on it. According to the interviewers' judgements, about one-fifth of the sample were very appreciative of being visited, and nearly a quarter not only appreciative but in some significant way dependent on their visitor. Just over one third enjoyed being visited, but in the interviewers' opinion were not strictly dependent upon these calls. For nearly a quarter the calls did not appear to have any significance or impact that could be discovered during the interviews with the old people.

Both these studies – one evaluating the activities and outcomes of a rather homogeneous group of young volunteers in the metropolis, and the other attempting to ascertain the effectiveness of a variety of visiting schemes employing volunteers of all age groups in 20 urban and rural areas – suggest that about two-thirds of old people visited by volunteers derive enjoyment from it. Both seem to attribute the failures to haphazard allocation methods and the inability to match care and need. Indeed, in a revealing passage Shenfield and Allen question the perfunctory judgements and assumptions that often underlie so-called need for 'friendly visiting'. For example, some housebound old people did not particularly want more visiting but did want help to get out of their four walls – that is to say 'transport more than conversation'.

Wisely these two studies, one based on a one-off survey and one on a repeated survey, did not attempt to assess what specific differences the volunteers had made to the old people's lives. Did they feel less lonely or depressed as a result of the contacts, were they less isolated and so on? In order to answer such questions one needs a control group of old people in similar circumstances, who were not visited by volunteers. However, there seems little doubt that the 20 successful relationships in the Task Force study, where the volunteers became an important quasi-grandchild or caring friend on whom the old people depended a great deal, did improve the quality of their lives. It emerges – as one would expect – that people of a similar class, where there is not too vast a gap in age, form more successful relationships than those in which these differences are very great. There was also a suggestion that volunteers with religious or political convictions who aimed at a career in the helping professions were more successful than others. There are also indications in the work of Abrams and his colleagues (to be discussed later) that religious affiliation plays an important part in successful neighbourhood care. (Abrams *et al* 1981 and 1982)

One study did attempt to assess the effectiveness of help provided by volunteers to a sample of old people aged 75 and over compared with a control group of similar old people not being offered this kind of help. This was Power's quasi-experiment in Weston-super-Mare (Power 1979, Power and Kelly 1981), outlined in Chapter 3, in which he recruited, guided and supported a group of volunteers from the base of a health centre which also was the source of his samples of old people. On the whole, the comparisons of outcomes between the experimental and control groups are somewhat disappointing and to a certain extent predictable. On the other hand some of the most interesting findings, such as observations over two years on the morbidity and mortality of different risk groups and availability and type of support given by volunteers of different age groups, were not dependent on the existence of a control group.

The old people (who ranged from those with relatively slight disabilities to those near the margin of requiring total care), who were visited by volunteers for period from six months up to two years, did not seem to be any better off in terms of personal or home care after the end of two years than the comparison group. But they were getting out more and experienced significantly less loneliness. Most of the old people were very satisfied with the kind of volunteer help they had received. Power and Kelly point out that these satisfactory results were achieved without the benefit of matching or shared interests or compatible personalities, since the only criterion used in pairing volunteers and elderly people was that of geographical proximity.

Power and Kelly throw a great deal of light on the input dimension: first, the experiment presents an object lesson in the establishment, support, encouragement and stimulation of a local group of new volunteers, followed by the gradual withdrawal of the professional's input. The volunteer group is still going strong after five years. The experiment also illustrates the idea of a partnership between the professional health and social services and the volunteer endeavour. Thirdly, the study documents what kind of help one might expect from volunteers in different age ranges at different stages of their life cycle.

Did this quasi-experiment establish 'the potential and the effectiveness of volunteer support to elderly people living in their own homes', as the researchers hypothesised?

The study certainly testifies to the potential of neighbourhood volunteer help in which people of all ages can participate under favourable conditions of imaginative recruiting and support. Two-fifths of the helpers stayed with the scheme throughout, formed many warm and lasting relationships and performed a variety of tasks reliably. The authors raise the question whether the volunteer scheme carried out services that the statutory social services might be expected to provide. The volunteer activities amounted approximately to the work of three full time social work assistants, but as the researchers point out themselves some of the old people did not have any particular needs that required social service input. What seems clear is that this volunteer scheme fulfilled monitoring, emotional support and neighbourly help functions in a way that the statutory social services could not hope to achieve.

Power set up a similar volunteer experiment in six residential homes – two large and two small local authority and two private ones (Power *et al* 1982). A survey of attitudes about volunteer support to old people's homes showed that residents, staff and local people living nearby welcomed the idea of volunteers befriending residents. What was required, the staff thought, was friendly contacts, especially with those who had few visitors, to take residents out, occasionally to take them to the volunteers' own homes, and so on. The staff were quite clear that volunteers should not be required to help with the physical care of residents, which they considered to be their own domain.

The six homes were split into three pairs in a quasi-experimental design, one of each pair being the experimental home with volunteer support and the other the control. About half the residents in the three experimental homes, amounting to 92, asked for a volunteer. As a first step all 171 residents in the six homes, experimental and control, were independently assessed for physical and mental functioning and rated by staff for social adaptation and behaviour (Clifton Assessment Procedures for the Elderly: Pattie and Gilleard 1979) and for their overall satisfaction with life (the Life Satisfaction Index B: Neugarten, Havighurst and Tobin 1961) before the volunteer scheme started. Many interesting observations were made on the elderly residents' functioning and attitudes to residential care, as well as on the regime and staff attitudes. The volunteers, recruited and supported by Power, were mostly married women over 50 years of age already busy with many other activities. Interestingly, although keen to help, those recently widowed, divorced or separated were not able, in the event, to take on the volunteer role. The volunteers' acitivities were monitored for a year; they visited residents, took them out, often to their own homes, and consequently many individual friendships ensued.

Despite these positive experiences and many anecdotes recounted by staff of residents 'being transformed', becoming less depressed and crotchety, repeat assessments one year later of the two-thirds of all residents still in the homes showed no statistically significant differences in Life Satisfaction, although in one home with volunteers there had been a small positive measurable gain. One explanation could be that on average about two hours' volunteer contact in a week was a 'drop in the ocean' of uncommitted time and too little to make a measurable difference in the rather global Life Satisfaction Index. It is a reminder that if the whole tenor of residents' lives is to be changed radically towards greater activity, autonomy and general interaction within the home it would be achieved by more fundamental modifications of regime rather than by outside intervention. However, these overall negative objective findings should not obscure the important fact that it proved possible within a reasonably short time to recruit older suitable volunteers who offered steady friendship without upsetting staff. There were many examples of such experiences improving the quality of the residents' rather passive and dependent lives, even if, overall, attempts at measuring these effects proved unsuccessful.

In these four studies which tried in the main to evaluate the contributions and the impact of individual volunteers contradictory conclusions emerge about the importance of matching of volunteers and clients: while Hadley and his colleagues and Shenfield and Allen lay great emphasis on this aspect and blame its neglect for some of the failures in the volunteer/old person relationships, Power took proximity as his main criterion. This is reminiscent of the different approaches adopted in the Thanet Community Care Project (matching) and the North Wales replication study (proximity). These differences run right through volunteer schemes and warrant further exploration. All four studies stress the importance of support for volunteers by a readily available organiser or co-ordinator and the need for recognition by professionals and formal agencies, as do Abrams and his co-workers in their most recent findings.

The studies suggest that the measurable impingement of the volunteers on the lives of most of the elderly people was not very great. We need to add that there is very little reason to believe or evidence to show that the impact of professional social workers, for example, would have been any greater except in special circumstances of intensive care. But possibly this is to be expected, since old people as a rule find it more difficult than younger people to form new intimate relationships with 'strangers' who have not shared any part of their past lives when there is little time left to build on the prospect of future shared experiences.

Neighbourhood care
We now want to widen the area of discourse of voluntary action towards the evaluation of neighbourhood care schemes in general. Important contributions have been made by Cheeseman *et al* (1972) in Nottinghamshire, Ferguson and McGlone (1974) in Manchester, and the Volunteer Centre (Leat 1979), followed by Abrams and his colleagues at Durham University who have carried out the most extensive evaluative study in this field so far. Arising from previous theoretical and empirical studies on neighbouring (Abrams and McCulloch 1976, Abrams 1978) they undertook a national survey of good neighbour schemes in England which explored their range of activities, their geographical distribution and their organisational patterns and tried to identify factors associated with success or failure of neighbourhood care (Abrams *et al* 1981). This extensive survey was largely based on postal enquiries, followed by telephone enquiries and visits to selected areas. A more intensive evaluation study – not yet published – of 12 distinct types of neighbourhood care ventures was also carried out (Abrams *et al* 1982). In addition to interviews with participants in schemes and 'clients' it included the views of residents in the vicinity. Since Abrams regarded neighbourhood care projects as 'crucial experiments in opening-up the frontier between formal and informal care', his main aim in the intensive exploration was to elucidate the relationship between neighbourhood care and formal welfare provision.

Why neighbourhood care?
Leat (1979) defines neighbourhood care as 'caring engaged in primarily because of geographical proximity', while Abrams says that 'a good neighbour scheme is simply any organised attempt to mobilise local residents to increase the amount or range of help and care they give to one another'. Thus both emphasise the local dimension (the word neighbour deriving from 'near dweller') but Abrams adds the element

of reciprocity in caring. Bayley (1981) prefers the concept of 'locally based care' which can include 'moral communities, such as the church, care and friendship groups, not necessarily resident within the immediate vicinity'. There may be in existence in Britain several thousand neighbourhood care schemes, of which about half were probably started since 1975. Four factors seem to be associated with this expansion of neighbourhood care.

(i) As already said, there are many personal, social and emotional needs, particularly among very old people, which the statutory services cannot meet. Hence flexible forms of locally based care available at times of maximal need, which can 'keep a monitoring eye' on old people, and which can mesh in with rather than substitute for the usual statutory domiciliary services, are being developed.

(ii) In addition to the practical necessity of making more immediate local help and support available to old people at low cost, there has grown up a conscious desire to create a better, more caring society. This was dramatically exemplified in the Good Neighbour Campaign started by David Ennals (the then Secretary of State for Social Services) in 1976 which aimed at sustaining and widening natural helping networks in the community. In addition to the wide-ranging publicity drive, general measures were worked out with the TUC and local authority associations as to how people whose work takes them to people's homes (milkmen, postmen and so on) can become more aware of needs for help and how they can bring these to the notice of the health and social services. A resource pack for schools was designed to encourage pupils to be more aware of and active in their neighbourhood. Leat has referred to this modern movement of 'love thy neighbour as thyself' as a 'moral imperative'. In this connection it is noteworthy that both Cheeseman and his colleagues and Abrams and his co-workers found the churches to be the foremost promotors of neighbourhood care schemes. In the Durham intensive study (1982) 70 per cent of neighbourhood care volunteers described themselves as 'religious'.

(iii) The third factor is probably associated with the growing movement towards decentralisation and participation which in the social field found strong expression in the Seebohm Report (1968) which aimed at a 'community-based and family oriented service' which would 'enable the greatest possible number of individuals to act reciprocally, giving and receiving service for the well-being of the whole community'. The report stressed that both 'the importance of community involvement' and 'the need to encourage informal good neighbourliness' were essential ingredients of the new pattern of social welfare which they envisaged.

(iv) The fourth possible contribution to the growth in neighbourhood care is satisfaction and fulfilment that contact with others in the neighbourhood can bring, not only to the helped but to the

helper. Abrams (1978) has written eloquently about the element
of reciprocity embedded in the idea of neighbourliness and the
new 'neighbourhoodism' which is trying to foster a sense of
community and belonging in a very mobile society. Power's
findings (1979) and Abrams' and his colleagues' survey (1981)
suggest that newcomers to a town or neighbourhood join
schemes as one way of making satisfying social contacts. The
retired, who form a considerable proportion (between 20 and 30
per cent) of the neighbourhood volunteer force, can find a way of
being useful and 'needed' in these activities.

Some facts about neighbourhood care
The national survey of about a thousand neighbourhood care schemes
shows that two-fifths were initiated by the churches, just over a quarter
by national voluntary agencies of whom the most important is Age
Concern, 16 per cent by local residents, while only 11 per cent were set
up by local authorities. Although these schemes are concerned with
many different kinds of people such as young families and pre-school
play groups, the largest 'client' group served by them is the elderly,
especially those who are housebound or handicapped. Most of the
schemes are small: nearly half have less than 40 helpers. In effect most
schemes are even smaller since they often contain a few committed
members who do a lot of work, a periphery of helpers who are occasionally involved, and a number of enrolled people who never become
seriously involved. Compared with population size, schemes are distributed fairly evenly throughout the country except for a slight clustering
in the south west and the south east of England and some under-
representation in the north and north west. However, when Abrams
and his colleagues related the distribution of neighbourhood schemes to
indicators of general deprivation such as numbers in receipt of unemployment and other welfare benefits, low household income and to some
specific indicators of need such as number of handicapped people, old
people living alone, single parents, households without cars or telephones, paradoxes emerged: although the south east scored lowest on
most of these indicators it had the highest prevalence of neighbourhood
schemes. The authors stress that the existence of good neighbour
schemes only partly reflects the level of need in a given environment but
more importantly the availability of helpers and organisers. Schemes
appear to develop most readily in areas where there is a large supply of
people – mainly women – who do not have full time work and who can
afford to meet the costs involved in being a good neighbour. The north,
though scoring high on indicators of need, is nevertheless reasonably
well provided with neighbourhood schemes. The explanation appears
to be that while neighbourhood schemes in the south east are relatively
independent of the state, and mainly flourish on the basis of private

prosperity, in the north the statutory authorities have played an active role in promoting, supporting and funding schemes. Thus while 70 per cent of the schemes in the north were either initiated or helped to start by the social services departments, this applied to only 42 per cent in the south east; and while in the north 25 per cent of the schemes had a paid organiser this was only the case in 14 per cent of the schemes in the south east.

Leat suggests that the identification of needs and of potential volunteers and the definition of aims and functions is not a once-and-for-all task but a continuing process as the neighbourhood schemes evolve and respond to the needs they uncover. She distinguishes at least three general types of aim: (a) promoting general social contact or integration; (b) providing help or services; and (c) promoting social awareness or action. The majority of schemes as described by both Leat and Abrams and his co-workers were primarily concerned with the second aim. They tended to concentrate on practical activities rather than on the more social tasks, such as relieving isolation and loneliness, which however may well turn out to be important by-products of practical help. Visiting and transport were the most prevalent activities of good neighbour schemes, but one-fifth of the respondents suggested that part of their activities was making connections, linking people to public services, thus acting as 'a half-way house between the informal world of care given by relations, neighbours and friends and the formal realm of organised social services'. Many organisers also said that their schemes existed to 'keep an eye on those at risk', or help out in emergencies only. Abrams and his colleagues observed that 'monitoring', popping in to see whether people are all right, is the function neighbourhood schemes fulfil particularly well. About ten per cent included organising social events, outings and social clubs for the elderly among their activities. Odd jobs comprised nearly one third of activities mentioned and appeared to include an enormous variety of tasks. Shopping, gardening and collecting prescriptions were mentioned often. (Leat's point that a good neighbour scheme is not necessarily one that involves actual neithbours but one that provides the sort of help that might be given by neighbours is particularly relevant here.) Two-fifths of the schemes were engaged in generating new social networks, especially self-help networks. However, the examples given such as forming clubs (mainly for the elderly), organising and running day centres, arranging outings and parties and other occasions for meeting others, may not necessarily promote self-help among an older population. On the other hand among younger age groups baby-sitting pools, community or residents' associations, neighbourhood information shops etc. probably do foster mutual help among local residents.

The diversity of organisational forms which can range from tightly organised warden schemes to very informal and loosely organised groups defies any attempt at a typology according to Abrams. However, he and his colleagues have found perceptive if somewhat provocative ways of describing the relationships between neighbourhood schemes and the surrounding community and between the formal welfare agencies and informal caring schemes. Relationships established by neighbourhood care schemes can be those of 'social patronage' or 'care as doing good' in which 'characteristically middle-class people offer services to working-class people out of a more or less well-defined sense of class duty'. 'Sympathy rather than empathy' appears to be the driving force. At the other extreme is a relationship of 'redundancy'. Here organised neighbourhood care merely formalises mutual patterns of help which existed anyway. The third relationship is one of 'isolation' in which a project 'simply fails to expand beyond its initial circle of supporters and to effectively penetrate the universe of local residents' (Abrams *et al* 1981). In the intensive study these researchers isolate a fourth pattern: 'paid caring' where paid warden or 'good neighbour' schemes result in friendships deeply rooted in shared working class experiences.

The relationships that can exist between formal systems of welfare and informal systems have been described as those of comparative *laissez-faire or neglect* where the authority considers its services as a safety net only, doing little or nothing to encourage bridge building between formal and informal systems. The relationship can be a *partnership* where the local authority acts as a springboard; it encourages, supports and contributes some funds to the schemes but respects their autonomy and informality. Thirdly there is the phenomenon of *colonisation*, encompassing a wide range of relationships in which informal systems of care are 'either directly invaded by statutory or voluntary services or indirectly dominated by them'. This kind of control, seen at its best in Sheffield's battery of complementary schemes based mainly on the local authority and on the Churches' Council for Community Care, can be a very effective way of promoting comprehensive neighbourhood care, possibly at the expense of the informal system.

Most good neighbour schemes received very modest financial support – only 13 per cent had a paid organiser and only 16 per cent of the helpers had their expenses paid. Financial support came from a variety of sources: from local authority grants in two-fifths of the cases; a considerable number of schemes (two-fifths) relied in part on donations and direct fund raising. All studies raise the problem that outside funding carries with it some obligation of accountability. How to reconcile a neighbourhood care group's philosophy of informality with the need for organisation and efficiency, including record-keeping, appears to be a key dilemma. How to strike the right balance between these different 'pulls' is one of the questions to which Abrams and his colleagues address themselves in their conclusions and to which Leat also attaches great importance. They suggest that organisers of schemes will have to learn to live with a measure of outside interference and with demands for accountability, and that they need to work out a dialogue with more formal organisations in which information, referrals, advice and support flow readily in both directions. 'It calls for considerable negotiation, experiment and compromise on both sides, if schemes are to become effective agents of social care without at the same time losing the distinctive local identity and energy that is the key to their ability to cultivate neighbourliness. And it requires both sides to recognise the limits to their own field of action.' The authors also point to the need for cash, and suggest that it is unrealistic to expect 'doing good' to be its own reward and that most people join good neighbour schemes on the basis of what Leat has called 'limited liability', having many other commitments and interests. Many schemes survive because of the extraordinary devotion and energy of one or a few 'central figures'. But the authors warn that the supply of such people is strictly limited – 'and even among them few can endure the burden of sustaining an effective scheme for very long'.

Success and failure of neighbourhood care
Abrams and his colleagues in their extensive survey and Leat in her case studies had to base their judgements of the success and failure of schemes mainly on the information supplied by the organisers or co-ordinators. However, as this book is going to press information from helpers, clients and residents in the Durham researchers' intensive sample of neighbourhood care schemes has become available and will be referred to, but should be regarded as preliminary findings.

Abrams and his colleagues approached the exploration of success and failure by asking the organisers about major problems encountered and what factors would enable good neighbour schemes to be more success-ful. Fifty eight per cent of informants had encountered major problems and 71 per cent thought that their schemes 'could be more successful'. As Table 8.1 shows, the most common problems were shortage of helpers and of finding helpers 'of the right type'. The researchers identify the root cause of this problem as 'matching the care and help they can offer to the needs that exist in their particular localities'. The problems militating against success are illuminated by their case studies and seem to be associated with the following factors:

(i)   The organiser's experience and personality. For example, a very active, indigenous organiser who starts a scheme with a group of close friends and neighbours and who wants to keep his finger on the pulse of the scheme may be unwilling to delegate organising

Table 8.1 Major problems of good neighbour schemes

Problem	Percentage of schemes
Shortage of helpers	43
Inappropriate helpers	21
Transport difficulties	20
Organisation/administration	19
Inadequate contact with external agencies (Social Services etc.)	19
Shortage of clients	15
Shortage of finance	14
Other	29
(N = 483)	

Source: Abrams *et al*, p. 39

functions to other volunteers in adjoining streets and thus tends to under-use people who do not belong to the core group.
(ii) The social composition of a mixed neighbourhood where middle class volunteers try to befriend working class 'clients' and find that they have little in common.
(iii) The failure to adjust tasks to the needs and capacities of available helpers. For example, some helpers feel comfortable cooking a meal in a small day centre where they have a definite role, can merge into a friendly group and do not have to make close one-to-one relationships in a visiting scheme.
(iv) A sense of isolation which volunteers may feel if they never meet as a group to share their experiences, especially if they have joined partly to find new like-minded friends among the volunteers as well as among those to be helped.
(v) The perennial problem of finding sufficient numbers of volunteers who will be prepared to enter open-ended long-term commitments, keeping in touch with very isolated, lonely and possibly difficult people.
(vi) Related to the last point is the problem touched on by Abrams and Leat that the need for a good neighbour scheme in an area may arise partly because some neighbours do not get on with each other and thus are not able to give support to each other. This also raises the question whether it is always advisable to have a scheme concentrated on a very small neighbourhood.
(vii) Finally, as the table indicates, there is also under-use of available volunteers which Abrams and his colleagues link to insufficient confidence that volunteers will help rather than interfere, which is particularly prominent in new, dispersed and socially mixed neighbourhoods.

What factors were found to be associated with success? Forty two per cent of the respondents in the national survey had not encountered any major problems. The authors doubt the reality of two types of success sometimes quoted by respondents: schemes that either succeed by deliberately restricting their aims, for example, transporting people to hospital only, or by merely formalising into a neighbourhood care scheme neighbourly relationships that already exist in a community. The authors suggest that the lack of problems experienced by such schemes seems to result from not having to struggle to advance and strengthen informal networks of social care.

If one takes the impact on the neighbourhood as a criterion of success then thought-provoking findings emerge from the Durham researchers' interviews with their samples of local residents who were non-participants. Although on average 50 per cent had heard of the neighbourhood schemes in question, not one person interviewed would resort to them in case of need. It simply did not occur to them. This suggests that most schemes did not as yet recruit 'clients' directly from the surrounding neighbourhood but from more official referral agents. Another reason may be that the residents interviewed identified neighbourly tasks with relatively minor things that need quick action like shopping, paying bills if one is ill, keeping an eye on the elderly, or in any emergency; and they may not have associated these neighbourly acts with an organised scheme. The residents interviewed saw 'visiting' as the most appropriate function for voluntary neighbourhood schemes in preference to any statutory or private source, in the sense of providing company and monitoring for very lonely and isolated people. Perhaps most of the residents interviewed did not feel themselves or admit to being isolated and in need of 'visiting' and hence the neighbourhood schemes were not for them.

The researchers found confirmation of the residents' views in the clients' opinions when asked about their most important social contacts. While the largest proportion of clients named their children (35 per cent), those who either had no close relatives or only saw them rarely (but even a few who saw their children regularly) regarded the home helps as their most important social contact (15 per cent). If one considers only those who received visits from home helps, then 31 per cent saw them as their most important social contact which the authors call 'impressive'; this leads them to the observation that 'there need not be an antithesis between paid welfare services and the establishment of close personal relationships'. (These findings are in great contrast to Abrams' earlier views.) Eleven per cent of the residents selected their voluntary visitor as the most important social contact and if only the clients who actually had visits from volunteers were considered this figure rose to 20 per cent. The authors call this also an impressive achievement and interestingly this figure is similar to the proportions of successful volunteer relationships identified by Hadley and his colleagues among the Task Force clients and in the PEP volunteer study.

If one takes the matching of care and need as a criterion of success in a broader sense then the extensive survey suggested that volunteers were most plentiful in fairly affluent and rather neighbourly areas where they were least needed, while there were few or no helpers in areas containing large numbers of old isolated poor people – except in those areas where helpers received some form of payment.

However, the central criterion of success the Durham researchers wished to test was whether neighbourhood care schemes can actually encourage ordinary neighbourliness. They tried to construct objective measures that would indicate a rise or fall in neighbourliness as a result of the existence of the scheme. They finally realised 'that the question was inextricably related to both the organisational framework of the particular scheme and the social context in which it exists'. Hence, they abandoned the idea of quantitative measures. Instead they produced a series of propositions about how different types of schemes can prosper within different social contexts. These propositions were based on an analysis of a mass of quantitative data on the residents' social class, beliefs, their work status, the helpers' characteristics and the clients' evaluation of the help received, and on the basis of their case studies. For example, in middle class areas voluntary schemes can be relatively effective providers of care, even within the context of a statutory authority which adopts a 'safety net' policy of laissez-faire. However, this does not seem possible in homogeneously working class areas where the economic need to work influences the woman just as much as the man. It is in these areas that payment of workers or neighbours becomes vitally important for any serious attempt to alleviate local problems. The authors consider that such a scheme is in turn dependent on a local authority that acts as a 'springboard', guiding statutory as well as voluntary and informal care into areas where they are most needed.

They suggest that such developments cannot happen within the context of statutory services which act as a safety net, performing minimal functions for those in greatest need and taking a laissez-faire attitude towards any developments of neighbourhood help. While the authors are convinced that in the long run paid organisers are essential for the success of most neighbourhood care schemes, they suggest that in working class areas, payment of indigenous residents will prove a necessity for successful neighbourhood care.

These hypotheses still need further exploration in relation to the question what is a 'successful' neighbourhood care scheme? This clearly depends on aims. Within the general framework just outlined, should it be one that manages to reach most isolated and lonely old people, one that really impinges on the neighbourhood and to which people will turn readily when in need, one that brings together and relieves strangeness and loneliness among newcomers to an area, one that gives older volunteers a sense of being useful – even if they have not got many 'clients', one that is readily available in emergencies reported not only by residents, but also by statutory agencies?

How justifiable is it to spend resources and effort on assessing the specific effectiveness of differently targeted neighbourhood schemes which at present consume relatively few resources in monetary terms, when we fail to assess the effectiveness of very expensive statutory services? Since aims of neighbourhood care schemes are so varied and often diffuse, and crucial inputs may consist of a mixture of practical tasks, dutiful monitoring, close friendships between helpers and helped, or even creating a feeling of belonging and solidarity among the helpers, the assessment of effectiveness may be even more hazardous than measuring outcome in more clearly circumscribed statutory services. However, it would be useful to push forward the work begun by the Durham researchers in identifying those factors which seem to be associated with a flourishing neighbourhood scheme which is continually renewing itself on the one hand, and with stagnating and moribund schemes and their eventual demise on the other. In this connection it may also prove helpful to work out, in close collaboration with neighbourhood care groups, some simple monitoring devices which the volunteers themselves could use. For example, they may be helped to clarify what their particular group is aiming at, whether their activities are related to these aims, what helpers and helped think about these activities, what the reason for drop-outs are, how the balance between supply and demand works out over time, and so on. Certainly we should follow the example of the Durham researchers and monitor from time to time how the neighbourhood scheme impinges on the neighbourhood.

It would be interesting to test Power's hypothesis of the 'staying power' of volunteers among different age groups which will be discussed below. It may also prove rewarding to take a closer look at the natural leaders that are emerging in neighbourhood care whose experience and personalities, while useful for the instrumental side of the work, may not always encourage participation in decision-making among the volunteers.

This brings us to a topic which has attracted research attention recently, namely the rewards of neighbourhood care.

The rewards of neighbourhood care

It is clearly important to establish what makes formalised neighbourhood care worthwhile and rewarding to the volunteers in the absence of substantial monetary compensation. First of all one might ask why volunteers join neighbourhood schemes instead of just trying to be good neighbours. One must not forget that many – unsung as 'volunteers' – do just that, as testified by general experience, national studies (Hunt 1978) and local studies (Wenger 1981, Goldberg *et al* 1970, Abrams *et al* 1981). Some people, so Leat suggests, prefer to join a scheme because it removes the uncertainty about interfering and makes their desire to help legitimate. Also there is the phenomenon of what Abrams has aptly called 'latent neighbourliness' – people who are prepared to help but perhaps are too shy to do so on their own initiative or do not quite know how to set about it. Also joining a scheme establishes boundaries and removes the burden of an open-ended commitment. The volunteer can determine the nature, scope, frequency and duration of the contact, and this control over boundaries and the degree of intimacy is equally important to the recipient. Leat suggests that in this way volunteering is a means of creating a 'controlled belonging'.

In general there is no shortage of hypotheses which researchers have advanced about the motivation and rewards of volunteers. They can be roughly divided into three groups.

The first group contains four kinds of *personal satisfactions* people are looking for when engaging in neighbourhood care as suggested by Abrams (1978). First, there is status: public recognition matters to some people. Tradition is the second motivating force; about a quarter of all the good neighbours interviewed by the Durham researchers invoked long-standing family or community practice to explain why for them care is something one simply does. The third driving force which Abrams identifies is altruism, mostly found in church-initiated projects. 'There is a compelling obligation to give help to those worse off than themselves just because they are worse off.' The fourth most widespread expectation from neighbourhood care is reciprocity, regarding neighbourhood care as a 'vehicle for reciprocal advantage . . . part of a process in which care in diverse forms is both given and received'.

The second major group of motivations and rewards seem to relate to what one might term *role expansion*. Most studies of volunteers show that the majority are recruited from the economically inactive, namely school children and students, housewives, the unemployed and the retired. In the case of young people, there may be a deliberate element of socialising them into neighbourly caring roles, which in turn might bring their own rewards in terms of reciprocity or status. By far the largest group – usually well over half – are the young mothers and housewives. Although the volunteer role has much in common with their usual domestic role, they value the quasi-work role, though unpaid, since they are considered persons in their own right, and their

Voluntary Action 167

giving is not being taken for granted (Leat 1979). They are beginning to acquire an identity beyond the home and its immediate environs. Their volunteer role is often transitional, preparing for a future work role possibly in the field of social service. Qureshi and others, in their study of rewards systems of helpers in the Thanet Community Care Project, have called this a 'capital building role' (Qureshi *et al* 1981). Hadley and Scott, in a study of the elderly as volunteers (1980), and Leat, stress the work identity of the volunteer role for the retired as well as the social satisfactions derived from new contacts and interests.

Lastly we come to rewards which relate to what Qureshi has called *affiliation needs*. Several investigators have commented on volunteering for neighbourhood care as a means for newcomers to make contacts in a strange neighbourhood, or as a means for seeking new affiliations on the part of those whose life circumstances have changed through widowhood, separation or children leaving home.

Neighbourhood care thus appears able to fulfil a rich variety of needs and motivations in different social contexts. Further studies in progress on motivation and rewards will make a particularly useful contribution to the maximal use of resources if they can be related to the life circumstances and characteristics of the volunteers. For instance, over three-quarters of volunteers associated with social care are women. Power found that the husbands of his volunteers were very interested in the scheme but would not join because they did not consider themselves suited to visiting the elderly. In fact they provided much background support – 'drive a meals-on-wheels van willingly, but not talk to old ladies'. Thus volunteer roles congruent with people's self-image of their capacities would have to be found. Power also made interesting discoveries about the relation of age and life circumstances to the type of help given. The younger age groups were particularly outstanding in short-term crisis work necessitating a lot of intensive work. They were the age group that stayed the shortest time in the scheme because of domestic changes and work mobility. Older married women aged 30–59, though busy people, turned out to be the group that stayed the longest with the scheme. They were the 'generalists' with a 'maintenance role', giving long-term support on a regular basis. The group of retired people, amounting to nearly one third of the volunteer force, who had considerable leisure time, proved to be extremely conscientious volunteers, and an exceptional contribution in this age group were the husband and wife teams who combined a range of skills and understanding. However, only 16 per cent of this group were able to stay throughout the two years of the community care experiment, the main reason for withdrawal being the illness of the elderly volunteer or her spouse.

If Power's findings are confirmed in other studies, then they provide useful pointers to the deployment of men and women volunteers in different age groups. Qureshi, exploring the relationship between initial motivation and sustained involvement, found that previous experience was the much more powerful explanatory factor in drop-out: while only two out of 14 helpers with previous experience in the care of the elderly dropped out of the Thanet Community Care scheme, 17 out of the 26 with no such experience gave up. Both Qureshi and Leat stress that in establishing and sustaining the relationship between helper and helped the organiser's role in providing boundaries to caring was crucial in avoiding the danger of over-commitment and enabling individual helpers to obtain the rewards for which they hoped.

Neighbourhood care – a bridge between informal voluntary care and statutory services?

Leat, whose definition of neighbourhood care we have already quoted, makes the point that this excludes all caring in which the dominant factor is professional responsibility or payment or an interest in the problem itself, irrespective of the geographical proximity of those with that problem. However, some neighbourhood care schemes include paid 'good neighbours' and street wardens, for example in Islington (Islington SSD 1977), Manchester (Leat 1979) and Sheffield (Abrams *et al* 1981). Patch-based social services, in which the patch workers and home helps interact informally with the neighbourhood and its inhabitants, could also be regarded as verging on neighbourhood care schemes. Preliminary observations suggest that a high proportion of referrals are picked up in an informal manner as a result of neighbourhood contacts (McGrath and Hadley 1981). The Kent Community Care models provide social, household and personal services for the clients largely on a neighbourhood basis for relatively small payments. The Dinnington Project (Bayley *et al* 1981) helps statutory and voluntary services to reinforce natural informal networks, and these activities are based on neighbourhood patches. Thus there seems to be developing a continuum of care from schemes supplementing and supporting informal care on a purely voluntary neighbourhood basis to a professionally organised network of neighbourhood care which includes professionals, paid neighbourhood workers and volunteers. These developments foretell a possible merging and intermeshing of informal and formal neighbourhood care – notwithstanding some formidable problems of accountability and responsibility. Abrams used to suggest that there were distinct boundaries between two systems of social care:

> one, the public sector organised on principles that are in every crucial respect at odds with and incompatible with the principles governing the other, the private sector. There is the social care world of social administrators and their publics, or of social workers and their

clients; and set sharply against that there is the world of mothers and daughters, of caring neighbours and devoted friends.

However, as already indicated in their latest work, referring to home helps and also to the paid street warden scheme in Sheffield, the Durham researchers now emphasise that (possibly particularly in working class areas) 'organised wage work and the warm humanity of voluntary carers' can go hand in hand.

Most evaluative research into social care now in progress is inspired by the hypothesis that it is possible and desirable for the formal statutory and voluntary services to support, complement and strengthen the existing natural helping networks. Indeed, Power appears to have achieved, though on a small scale, a useful partnership between informal but reliable voluntary support and statutory services. It seems that the volunteer help in the community scheme enabled family and friends to keep their major contribution at the same level with the home help support unchanged, despite the elderly person's deteriorating personal and household capacity over a period of two years. In the residential experiment volunteers complemented and supplemented the help of care staff.

The suggestion that statutory, voluntary and semi-voluntary neighbourhood services can mesh into each other still does not answer the question whether there are important differences in accountability and in the nature of the job between informal neighbourly help with its potentiality for a mutually satisfying friendship and the professional services of a local authority agent. And where the one ends and the other begins is also a moot question. What about the 20 per cent or more of the home helps who say that they are doing neighbourly acts for their clients in their own time? How many social workers and social work assistants do this? What about the suggestion implied in some of the research findings on long-term social work that social workers need their clients (and their dependence) at least as much as their clients need them? The theory is that professionals are trained to be aware of their own needs and to keep these in check rather than to use their clients for the fulfilment of their own needs. In practice, reciprocal needs between clients and helpers are probably satisfied in 'successful' cases whether they involve volunteers or professionals working in bureaucratic settings.

Problems and limits of neighbourhood care

Some studies highlight a conflict between the concept of locally based neighbourhood care and the inability, particularly in working class areas, to recruit volunteers from the neighbourhood. This often meant that volunteers were imported from surrounding middle class areas. Some schemes associated with social services departments have sought to overcome this difficulty by introducing token payments for volunteer services as 'good neighbours'. For example Islington Social Services Department pays good neighbours, of whom two-thirds are drawn from the catchment area. Less than 10 per cent of the volunteers belong to the professional and managerial classes and 25 per cent are or have been clients. The suggestion has been made that it is not so much the money itself that is important as the recognition it conveys, especially to working class people who otherwise might consider volunteering as interfering nosey-parkering. However, in the Thanet Community Care Project out of 40 helpers studied, 14 stated that they were definitely attracted to the payment, though they emphasised that money was not an overriding initial motive but the payment enabled them to participate. Similar views were expressed by the neighbourhood wardens in Sheffield. Here we come upon another contradiction between neighbourhood theory and practice: will it lead to a potential social cleavage if the middle class volunteer does it for nothing and the working class volunteer gets a 'token' payment or even a full wage?

It is only a short step to suggest that in the face of mounting and permanent structural unemployment, neighbourhood care should be reserved for those who need paid work, rather than to encourage voluntary work. Where should the line be drawn between relatively straightforward neighbourhood work as done by paid 'patch' workers in Normanton, the semi-voluntary helpers in the Community Care models, and the volunteer good neighbours carrying out very similar functions in the community experiment set up by Power?

The conflict which arises overtly or covertly in most of the studies and discussions of volunteer neighbourhood schemes is that between informality and efficiency. Although responsiveness and informality, sometimes blending into sustained friendships, are a hallmark of neighbourhood care, yet the relationships emanate from an artifically created network which often relies on statutory or voluntary funds for its existence and for 'referrals' to keep it going. How accountable should these neighbourhood care schemes be, and to whom? Interestingly Leat called her monograph *Limited Liability*. The question opens up serious problems. If, as seems to be the case now and will be even more so in the future, these schemes are in touch with very incapacitated and frail elderly people originally referred to them by the personal social services or the health services, should not the statutory authorities ensure that these clients are being visited and supported? The results of Abrams' national survey, which often refer to the lack of contact between most schemes and the statutory authorities, would throw doubt on this proposition. (One wonders what the general public would say if children at risk were handed over to a friendly neighbourhood care group without any kind of mechanism for reporting back or supervision.) Those schemes which are associated with paid street wardens who in turn relate to the area office of the social services department have a clearer channel of communication than independent schemes. Should we try to distinguish more clearly between those clients whose main need is for an extension of their informal networks and where neighbourly contacts need not be the concern of statutory services, and those in which some form of collaboration between informal neighbourhood care and the statutory services is essential?

There seems to be a further contradiction: evidence from surveys suggests that there are many very disabled, elderly, mentally handicapped and other groups in the community who would welcome more neighbourhood contacts, and yet repeatedly, particularly at the beginning of schemes, volunteers outnumber potential recipients. In this way much goodwill, enthusiasm and potential neighbourly help is lost. This imbalance between needs and resources is possibly a management problem, calling for the development of techniques of publicity and recruitment which stagger the supply of volunteers in proportion to the detection of needs. Most writers on the subject also stress that publicity and recruitment should be an ongoing process rather than a once-and-for-all activity, since – as Power has shown so clearly – people in various age groups weave in and out of neighbourhood activities in accordance with their changing life circumstances.

Finally, where are the limits to what friendly neighbourly acts and relationships can achieve? Should we attempt to define these by empirical investigation, building on suggestions arising from a number of studies? McGlone (1974) suggests that situations referred by social services departments on occasion proved too difficult for good neighbour schemes to tackle. One would like to know more about the background of such referrals and the nature of the assessments that had been made prior to referral.

Abrams (1978) refers to the number of clients who are not 'taken on' by volunteers. That is to say, some clients are never visited at all, some are only seen once and never again, while others receive a good deal of attention and care. There are reasons to suppose that those who are rejected are the difficult, smelly, and possibly most deprived people who are in greatest need of help. While a trained professional is expected to be able to overcome feelings of revulsion and antagonism towards some of the more unpleasant clients, it is understandable that ordinary 'neighbours' need a great deal of altruism and moral conviction to persevere with clients who arouse strong negative feelings in them.

Power also discovered some limiting circumstances: out of 20 cases of very elderly and frail clients who lived with their children and to whom volunteers were introduced, only five materialised into ongoing relationships. He thinks (personal communication) that the fraught family situations where an elderly person has come to live with his or her children are too complex for 'good neighbours' to cope with. He suggests that the defensive pride of the relatives who feared that they were being accused of not looking after their elderly mother properly, and the lack of understanding and skill on the part of the volunteer in the face of hostile family relationships, resulted in withdrawal. He feels that work with family problems needs a trained social worker, at any rate initially. The work of Nissel and Bonnerjea, and of Levin, would tend to confirm these hunches, particularly where families are caring for severely mentally disordered relatives (Nissel and Bonnerjea 1982; Levin personal communication).

It seems that further investigation, and the kind of dialogue Abrams and his colleagues (1981) advocate between neighbourhood care schemes and statutory services, is needed to delineate some of the boundaries. In their words: 'There is much Good Neighbour Schemes cannot do, and there is much that statutory authorities need not do.'

Older people as volunteers and as members of mutual help and pressure groups

Reciprocity and mutual help is the ideal towards which many neighbourhood care groups strive and which they sometimes attain. Since so many who come to the attention of neighbourhood care schemes are very frail and elderly, their ability to give is often severely curtailed and reciprocity difficult to achieve. Still, young volunteers have learnt much from listening to old people's reminiscences and 'what it is like to be old', non-literate people have benefitted and struck up friendships with old volunteers teaching them to read and write, and many younger volunteers envisage what Richardson (1982 a and b) has called 'serial reciprocity': 'I trust someone will do the same for me when I am old and frail.'

However, physical and mental frailty does not generally begin to take its toll till the late seventies, and potentially many retired people could engage in vigorous mutual help and pressure group activities, either to advance their own or other people's causes. As far as can be ascertained, only a small minority do so explicitly, but many other voluntary activities carried out by older people can be regarded as a form of mutual help since they are often directed towards helping other old people.

Although one in five people over 65 seem to be doing some regular voluntary work in the United States, the figures for Britain are considerably lower: according to the 1977 General Household Survey nine per cent of retired people are engaged in voluntary activities, which peaks at 13 per cent among women aged 65 to 69 (Hadley and Scott 1980).

However, retired people form a considerable proportion of the volunteer force supporting old people. A small study of older volunteers in a northern town (Hadley and Scott 1980) showed that several organisations such as WRVS, Age Concern and Oxfam seem to rely almost entirely on the retired for their volunteers. In Abrams' intensive study people over retirement age formed 24 per cent of the helpers, and in Power's studies 30 per cent. While worker satisfaction is always an important ingredient in evaluative studies, among elderly volunteers work satisfaction and enhancement of self confidence can legitimately be considered a vital outcome measure. For example, a study of the impact of an American Foster Grandparent Programme was focused on the life satisfaction of the foster grandparents rather than on the benefits accruing to the foster grandchild (Gray and Kasteler 1970). Older people who participated for about a year as foster grandparents to institutionalised mentally handicapped children were better adjusted both personally and socially and were more satisfied with their lives than a comparative group of older persons who did not participate in the project. Thus, among older people voluntary work can be considered as a therapeutic measure enhancing self-esteem and life satisfaction.

The British literature on mutual help among older people is as yet small, but a beginning is being made: Hadley and Scott (1980) have tried to evaluate some 20 mutual benefit and service schemes run by retired people attached to a variety of statutory and voluntary agencies in England and Wales. Richardon (1982 a and b) has carried out evaluative surveys of four mutual aid organisations in England, of which two – the National Association of Widows and the National Council for the Single Woman and her Dependants – contain a majority of older people. In relation to pressure groups, community workers from Task Force (Buckingham *et al* 1979) have evaluated work with pensioners' community groups in a series of six case studies. Similarly Butcher and his colleagues (1980) have assessed the achievement of a Senior Citizens Action Group formed in conjunction with a Community Development Project in Cumbria. The focus of this inquiry was the group's own effectiveness in relation to the formulation of aims, organisation, selection and implementation of strategies and the use of both internal and external resources. The development of an evaluative tool – a checklist built on the Gulbenkian framework of analysis (1973) – is an important element in this study, since it adapts the basic evaluative questions of aims, needs, inputs and outcome to the practice of community work.

The common thread that runs through all these studies is the great need for older people (including the 'young olds' who form the bulk of the actors in these studies) to feel useful, to meet and relate to other elderly people and to support each other, rather than to take up issues with outside bodies for the general improvement of conditions that directly impinge on their own well-being and that of other citizens experiencing similar problems.

Hadley and Scott focused on older people as a volunteer resource in a great variety of settings and roles: as probation associates, hospital volunteers, community wardens, telephone volunteers; as members of pensioners' associations and action groups; running voluntary clubs and day centres and a volunteer bureau for the retired. In their evaluation the authors point to a marked lack of stimulation of voluntary activity among the elderly by the statutory sector; they were unable to find any old people's homes or day centres where the clients were encouraged to play an active part in running the organisation, although there are now a few promising developments in this direction, notably in Stockport. Nor did they find any social services department that stimulated mutual aid among retired people living at home. In the 20 projects studied the older people's experience of life, their expertise in many different fields and the time at their disposal were often mentioned as advantages, but some organisers suggested that volunteers of retirement age needed more support than younger volunteers and some doubts were expressed about their growing physical frailty and occasionally about their rigid attitudes. It seems that most schemes had little difficulty in recruiting older volunteers, and the authors suggest that there is a reservoir of volunteers among the 91 per cent of old people not engaged in voluntary work so far, especially if more attention is paid to their positive attributes, and if expenses were met and token payments made in order to draw in more working class volunteers. Most importantly, drawing more elderly people into volunteer or semi-volunteer activities would provide them with more recognition and a greater sense of their own role in society. The case studies which included interviews with volunteers not only convey individual fulfilment and pleasure from helping others, but also enjoyment derived from companionship with other volunteers and from the status achieved by associating with, for example, the probation service and other welfare organisations. However, Hadley and Scott found very little participation by older volunteers in the decision-making and management of the organisations with which they were associated, and the volunteers hardly ever felt impelled to take up any issues that arose from their voluntary experiences. The authors put this down to the older generation's largely passive role in public affairs, which also helps to explain the very small core of activists in the pensioners' action groups.

The Task Force case studies illustrate vividly how difficult it is to encourage active participation, let alone public action and campaigning among pensioners, many of whom prefer to settle down into a mutually congenial social club. Yet it was the aim of the Task Force community workers to develop community groups which would give older people more control over the groups and over decisions which affect their lives locally or nationally. Possibly it was not only the reticence old people show in exercising more active control over broader aspects of their lives, but also the mistakes the young and inexperienced community workers made in their strategies, as the authors freely admit. For example, they were often in too much of a hurry to get a pensioners' action group going without being familiar with the area and the issues that were of importance to pensioners. Nor were they very clear or explicit about their objectives, not infrequently trying to keep an uneasy balance between those pensioners who wanted to use the group for meeting people and engaging in social activities and those – usually a minority – who wanted to participate in action about particular local or national issues affecting pensioners. The studies are also an object lesson in groups pursuing ambitious goals for which they have neither the resources nor skills, such as trying to run a five-day-a-week pop-in parlour with a group of 15 members, or setting up as a welfare rights advice group without any special preparation. Another point to emerge clearly is the necessity to be open about objectives so that the members of a group can make a choice: 'the group thinks that it has got together for a friendly chat and a cup of tea, but the worker is trying to get them to write poetry' and the authors conclude: 'it is obviously hypocritical to get people to express their needs on the basis of self-determination, and then to try to influence indirectly their decisions and activities.'

What is so fascinating about these shortcomings in community work is that they mirror exactly the obstacles that have been identified as inhibiting success in individual casework, namely failure to be explicit about objectives often concealing a double agenda, lack of agreement on tasks to be undertaken, and failure to limit goals to what is achievable. The authors' refreshing openness about naivity, errors of judgement and over-ambitious aims must not conceal the achievements. All the groups that survived were eventually run by the pensioners themselves, although – as in neighbourhood care – usually by a small core of stalwarts. A number of groups achieved small objectives in gaining greater control over decisions which affected their lives and their localities: pavements were repaired, bollards erected to prevent lorries parking, and heating installed in cold chalets to which old people were sent on holiday in October. Self-help objectives were also achieved in terms of self-run social activities, advice and support, food co-operatives and so on. Similar types of achievements are reported in the Cumbrian study. Butcher and his colleagues are critical of old people's tendencies to look mainly towards self-help before taking up issues with outside agencies, such as councillors, MPs and so on, since mutual help does not usually result in the transfer of resources to low income pensioners. For example, Butcher and his colleagues argue that food co-operatives would not be necessary if people had reasonable pensions. But is this not underestimating the sense of achievement and control over one's own destiny that result from pooling and maximising resources, and the feeling of camaraderie that arises from mutual help? Possibly older people need to build up confidence from successfully running such semi-public activities before being able to launch into more political struggles with local or even national decision-making bodies that control resources.

In any case the desire of people experiencing common problems or conditions to band together in mutual help or self-help groups has grown in popularity in recent years, as evidenced in the proliferation of such organisations. Interestingly, the people who joined two of the organisations studied by Richardson, the National Association of Widows and the National Council for the Single Woman and her Dependants, were seeking companionship among the former and information and advice among the latter, rather than the receiving and giving of help (Richardson 1982 a and b). Among the main aims of the National Association of Widows was to provide an active social life for its members. The aims of the organisation for the single carers were less clear: none of the branches was very active, since many carers felt unable or unwilling to leave their homes even for short periods; branches had run into resistance from members if they tried to provide services, as members were sensitive about accepting charity. Even sitting-in help or holiday relief for carers found little response. Nor was a 'phone-a-friend' or a telephone counselling service much use. Thus a newsletter issued by head office seemed to represent the principal contact with the organisation for many members. There was a common assumption that former carers should remain members in order to give help, but they found little call for their services.

Originally these two organisations were launched not only as mutual help groups but with predominantly political aims of improving conditions for widows and single carers. But although over two-fifths in both these organisations alleged that they had joined the group to work to improve the situation of similar people, there was only limited evidence of any such pressure group activity.

However, the mutual help element does emerge over time: the propensity to give help was regularly greater among those who had experienced the relevant problem for some time compared with those who were new to it. Individuals join in order to get emotional support, companionship or advice; they may receive it and then if they stay on they are in turn able to pass on help to others. But in order to effect such 'serial reciprocity' the organisations need to retain their experienced members and ensure a sense of commitment among them. This does not always happen. For example, many widows, having received support and companionship, pass on to other social activities. And among the single carers opportunities for passing on help were small.

How is one to evaluate the success or effectiveness of these mutual help organisations? First, in order to gain some perspective it is important to realise that only a tiny proportion of older people participate in such activities. Thus out of the three million widows in this country the membership of the National Association of Widows amounted to approximately 4,000 in 1981 – over half of them were 60 years and over. Only nine per cent were very active. Nor can one take the numbers who stay with the organisation as an index of its success, since the high turnover in the National Association of Widows may be a healthy sign of people finding other contacts and interests. The opposite tendency of a clinging-on of single carers long beyond the death of their dependants may be an indication of their isolation and loneliness occasioned by many years of confinement to their own homes while concentrating on the care of their relatives. What about the members' own views on what they gain from involvement with a mutual help organisation? Nearly all the members (85 per cent) of the National Association of Widows had gained something, most important of all companionship and support. The newly bereaved were more likely to stress emotional support, especially 'helping me to come to terms with my grief' (33 per cent) and 'having people to understand how I feel' (41 per cent), while for the longer-term widows social activities and giving help to others in the same situation became more important. Not surprisingly from what has already been said, fewer among the single carers seem to have gained from their involvement. However, one quarter of the members indicated that they had gained advice, and nearly as many (48 per cent) had gained some support. However, one-quarter of the single carers indicated that they had gained nothing from their involvement. The number of inactive members was also very much higher (46 per cent) than among the widows (26 per cent).

Thus it seems while a high proportion of the widows who join the NAW seem to give and receive companionship and mutual support at any rate for a period of time, the National Council for the Single Woman and her Dependants appears to have made a much smaller impact on the carers' lives. This raises the question how much such an organisation originally founded to improve the lot of single carers financially and socially, can really fulfil its other purpose of mutual help? Would the carers, particularly during the period of maximal burden, find more help and support and opportunities for sharing troubles in non-specialist neighbourhood care schemes which may also gradually draw them out of their often somewhat embittered isolation? Or is the element of all being in the same boat of paramount importance?

Some conclusions

Evaluative research in the voluntary sector is still at the exploratory stage and many questions have been raised in this chapter about its functions, aims, scope and achievements.

The modest results emerging from the four studies that examined the outcomes of voluntary visiting possibly signify that we should look for enrichment rather than significant changes in old people's lives as a result of these experiences. It is also possible that the measuring instruments used to assess change were not entirely appropriate to capture the effects of neighbourly acts and friendly relationships which are enjoyed but may not impinge deeply on either partner. Perhaps the enjoyment and satisfaction of the 'giver' as well as the 'receiver' should receive greater attention in assessing outcomes.

Until the more definitive results of the intensive case studies carried out by the Durham researchers are available we know as yet little about how different kinds of neighbourhood schemes impinge on older clients and older helpers. What can already be discerned is the satisfaction and stimulation that voluntary and mutual help activities bring, albeit inspired by different motives in different social contexts, to members who are actively involved in them. This includes elderly people who form about a quarter of these groups. There seems to be ample scope for the expansion of voluntary and semi-voluntary work on the part of older people, bringing into play the skills, talents and experience they possess. This does not only apply to neighbourhood care schemes but to the running of clubs, day centres and other voluntary enterprises. Power's residential experiment suggests that here too is an enormous field for volunteers enriching the lives of very old people, many of whom have few if any relatives and friends left.

Since common experience and the results of several studies suggest that people of similar background and habits of living get on better than those living in very different circumstances, ways of drawing in more working class volunteers will have to be found. This may mean small payments which have already proved their worth in a number of different schemes. Clearly the anomalies arising from different types of monetary rewards for roughly similar help will have to be faced.

If voluntary activities are to flourish and to complement and supplement statutory services, then a great deal more thought and experimentation will have to be devoted to working out patterns of fruitful relationships between statutory, organised voluntary and informal neighbourhood activities in different local circumstances. Simple ways of monitoring voluntary activities need to be developed not only for purposes of accountability to the funding authorities which in some instances will still carry ultimate responsibility for the clients they refer, but also to give the volunteers themselves some idea of how they are doing, and where they are going. It is also desirable that the research begun on rewards derived from volunteering should be developed, as well as research on users' perceptions of volunteer as opposed to professional help and what distinctions if any they make between them.

References

Abrams, P. (1978) *Neighbourhood Care and Social Policy: A research perspective*, Berkhamsted, The Volunteer Centre.

Abrams, P. and McCulloch, A. (1976) *Communes, Sociology and Society*, London, Cambridge University Press.

Abrams, P., Abrams, S., Humphrey, R. and Snaith, R. (1981) *Action for Care: A review of Good Neighbour Schemes in England*, Berkhamsted, The Volunteer Centre.

Abrams, P., Abrams, S., Humphrey, R. and Snaith, R. (1982) Patterns of neighbourhood care: End of project report, University of Durham Rowntree Research Unit, Unpublished report to DHSS.

Aves Report (1968) *The Voluntary Worker in the Social Services*, Report of a Committee jointly set up by the NCSS and NISWT under the Chairmanship of Geraldine M. Aves, London, George Allen and Unwin.

Bayley, M. (1981) Neighbourhood care and community care: a response to Philip Abrams, *Social Work Service 26*, 4–9.

Bayley, M., Parker, P., Seyd, R. and Tennant, A. (1981) *Origins, Strategy and Proposed Evaluation*, Neighbourhood Services Project – Dinnington. Paper No. 1, University of Sheffield Department of Sociological Studies.

Beveridge, W. (1948) *Voluntary Action*, London, George Allen and Unwin.

Buckingham, G., Dimmock, B. and Truscott, D. (1979) *Beyond Tea, Bingo and Condescension*, Stoke-on-Trent, Beth Johnson Foundation.

Butcher, H., Collis, P., Glen, A. and Sills, P. (1980) *Community Groups in Action: Case studies and analysis*, London, Routledge and Kegan Paul.

Cheeseman, D., Lansley, J. and Wilson, J. (1972) *Neighbourhood Care and Old People: A community development project*, London, Bedford Square Press.

Ferguson, J.H. and McGlone, P. (1974) *Towards Voluntary Action*, Manchester Council of Voluntary Service.

Goldberg, E.M. with Mortimer, A. and Williams, B.T. (1970) *Helping the Aged: A field experiment in social work*, London, George Allen and Unwin.

Goldberg, E.M. and Hatch, S. (eds.) (1981) *A New Look at the Personal Social Services*. Discussion Paper No. 4, London, Policy Studies Institute.

Gray, R. and Kasteler, J. (1970) An evaluation of the effectiveness of a foster grandparent project, *Sociology and Social Research 54*, 181–189.

Gulbenkian Foundation (1973) *Current Issues in Community Work*, London, Routledge and Kegan Paul.

Hadley, R. and Scott, M. (1980) *Time to Give? Retired people as volunteers*, Berkhamsted, The Volunteer Centre.

Hadley, R., Webb, A. and Farrell, C. (1975) *Across the Generations: Old people and young volunteers*, National Institute Social Services Library No. 28, London: George Allen and Unwin.

Hatch, S., Smolka, G. and Mocroft, I. (1981) Social Services Departments and the Community, Unpublished report to DHSS.

Holme, A. and Maizels, J. (1978) *Social Workers and Volunteers*, London, BASW and George Allen and Unwin.

Hunt, A. (1978) *The Elderly at Home*, London, HMSO.

Islington Social Services Department, Research and Development Section (1977) The use of volunteers in the Social Services Department.

Leat, D. (1979) *Limited Liability? A report on some good neighbour schemes*, Berkhamsted, The Volunteer Centre.

Leat, D., Smolka, G. and Unell, J. (1981) *Voluntary and Statutory Collaboration: Rhetoric or Reality?*, London, Bedford Square Press.

McGlone, P. (1974) The neighbourhood care project, Section II of J.H. Ferguson and P. McGlone, *Towards Voluntary Action*, Manchester Council of Voluntary Service.

McGrath, M. and Hadley, R. (1981) Evaluating patch-based social services teams: a pilot study, in E.M. Goldberg and N. Connelly (eds.) *Evaluative Research in Social Care*, London, Heinemann Educational Books Ltd.

Neugarten, B.L., Havighurst, R.J. and Tobin, S.S. (1961) The measurement of life satisfaction, *Journal of Gerontology 16*, 134–143.

Nissel, M. and Bonnerjea, L. (1982) *Family Care of the Handicapped Elderly: Who pays?* PSI Report No. 602, London, Policy Studies Institute.

Pattie, A. and Gilleard, P. (1979) *The Manual of the Clifton Assessment Procedures for the Elderly* (C.A.P.E.), London, Hodder and Stoughton.

Power, M. (1979) The home care of the very old, Unpublished report to DHSS.

Power, M. and Kelly, S. (1981) Evaluating domiciliary volunteer care of the very old: possibilities and problems, in E.M. Goldberg and N. Connelly (eds.) *Evaluative Research in Social Care*, London, Heinemann Educational Books Ltd.

Power, M.J., Clough, R., Gibson, P., Kelly, S. with the assistance of Kaul, E. (1982) Helping lively minds – a volunteer experiment in residential care of the elderly, Unpublished report to DHSS, University of Bristol, Social Care Research.

Quereshi, H., Challis, D. and Davies, B. (1981) *Motivations and Rewards of Helpers in the Kent Community Care Scheme*, Discussion Paper No. 202, University of Kent Personal Social Services Research Unit.

Richardson, A. (1982a) The Diversity of Self-Help Groups, in S. Hatch and I. Kickbush (eds.) *Involvement in Health: Self-help and self-care in Europe*, In press.

Richardson, A. (1982b) *Mutual Aid and Social Welfare*: The self-help experience, London, Policy Studies Institute, forthcoming.

Seebohm Report (1968) *Report of the Committee on Local Authority and Allied Personal Social Services*, Cmnd. 3703, London, HMSO.

Shenfield, B. and Allen, I. (1972) *The Organisation of Voluntary Service*, Broadsheet 533, London.

Wenger, G.C. (1981) The elderly in the community: help and helpers, University College of North Wales, Bangor, Department of Social Theory and Institutions, Draft paper, unpublished.

Wolfenden Report (1978) *The Future of Voluntary Organisations*, Report of the Wolfenden Committee, London, Croom Helm.

Part Three
Evaluating Special Accommodation

9 Assisted Lodgings and Sheltered Housing

Public and voluntary agencies have developed special kinds of housing and other residential facilities for elderly people, although the vast majority, of course, go on living in ordinary dwellings in the community. The options range from purpose-built bungalows, flats or 'granny annexes', through various forms of assisted lodgings and sheltered or residential accommodation, to hospital care and hospices for the dying. In this and the following chapter we consider evaluative research related to the social care section of the continuum, rather than to general housing or medical care.

Balance of provision
In order to evaluate the effectiveness of different kinds of accommodation for old people, each must be seen in relation to other ways of providing care. The various forms of care are not discrete: similar types or levels of care may be provided in different forms of accommodation. An authority may set up a new sheltered housing scheme with a warden, or may arrange for peripatetic wardens to visit elderly people in ordinary housing on a regular basis. For frail tenants of a sheltered housing scheme, a range and intensity of domiciliary services may be supplied almost equal to that which would be available in residential care. Increasing disability of sheltered housing tenants has led some authorities to provide 'very sheltered' housing, halfway between traditional sheltered housing and residential homes; increasing disability of those in residential homes has led social services departments to join with health authorities in providing 'high dependency' homes, with considerable nursing care. Another approach is an administrative one: housing departments and other voluntary and statutory agencies can provide for the housing of elderly people near relatives, and thus reduce the need for sheltered accommodation (Tinker 1980).

Researchers have noted that many of those continuing to live in ordinary domestic housing are as frail as those in any of the forms of special accommodation, and they have also observed people of similar levels of disability among those in the various forms of sheltered housing, residential homes and hospitals (for example, Plank 1977 and

1978; Alexander and Eldon 1979; Clark *et al* 1979; McDonnell *et al* 1979; Pattie *et al* 1979; Dodd *et al* 1980). This situation arises for many reasons, including undiscovered need and variations in 'coping ability', but also from lack of the most appropriate types of accommodation in a particular area at a particular time. Those who arrange care may lack knowledge of alternatives, or administrative barriers may militate against effective co-ordination of housing, social services and health resources. Many admissions to residential care occur as a result of an emergency. Those who live in sheltered housing or residential homes may become increasingly frail as they age, or they may improve in health and mobility with rest and treatment.

Some overlap may be desirable, providing necessary flexibility to the system; a large amount may be inevitable. However, there seems little agreement about what could and should be done to encourage or limit it. One reaction has been to urge that more clear-cut divisions between different types of caring environments be (re)instated, ignoring the understandable reluctance of many old people to move on from one place to another, even though the new accommodation may be better adapted to their current need. Another reaction has been to accept a certain degree of overlap in the long run but to limit it by carefully planned allocation policies – for example, by choosing new tenants for sheltered housing from those who are in housing need but not greatly (as yet) in need of social care. Yet another suggestion has been to make sheltered housing the basic provision, since many elderly people appear to have a preference for this, and to provide social and nursing services at a level sufficient to meet the needs arising from increasing frailty of tenants.

The existence of these overlaps complicates the difficult questions concerning balance of care. What is the 'right' balance in any locality between accommodation provided by housing departments, social services departments and health authorities? What are the appropriate roles of the private, voluntary and statutory sectors? Even on the assumption that community care of old people in their own homes is 'best', is there an irreducible proportion of resources that must be devoted to accommodation in residential homes? Any evaluation of particular types of accommodation must take into account these more general questions, with their implications for co-ordination among agencies in planning and decision-making, for administrative structures which allow for communication in day-to-day working, and perhaps for common assessment procedures.

A number of studies have looked at current use of various services and the flow between them (see, for example, Canvin *et al* 1978; Mooney 1978; Vaswani *et al* 1978; Cormell and Coles 1979). Others have described attempts at joint health/social services assessment

(Camden SSD 1978). An important ingredient in any discussion of the balance of care ought to be the wishes of elderly people themselves, but attempts to ascertain these meet the usual difficulties when hypothetical situations are at issue, and when elderly people are asked for their opinions *before* they are faced with choices in reality. To take a subject of current concern: how are the short-term care needs of frail elderly people best met? Should social service departments, in conjunction with health authorities, be considering domiciliary services, a temporarily resident aid in assisted lodgings, short-stay care in a residential home or hospital ward? How much choice can be afforded to individual people, and on what basis can an authority plan its resources and arrange its assessment and allocation procedures to offer such choices? What are the costs (financial and otherwise) of any particular balance, and on whom do they fall?

Framework for evaluation
By no means all of the questions about the 'right' degree of overlap, the 'right' balance of provision, can be answered by research; but these issues can, at least, be raised by researchers for consideration by policy makers. Evaluation seems to us critical in relation to accommodation. For the elderly person, the emotional and other implications of moving to another environment may be drastic, and the cost of allocation to different kinds of accommodation may vary widely (Wright *et al* 1981). In the following sections we will be looking at the aims of different ypes of accommodation, the needs they are intended to meet and how they are assessed, what the inputs are, and what can be said about outcomes.

Assisted lodgings
Assisted lodgings are a form of accommodation available at present on a minute scale, but are seen as having potential for an important role in meeting some kinds of care needs. Accommodation is arranged by a voluntary or statutory agency in the home of someone willing to provide more support than would normally be expected from a landlord or landlady, although the level of care may vary from little additional support to virtual incorporation into the family unit. The choices open to elderly people and those with some responsibility for their welfare can in this way (at least in theory) be widened considerably. Such lodgings can provide an alternative to residential home or hospital for short stays, for example for convalescence or while caring relatives are on holiday; they can provide a long-term base for those who have spent many years in an institution and have no home of their own to return to, or who need to unlearn habits of dependency before being able to function independently. For those who cannot live any longer in their own homes without a very great deal of support from domiciliary

services, a move to a lodging of this kind can provide a basis for continued living outside an institution.

A number of those organising such schemes have written accounts of them, and two recent studies have explored the rationale and achievement of assisted lodgings more fully. Neither study was able to compare these achievements with those of other types of special accommodation. The aim of the action-research project in North Yorkshire, Family Homes for the Handicapped (supported jointly by the DHSS and the Joseph Rowntree Memorial Trust), was to explore the possibility of placing handicapped adults with ordinary families, and 12 of the 38 people placed were aged 60 or over (Penfold 1980). The DHSS project Assisted Lodgings for the Elderly at Leeds University had a wider brief: to survey the scope of formal arrangements for assisted lodgings in private households in England and Wales. The full report (Thornton and Moore 1980) outlines the schemes located, describes different models of practice, raises issues for policy and practice, and discusses the scope for expansion. A summary of this report provides a more concise picture of the study and its findings (Greve 1981).

Background

According to Thornton and Moore, assisted lodgings schemes for the 'mainstream' elderly began to achieve popularity in the 1950s and early 1960s. However, only 23 schemes run by voluntary organisations or social services departments were located by them in England and Wales in the late 1970s, and all but two of these had been set up since 1974. In comparison with earlier schemes, they were more likely to be organised by the social services department than a voluntary agency, to cater for more dependent people, and to provide more continuing support for both elderly person and carer; sometimes payment of a fee to the carer was part of the arrangement. Thus there seems to have been some movement from arranged lodgings as housing to arranged lodgings as care.

The tiny proportion of the elderly population at present reached by such schemes can be seen in the Leeds researchers' estimates of 50 people in long-term placement in April 1980, and 285 who had had short-term stays in 1979. Frequently agencies had made a deliberate choice to restrict numbers in order 'to test the viability of the concept and its operation, to complement other resources for elderly people, to provide a service where quality rather than quantity is the measure'. Additionally, some schemes started with small resources and 'the battle for further resources has proved difficult to fight'.

Aims

Some short-term schemes have quite clear aims. The boarding-out scheme of the Liverpool Personal Service Society, for example, was set up to provide respite for those who look after an elderly relative, and rehabilitation for an elderly person after hospital care (Newton 1979 and 1980). Thornton and Moore, however, refer to 'the diversity of stated objectives' among schemes nationally. In general, aims are defined in terms of extending the number and range of care places available. Living in a private household is seen as more 'normal', providing a suitable combination of protection, independence, and exposure to risk, and making individual care and attention possible for those who need it. In long-term placements, the usual questions arise about whether encouragement of independence is an appropriate and realistic aim. In a study in New York, Newman and Sherman (1977) noted that carers frequently acted in a 'maternalistic' way, 'much as if they were housing foster children' and suggested that 'training might facilitate the incorporation of these elderly individuals on an adult basis'. Those who volunteer care within an organised assisted lodgings scheme (rather than taking in lodgers in the usual way) may, however, resist encouragement of independence, despite training.

Needs

For what type of elderly people is such accommodation considered appropriate? No clear picture emerges from the studies. This may be partly because of the relative novelty of this form of care: few elderly people or their carers request it as yet, and schemes are still gaining experience of what kinds of people seem to cope well in this environment and what degree of support works best. Additionally, as Thornton and Moore point out:

> almost all long-term placement schemes have found that the supply of carers falls behind the demand for placement. . . Accordingly, clients are chosen to fit the carers, rather than vice versa. As a result, clients to whom the scheme might wish to give priority can be passed over in favour of other clients who can be more suitably matched.

Long-term schemes generally tended to look for users among people for whom hospital or residential care was no longer required, but who needed some help in daily living; people living alone who, with increasing frailty, required supervision, help with self-care or company; and people with accommodation needs arising from a variety of circumstances. The social workers in the North Yorkshire project attempted to recruit elderly people (without any specific handicap) from old people's homes and from the community, with little success; a number of factors were thought to be involved, including disinclination to move, and the uncertainties of the scheme in its initial stages. Thus, elderly people placed by the scheme were those with particular physical and/or mental disabilities (Penfold 1980). Short-term schemes are usually intended as respite for caring relatives, rather than to meet any specific 'need' on the part of the elderly person, or else as an alternative to short-term stays in residential care, whether for relatives' respite or other reasons.

Because of the concern to match users with existing carers, little in the way of systematic assessment procedures seem to be used. Thornton and Moore note that

> those in use concentrate mainly on the clients' physical state and self-care capacity, but some fuller forms cover temperament, habits, hobbies, likes and dislikes, as well as home background. Such information tends to be used as indicators of the suitability of possible host families, rather than as a measure of the priority of need.

The 'intuition' of schemes' officers of what was acceptable to individual carers seemed to be the most common assessment device.

Inputs

As in day care, some physical aspects of the environment are important. Other inputs are: the organisation and financing of schemes; the characteristics – including adaptability – of the elderly people; and the characteristics – including caring and coping abilities – of the carers.

The physical aspects of the dwelling, and its geographical location, may affect the appropriateness of the placement; this is probably less so in short-term than long-term care, although some of the intended advantages of short-term care can be vitiated if excessive physical strain is involved. In considering organisational factors, Thornton and Moore concluded that no model of organisation could at present be said to be the 'right' one for a form of provision which is still in its infancy. As noted above in relation to 'need', the group for whom care is intended is rather ill-defined; however, some striking facts emerge from the various reports about the age and disability levels of the people placed. In the Liverpool short-term scheme, the average age was 78 (Newton 1979); in the short-term scheme run by Leeds Social Services Department (1979) it was 79 (of the first 51 persons accommodated, 9 were over 90). Those in long-term placements were, on average, much younger; Thornton and Moore think this is related to the proportion of old people who have come from long-stay hospitals. Carers were found who were willing to accommodate elderly people who were confused, or very frail, or incontinent, and Thornton and Moore note that many carers stated their willingness to undertake more physical care than had been required of them so far.

In the case of carers, the situation appears too diffuse for easy generalisation, although married women whose children have left home predominate. Previous experience in caring for an elderly person, either within the family or as nurse, home help, or similar occupation seemed relatively common: Anstee (1978) commented that over half the landladies taking patients from a Salisbury hospital were qualified nurses. Newman and Sherman (1977) found in New York that 'family-type interaction' seemed *more* likely when fewer 'natural' family members were present, and suggested that 'foster care might provide caretakers who are themselves in their 50s and older with a meaningful role in their later years'. The North Yorkshire project attempted a careful analysis of many variables, but concluded that the most striking fact was how varied the carers were, and therefore how difficult it was to predict success on the basis of their characteristics (Penfold 1980).

Preparing and supporting the carers is frequently considered to be an important input, as is some assurance of back-up should the placement break down. Opportunities for informal discussion of mutual problems among carers were provided by the Leeds, Liverpool and North Yorkshire schemes.

Outcome

Thornton and Moore found that, in general, the organisers of the schemes did not consider evaluating the outcome of individual placements, and they noted that number of placements could not be taken as an index of success of a scheme as a whole, where quality rather than quantity was so often an expressed aim. The fact that long-term placements have been achieved and have lasted, that short-term placements have effected their purpose of giving respite to relatives or a brief break to elderly people, that some closer relationships have come about, seem to have been taken as reasonable indicators of successful outcome, at least in the absence of time or resources for more sophisticated measurements. Barley and Wilson, in a report on the East Sussex long-term scheme (1979), defined success as 'those placements where both the host family and the client were prepared to continue the placement indefinitely'. Newton (1979), in reporting on the first year's operation of the Liverpool scheme, refers to the elderly users' enjoyment of the experience, their appreciation and that of their relatives at the personal attention offered by carers, and the pleasure the carers themselves took in exercising their skill and dedication in this way. The Leeds Social Services Department report (1979) refers to 'the forging of relationships . . . continuing beyond the actual period of the placement' as having been 'one of the outstanding features of the scheme'. Thus mutual emotional satisfaction with the relationship was regarded as an important criterion of success. Detailed evaluation based on functional, behavioural and attitudinal criteria was an integral part of the North Yorkshire action/research project, and the *Final Report* (Penfold 1980) gives details of the method of evaluation used, based on data collected

188 Social Care for the Elderly

initially and then periodically during the course of each of the 38 placements. One set of measures concerned changes in condition, performance, activities and social relationships; where possible, scales relating to specific disabilities were included (for the physically handicapped, for example, there were scales measuring self-care and mobility). A further set of measures was concerned with clients' feelings and views: 'first, how the clients felt during placement – were they happy, sad, anxious, relaxed, etc.; secondly, how they saw their environment – did they regard themselves as well cared for, encouraged and surrounded by opportunities; thirdly, the preference of clients for different living situations.' Finally, an attempt was made to evaluate various aspects of the care given and 'the opportunities and restrictions of the environment'. However, the researcher was aware of the value judgements entering the assessments and the difficulty of establishing just which changes were brought about by the family placement, in the absence of a control group. Development of the measures must, in any case, be regarded as a pilot exploration, as so few people, with such a range of disabilities, were placed.

Thornton and Moore were able to collect some 'impressionstic' views about outcome from users, a few relatives, carers, and social workers organising schemes. They found that most of the short-term users expressed great satisfaction with the personal qualities of the carer and the trouble taken to please them; they would be 'happy to use the service for a further stay' (about half had previously been for short stays in residential homes – most preferred assisted lodgings). About one-third, however, found themselves unsettled or lonely on return home.

'With long term clients their satisfaction tended to relate to the care with which they and the carers were prepared for the placement.' Although they seemed pleased also with their standard of living in the placement,

> it was difficult to elicit comments from clients on their attitudes to the more intangible support offered to them: often clients preferred to look on the arrangement as a type of lodgings and to avoid consideration of the fact that they required supervision or support. A small number of clients were initially overwhelmed by the level of care and attention and found it difficult to work out their status in the household.

Those relatives approached 'appeared to have confidence both in the efficiency of the scheme and the capabilities of the carers, and to have no qualms about leaving the clients in their care'.

Carers and social workers noted marked differences in outlook of previously institutionalised or isolated people, and 'the most striking change . . . was in the social competence of subnormal and institutionalised elderly people. The extent of improvement related clearly to the sensitivity of the carers and the encouragement they gave to clients.' This was related, in the view of the researchers, to the guidance and support given by the social workers. However, these are subjective judgements, and no independent before-and-after assessments are available.

In any discussion of outcome, the question of aims is all-important: is the aim the provision of caring accommodation, or is there some therapeutic intent beyond this? What is meant by the term 'caring accommodation'? What are the implications of various ways of answering these questions for the organisation of schemes, recruitment and training of carers, matching processes, the elderly people's *own* views of their requirements, commitment by agencies to long-term social work support (as Thornton and Moore point out, not otherwise usual with elderly clients), and so on?

If knowledge of this type of care grows, and carers become easier to recruit and to hold, some of the difficulties in matching may be eased. These difficulties might also decrease if planning of care and moves to new accommodation could be considered gradually, over a period of months if necessary, rather than – as so often at present – at a crisis point in the elderly person's life. Even so, the apparently problematic nature of matching for long-term placements, together with the real dilemmas which such placements raise about the continuing responsibility of the organising agencies, may mean that resources are best devoted to short-term placements. (Some of these, of course, may turn into long-term placements.)

The considerable amount of information now available about assisted lodging schemes makes clear the need for individual agencies to look critically at planned or expanding schemes in terms of what they can achieve, and at what cost, in relation to other ways of providing accommodation and/or care for elderly people.

Sheltered housing

The term 'sheltered housing' is used to refer to specially designed or converted houses, flats or flatlets – grouped, and with a resident warden; there may or may not be an alarm system and communal facilities such as a common room, laundry or eating facilities. Local authority provision of such dwellings rests with housing departments, and those who live in them are tenants, like other people renting local authority housing. Social services departments may take responsibility, however, for the provision of warden services or their costs. In some authorities the social services department has little or no say in allocation of tenancies, while in others it largely controls allocation.

There is a considerable research literature on sheltered housing, as well as working party reports and discussions of policies and problems by housing managers and other practitioners. Research has dealt with allocation, the size and design of schemes, the role of the warden, the views of tenants on design and functioning, and so on. A study at the University of Leeds, sponsored by the Joseph Rowntree Memorial Trust (Butler *et al* 1983), includes a survey of 600 tenants and 280 wardens of local authority and voluntary association schemes in 12 housing areas; some data available from the study are referred to later. Besides this, the Leeds sheltered housing researchers have prepared a *Critical Review* (Butler *et al* 1979) which brings together and discusses within a policy context much of the available literature.

Background

Sheltered housing schemes were originally envisaged as a useful form of housing midway between an elderly person's ordinary dwelling (perhaps now unnecessarily large or inconvenient) and care in a residential home. A number of Acts and Circulars in the late 1950s and early 1960s gave power and encouragement to housing authorities to provide special housing for the elderly, and to welfare authorities to provide warden services. A 1969 Circular classified such housing as category 1 (self contained dwellings) and category 2 (grouped flatlets for the more disabled, with certain common facilities) – the assumption was that more mobile elderly people would inhabit the former, the less mobile, the latter.

In 1963 only about 36,000 people were thought to be living in sheltered housing. Subsequently this form of accommodation has grown in popularity – at least partly as a reaction against the institutional nature of much residential care; about five per cent of the elderly population, roughly 300,000 people, were thought to be living in such schemes by 1976 (Hunt 1978), with a more recent estimate of 400,000 (Butler and Oldman 1980). Most sheltered housing is provided by local authorities, with a growing proportion – perhaps now 20 per cent – provided by voluntary organisations or voluntary housing associations (Butler 1980).

Originally it was thought that tenants would need only a little special care. A London working party on the role of the warden agreed in 1970 that the aim should be 'to re-create for old people a kind of family life, with opportunities for neighbourliness, but offering always maximum privacy and independence' (Greater London Conference on Old People's Welfare 1970). A working party report by Age Concern in 1972 on the role of the warden preferred to use the term 'grouped housing' rather than 'sheltered housing', as this suggested to them 'a degree of care and support not really found or indeed desirable . . . the use of "sheltered" may mask the basic aim of maintaining independence as fully and for as long as possible and could even discourage would-be applicants'. The working party saw the aim as providing 'convenient, well-planned self-contained dwellings for elderly people which offer them the opportunity of retaining their independence and yet give security, the background support of a warden and help in an emergency. Privacy is assured by each dwelling having its own front door'. The role of the warden was said to be one of 'underlining rather than undermining the independence and relative normality of the tenants'.

However, once people moved into such dwellings they were reluctant to leave them, and increasing age and infirmity of existing tenants has meant a growing dependent population, with the boundaries between tenants of the two 1969 categories becoming blurred. In addition, recent emphasis on delivery of domiciliary services to people in ordinary domestic housing has meant that by the time tenancies are sought in special housing, the people involved may be more disabled than had originally been envisaged. Attempts to deal with this have contributed to a vicious circle: as greater responsibilities are shouldered by wardens, relief wardens appointed, and more domiciliary resources allocated to schemes, so these services become an expected part of sheltered housing. Those nominating elderly people from the community, and those responsible for intake and discharge from hospitals and residential homes, assume a high level of care in sheltered housing, and tenancies are requested for more severely physically or mentally disabled people. Tenants may be sent back to such schemes from hospital sooner than they would be otherwise; tenants may be refused admission to residential homes on the grounds that they are too frail. Those younger and more active elderly people whose presence could in many ways ease the problems of the older schemes may refuse tenancies, considering the atmosphere too similar to that of a residential home.

There has been a range of reactions to this situation – the severity of which, of course, varies from one area to another, depending on when schemes were built, what other resources are available, and so on. The impression received by Bytheway and James in their study of allocation policies (1978) was that while both housing and social services departments recognised the 'drift', the former tried to fight it while the latter accepted it as inevitable. One response has been the substitution of 'very sheltered' for 'sheltered' housing: accommodation designed without stairs, with rooms and door openings large enough to ease use of wheelchairs and walking aids, and with specific commitment to high levels of staffing. Another has been the deliberate choice of 'fitter' candidates from the waiting lists when vacancies occur: elderly people whose bad housing conditions might be exacerbating a health problem, but who are unlikely, at least initially, to generate many demands upon the resident warden, and who seem likely 'to make a contribution towards the life of the community' (Thompson 1981).

Aims and needs

It will be apparent from the discussion thus far that sheltered housing may have three kinds of aims, within the more general objective of helping maintain independence: to fill a housing need; to fill a 'social' need for security, neighbourliness, general support; and to fill a social care need. Any particular scheme may encompass all these aims, and may be successful in meeting them. Difficulties arising from differences of view about the order of priorities of the aims are, however, likely to occur in designing schemes, in determining staffing levels and roles, and in allocation of tenancies. When a new scheme is being opened, and applicants far outnumber the units available, to what extent will social services or health personnel be involved or consulted, and how will housing department procedures weight one 'need' against another? If the greatest need is one for accommodation, is *sheltered* housing required or is it allocated unnecessarily because of lack of other small dwellings, or lack of imagination or funds for alterations to the existing dwellings? If the greatest need is social, would assisted lodgings, or opportunities to attend clubs or day centres be at least as suitable as a move to sheltered housing? Where the main need is for social care, will a sheltered housing scheme be able to provide this at an appropriate level?

Butler (1980) wryly quotes a warden as saying 'If an applicant is fit he doesn't need sheltered housing. If he is incapacitated in any way he is unsuitable'. Butler goes on to note that the tenant, the warden, the housing manager, the social services director may all quite legitimately have different views about the role sheltered housing does and should play. Who, then, become tenants?

A number of studies have examined the reasons given by tenants for moving to sheltered housing, and these give some indication of the 'need' involved. Inadequate housing conditions (perhaps especially in the private rented sector) are an important reason for moving: cold, damp, inadequate facilities, or the elderly person no longer being able to cope with stairs or other aspects of the dwelling. This last, however, is presumably related to failing health – another important reason given for the move. This again is related to a third type of reason: the felt need for security such as a warden and an alarm system may provide.

Oldman and Butler (1980) have suggested that the use of systematic assessment procedures based on points systems or 'need scales', while apparently fairer than more *ad hoc* procedures, may inadequately reflect the 'real' preferences of the elderly people themselves, which may not be for sheltered accommodation at all. In their study of 600 tenants they found that 30 per cent had, before the move, considered other council housing as an alternative; and that 23 per cent said they would have preferred to stay in their own home if improvements had been possible (Oldman 1980). They point out that, increasingly, housing associations are devising formal methods of assessment comparable to those used by local authorities.

Inputs
Among the important inputs influencing the effectiveness of sheltered housing are physical factors: the size and design of the individual dwellings, heating arrangements, the location of schemes, the number of units involved, the inclusion of communal facilities, and so on. Those studies which have sought tenants' views on aspects of design have found fairly general satisfaction, tempered by criticism of some features which date from earlier concepts of sheltered housing which are now less acceptable (e.g. shared bathrooms, toilets in blocks across corridors); some features which are not uncommon in ordinary housing, and are probably equally exasperating to younger tenants (tiny kitchens, inadequate storage space, too few and badly placed electric points); and some features which are not suitable for the more disabled tenants in a scheme. Department of the Environment Circular 8/80, *The Housing Cost Yardstick and Lifts in Old People's Dwellings* (DoE 1980) has recognised the changing situation by sanctioning installation of lifts in two-storey buildings. One of the major planks in Warwickshire's very sheltered housing policy is 'all parts of the complex to be accessible without having to climb steps and stairs'; even a single step to the front door of a bungalow can be a barrier to someone in a wheelchair (Reed and Faulkner 1980).

The design of a scheme as a whole has been looked at from the point of view of optimum number of units (see especially Griffin and Dean 1975), location, views, noise levels, security of premises, and so on. As might be expected, a range of views usually emerges. All these aspects undoubtedly have some influence on how satisfactory tenants find the housing overall, but location is now recognised to be of special importance on a number of counts. If maintenance of independence is to be the aim, there must be easy access to shopping facilities and pub, church, library, and so on. The Warwickshire study found, for example, that the majority of tenants in the six schemes left the complex at least once a week, and 'shopping' was the destination most frequently quoted; most of the schemes were near shops and village or town centres (Reed and Faulkner 1980). Of at least equal importance with respect to location is whether the scheme is in or very near to the tenant's former neighbourhood, or, alternatively, was chosen because of its proximity to relatives or friends. It is, of course, unrealistic to expect applicants always to be able to have a choice of schemes which includes one in their own neighbourhood. One of the reasons why some authorities have instituted peripatetic warden schemes, and installation of alarms in ordinary dwellings, is the disruption of social and support networks which can be caused by a move of only a mile or two; recognition of this has led to a number of such initiatives by the London Borough of Hammersmith and Fulham, described by Chapman (1981) and Tunney (1981).

Because of the shared responsibility of housing and social services departments, the relationships between the two and the allocation procedures which result is an important organisational and administrative input. In non-metropolitan counties, housing is a district responsibility and social services a county one, which may make co-ordination somewhat more difficult than in metropolitan districts and London boroughs. The national study by Bytheway and James (1978), which explored the subject of allocation, asked about procedures, and about the views of housing and social services staff on the role of sheltered housing, relationships with the other department, and so on. Diverse views emerged, and a wide range of practices, from virtually no social services involvement to very substantial control. The Leeds University study hoped to build on this by including more detailed observation of how referral and allocation actually work, and what the processes are by which somebody 'emerges' as a sheltered housing tenant (Oldman 1980). Reed and Faulkner suggest that application forms for sheltered housing and residential care 'which have common questions on relevant factors such as dependency' may facilitate co-operation.

Originally, it was usual for only one warden to be assigned to a scheme, and she was on call virtually 24 hours a day, seven days a week. This probably was never a satisfactory system, but it has become less viable as residents have become more disabled, so that the employment of assistant wardens and relief wardens as well as provision of domiciliary and nursing care have become necessary.

Tenants of sheltered housing are generally thought to receive more care than those of equal disability in ordinary housing. Although this seems inequitable to some observers, it is perhaps inevitable, given the greater 'visibility' of such concentrations of need, the greater knowledge among tenants of possible aid when they observe their neighbours receiving such help, the role of the warden in liaising with the agencies involved, and the possibility of more efficient use of, for example, home help time when no travelling is necessary between clients. The Leeds University study has found that of the 600 tenants studied, 16–17 per cent were receiving meals-on-wheels and approximately 30 per cent home help; in a study of 129 tenants in ten schemes in Hillingdon 20 per cent were found to be receiving meals-on-wheels and 59 per cent home help (Hillingdon Housing Department 1978). The relative intensity of this provision may be seen by comparison with the proportions found in Hunt's 1976 study of *The Elderly at Home*: overall, 2.6 per cent had received meals-on-wheels within the past six months, although the figure was 8.5 per cent for those aged 85 and over; overall 8.9 per cent had received home help services, with 15.8 per cent of the 75–84 age group and 27.3 per cent of those aged 85 and over receiving such help.

A useful source of information about client characteristics is the *Critical Review* of sheltered housing by Butler *et al* (1979), which compares the findings of ten previous studies. Some of the findings of the national survey are given by Butler (1980). Just over half of the 600 tenants were over 75 years old. Age was associated with the age of the particular scheme: 64 per cent of those living in schemes opened between 1965 and 1969 were over 75, whereas only 44 per cent of those in schemes opened since 1975 were over 75. The study provides some confirmation that the average age on entry is now higher than it used to be: women who have been in sheltered housing less than one year average 75.8 years, while those who have been tenants for over eight years average 77.6 years. In areas where sheltered housing was particularly scarce, age on entry was found to be higher than where such housing was more plentiful.

Poor housing conditions seemed to be 'a powerful reason' for allocation of a sheltered housing place, as 25 per cent had previously had no running water, 22 per cent no bathroom, and 23 per cent no inside toilet; in Hunt's 1976 study of *The Elderly at Home* the comparable figures were 8 per cent, 11 per cent and 12 per cent. However, 69 per cent of those moving to sheltered housing recently had done so for 'health reasons', whereas the figure was 41 per cent for those moving over 8 years before.

Considerable information is available about the warden and her role. Boldy and others, in a number of studies in Devon, have provided some details about what wardens actually do (Boldy *et al* 1973; Boldy 1976 and 1977). The changes taking place are indicated in diaries kept by wardens: in 1973 wardens in the schemes Boldy surveyed were spending on average 20 hours a week in general support of tenants and 'emergency' activities such as cooking and nursing, whereas in 1977, for the same schemes, this had risen to 28 hours. These figures do not include time spent in 'chat' or on call; in 1977 nearly one third of these wardens were not officially allowed any time off.

Heumann (1980) has carried out a study of wardens of 34 voluntary and local authority schemes in the West Midlands. A list of 29 duties was derived from earlier studies, and wardens were asked whether these duties were required by management, not required but done anyway, or specifically *not* to be done. All wardens provided 'neighbourly services' (paying regular calls on tenants, contacting relatives, arranging doctors visits) whether required to or not; there was more variation in relation to caretaking and organisational services. Thompson (1981) has described the way in which wardens in Hammersmith were relieved of some of their excessive burden of individual caring, and helped to move into a more enabling role, encouraging less frail tenants to provide assistance to the more frail.

Heumann stresses the 'strong socio-economic compatibility between wardens and residents in all the schemes', and notes that 'from observation of the sheltered housing schemes, the average warden was an acceptable proxy for the average resident's own daughter'. Views about characteristics of the 'good warden' were sought from wardens and managers, and three answers accounted for 60 per cent of the replies: 'loving and tolerant', 'patient', and 'shows good common sense'. In addition, managers were concerned with the warden's ability to spot changes in 'physical health, hygiene, social activity and personality; project a sense of trust and authority among the residents, especially during emergencies; and call in appropriate help for further diagnosis, support or assistance'. Managers were in complete agreement about what constituted a model warden (92 per cent of the 128 wardens were said to fall into this group): 'someone who keeps the residents independent and actively engaged in society'. The ineffective warden was one who 'undercares', who is 'elderly dominated', or who 'overcares by choice'. These concepts strike one as rather global and unrealistic.

The tendency of some wardens to encourage dependency has been noted with concern by a number of researchers. For example, Griffin and Dean, in their study of the size of grouped schemes (1975), suggest that the close contact between warden and tenants in some of the smaller schemes 'encouraged overdependence on the warden and occasionally resulted in a situation of conflict between warden and tenants, making all concerned unhappy'. Butler has referred (1979) to 'the rather proprietal role adopted by some wardens'. The frequent use of the phrase 'warden-controlled housing' as a synonym for 'sheltered housing' may be of some significance!

Outcome
Given the various aims of sheltered housing, what are appropriate indicators of outcome? The Warwickshire study includes a chapter called 'The question of happiness'; the authors comment on the difficulty of judging this, but suggest that 'information which at least touches on the subject is available from various sources, namely comments from interviewers, observations made when visiting schemes, questions about the accommodation, and direct questions about whether tenants were "glad" to have made the move to sheltered or very sheltered housing.' (Reed and Faulkner 1980). Happiness, perhaps, is too complex an emotion to be readily used as an indicator of

outcome, but the opinions of tenants about various aspects of living in sheltered housing, and the views of wardens on how adequately schemes function (together with views of policy makers and administrators as to the value of schemes as a contribution to accommodation for the elderly) are useful subjective indicators in evaluating the effectiveness of sheltered housing.

Taking account of the general aim of helping people stay in their own homes for as long as possible, some researchers looking for 'harder' data have considered the numbers of those moving out of schemes to live in hospital wards or residential homes (a negative indicator), and the number of those whose death occurs either in the sheltered accommodation or else after a very short period in hospital care (a positive indicator). Boldy and his colleagues, in the Devon study (1973), found that only 13 per cent of tenants who were no longer in the schemes had entered long-stay hospital care, residential homes or nursing homes, while 53 per cent of those who were no longer in the schemes had died either in their sheltered home or soon after admission to hospital. A number of other studies have found comparable encouraging results.

The evaluation by Hampshire Social Services Department of Kinloss Court very sheltered housing scheme (Brown 1978) includes monitoring of the progress of residents, some of whom suffered from dementia. Information on psychological state and physical capacity was collected as three-monthly intervals during the first year and subsequently four-monthly, under the headings wandering, dependency, practical ability, incontinence, behaviour problems, mobility, depression and confusion. The extent to which external support services, such as home help, were being made available to residents at Kinloss Court in comparison with tenants of other sheltered units was examined. How much these additional elements of support enabled those at Kinloss Court (who were on admission a frailer group) to maintain their independence and level of functional ability was assessed. Because of the small numbers in the first year, it was not possible for the reseacher to draw very firm conclusions about functioning, although the relative 'volatility' (great swings in condition) of the Kinloss Court residents was observed: almost as many people improved on various measures as deteriorated. Despite the value of such detailed individual monitoring of an innovative scheme, it is likely to prove impracticable for the 'mainstream' elderly tenants of most sheltered housing schemes, who might well see regular 'assessment' as an invasion of privacy.

Consumer views

Local authority departments, voluntary housing groups, and the Department of the Environment have all investigated in some detail the views of tenants, often with the specific intention of improving the design of future schemes. Some of this information, for example about design faults, has been referred to. Surveys usually ask also for overall feelings about living in the scheme. The questions vary in form and in sophistication, but satisfaction appears widespread. Ninety-two per cent of the Warwickshire tenants were glad to have moved to their sheltered homes and 89 per cent were satisfied with the warden service (Reed and Faulkner 1980). In Hillingdon, 42 per cent were 'very satisfied' with their flats and 52 per cent were 'satisfied'; 87 per cent were 'very satisfied' with the way the warden performed her role (Hillingdon Housing Department 1978). In a study of tenants of 23 Merseyside Improved Houses sheltered schemes, 63 per cent of tenants said they were 'very happy' in their accommodation and 33 per cent that they were 'satisfied' (Scott 1978). In the Department of the Environment study, 77 per cent of tenants expressed themselves as 'very satisfied' with their individual dwelling, and 73 per cent as 'very satisfied' with their scheme, although 'satisfaction ratings varied enormously between schemes, with from 30 per cent to 100 per cent being "very satisfied" ' (Griffin and Dean 1975).

The recent national survey found 63 per cent of local authority tenants 'very satisfied' and 26 per cent 'fairly satisfied'; for housing association tenants (whose schemes were newer) the figures were 76 per cent and 18 per cent (Butler and Oldman 1980). Tenants were asked whether they would advise friends or relatives to live in similar housing, and 88 per cent said they would.

Warden satisfaction
Boldy (1977) has said that his impression is that 'the vast majority of wardens . . . obtain considerable satisfaction from their job' and low turnover rates (although perhaps to be expected where housing is provided) give some support to this view. More recently, Reed and Faulkner found that 'wardens in the scheme surveyed gave the impression, on the whole, that they were satisfied'. Other fragmentary information, and the satisfaction of tenants with wardens noted above, suggest that the warden–tenant relationship probably works quite well in general. As the Hillingdon researchers comment, 'tenants obviously get used to different personalities' – and, no doubt, vice versa.

Reed and Faulkner point out that as the 'extras' (such as warden cover) of very sheltered housing are a response to perceived problems in existing schemes, an important part of evaluation must be to ask about the extent to which such problems are alleviated. Discussions with the Warwickshire wardens showed that although the few tenants with behavioural difficulties presented continuing problems, in general the wardens felt able to cope with even quite dependent or severely handicapped tenants, 'as long as they do not require constant supervision because they are likely to fall or in some other way injure themselves'.

Social environment
Little information is available about how successful schemes are in providing an environment in which neighbourliness and mutual support flourish. One of the aims of increasing warden cover in the Warwickshire very sheltered schemes was to reduce the burden on wardens, 'thus enabling them to manage the schemes better and develop the community facilities there'. This aim seems to have been achieved: in the sheltered schemes there were an average of 1.75 activities per scheme per week, whereas for the very sheltered schemes the figure was 6 – 'furthermore, many of the activities at the very sheltered schemes are organised by the tenants themselves . . . whereas in general it is the warden or volunteers who organise them in other schemes'. The common rooms of the very sheltered schemes are used more, not only for such formal activities, but 'as a place to go and sit and have a chat with friends or read a book, etc.'

Size and design – as well as the atmosphere engendered by the warden and the general sociability of tenants at entry – may well play a part in encouraging or discouraging relationships within schemes. As always the question of dependency arises: when do supportive arrangements, with the warden or with other tenants, result in over-dependence? Scott, in his study of voluntary sheltered housing in Liverpool (1978), 'wondered . . . whether the sheer neighbourliness didn't reduce the physical mobility of some tenants. Often tenants shopped for their neighbours who in their absence could probably have made it to the shops.'

Conclusion
Sheltered housing is clearly a popular form of accommodation. It fulfils a number of essential needs and functions in the total social care system. The first reports of very sheltered schemes indicate optimism about this development as a satisfactory method of care. Depite this, critical questions raised earlier still remain unanswered. If the main need is housing why is a special age-segregated scheme necessary, rather than small dwellings of appropriate design within the general housing stock? If the main need is a general one for support and security, is a housing solution the most appropriate one? When the level of disability is such that domiciliary and health services are required on a very intensive scale, is provision of these in sheltered housing really a more efficient and acceptable use of resources than life in a relaxed residential home with carers on the premises, and the possibility of help from other residents?

200   *Social Care for the Elderly*

References

Age Concern (1972) *Role of the Warden in Grouped Housing*, London, Age Concern.

Alexander, J.R. and Eldon, A. (1979) Characteristics of elderly people admitted to hospital, Part III homes, and sheltered housing, *Journal of Epidemiology and Community Health 33*, 91–95.

Anstee, B.H. (1978) An alternative to group homes, *British Journal of Psychiatry 132*, 356–360.

Barley, M. and Wilson, J. (1979) Boarding out officer helps the old, *Community Care*, 11 October.

Boldy, D. (1976) A study of the wardens of grouped dwellings for the elderly, *Social and Economic Administration 10*, 59–69.

Boldy, D. (1977) Is sheltered housing a good thing? In Institute of Social Welfare, *Some Unresolved Aspects of Sheltered Housing for the Elderly and Disabled*.

Boldy, D., Abel, P. and Carter, K. (1973) *The Elderly in Grouped Dwellings: A profile*, University of Exeter Institute of Biometry and Community Medicine, publication no. 3.

Brown, D.M. (1978) *Kinloss Court Sheltered Housing Scheme: A report on the first year's monitoring*, Hampshire Social Services Department, Research Report no. 17.

Butler, A. (1979) Sheltered housing in the 1980s: some implications for policy and practice, *Welfare 9* no. 5, i–iv.

Butler, A. (1980) Profile of the sheltered housing tenant, *Housing 16* No. 6, 6–8.

Butler, A. and Oldman, C (1980) The design and siting of sheltered housing: the consumers' view, *Housing 16* no. 10, 18–20.

Butler, A., Oldman, C. and Wright, R. (1979) *Sheltered Housing for the Elderly, A critical review*, University of Leeds Department of Social Policy and Administration.

Butler, A., Oldman, C. and Greve, J. (1983) *Sheltered Housing for the Elderly*, London, George Allen and Unwin.

Bytheway, W.R. and James, L. (1978) *The Allocation of Sheltered Housing: A study of theory, practice and liaison*, University College Swansea, Medical Sociology Research Centre.

Camden Social Services Department (1978) *Joint Assessment of the Elderly: The first six months*.

Canvin, R., Hamson, J., Lyons, J. and Russell, J.C. (1978) Balance of care in Devon: joint strategic planning of health and social services at AHA and county level, *Health and Social Services Journal*, 18 August.

Chapman, P. (1981) Hammersmith's initiatives: community care of the elderly, *Housing Review 30*, 95–98.

Clarke, M., Hughes, A.O., Dodd, K.J., Palmer, R.L., Brandon, S., Holden, A.M. and Pearce, D. (1979) The elderly in residential care: patterns of disability, *Health Trends 11*, 17–20.

Cormell, M. and Coles, R. (1979) *Planning the Care of the Elderly*, West Sussex Area Health Authority and West Sussex County Council.

Department of the Environment (1980) *The Housing Cost Yardstick and Lifts in Old People's Dwellings*, Circular 8/80.

Dodd, K., Clarke, M. and Palmer, R.L. (1980) Misplacement of the elderly in hospitals and residential homes: a survey and follow-up, *Health Trends 12*, 74–76.

Greater London Conference on Old People's Welfare (1970) *Wardens of Sheltered Housing Schemes for the Elderly*, Report of a working party.

Greve J. (1981) Assisted lodgings for the elderly: summary report, University of Leeds Department of Social Policy and Administration.

Griffin, J. and Dean, C. (1975) *Housing for the Elderly: The size of grouped schemes*, Department of the Environment Design Bulletin No. 31, London, HMSO.

Heumann, L.F. (1980) Sheltered housing for the elderly: the role of the British warden, *Gerontologist 20*, 318–330.

Hillingdon Housing Department (1978) *Tenants' Satisfaction with Sheltered Housing in Hillingdon*, London Borough of Hillingdon.

Hunt, A. (1978) *The Elderly at Home*, London, HMSO.

Leeds Social Services Department (1979) *A New Approach to Caring for the Elderly*.

McDonnell, H., Long, A.F., Harrison, B.J. and Oldman, C. (1979) A study of persons aged 65 and over in the Leeds Metropolitan District, *Journal of Epidemiology and Community Health 33*, 203–209.

Mooney, G.H. (1978) Planning for balance of care of the elderly, *Scottish Journal of Political Economy 25*, 149–164.

Newman, E.S. and Sherman, S.R. (1977) A survey of caretakers in adult foster homes, *Gerontologist 17*, 436–439.

Newton, S. (1979) *The Liverpool Personal Service Society Short-Term Boarding Out Scheme for the Elderly: Report on the first year of the project*, Liverpool: LPSS.

Newton, S. (1980) What shall we do with granny? *New Age*, Summer.

Oldman, C. (1980) Becoming a sheltered housing tenant, in M. Johnson (ed.) *Transitions in Middle and Later Life*. London, British Society of Gerontology.

Oldman, C. and Butler, A. (1980) Who knows best? *Voluntary Housing 12* no. 10, 27–28.

Pattie, A.H., Gilleard, C.J. and Bell, J.H. (1979) *The Relationships of the Intellectual and Behavioural Competence of the Elderly to their Present and Future Needs from Community, Residential and Hospital Services*, York, Clifton Hospital Department of Clinical Psychology.

Penfold, M.E. (1980) *Family Homes for the Handicapped: Final Report*, North Yorkshire Social Services Department.

Plank, D. (1977) *Caring for the Elderly*, London, Greater London Council Research Memorandum 512.

Plank, D. (1978) Old people's homes are not the last refuge, *Community Care*, 1 March.

Reed, C.A. and Faulkner, G.J. (1980) *Your Own Front Door: A study of very sheltered housing in Warwickshire, 1979–80*, Warwickshire Social Services Department.

Scott, M. (1978) *The Elderly in Sheltered Housing: A case study of Merseyside Improved Houses*, Liverpool Personal Service Society. (Shortened version published 1979 in *Social Service Quarterly 52*, 128–32.)

Thompson, L. (1981) Hammersmith's initiatives: housing management in practice, *Housing Review 30*, 98–99

Thornton, P. and Moore, J. (1980) *The Placement of Elderly People in Private*

Households: An analysis of current provision, University of Leeds Department of Social Policy and Administration, See also their *Bibliographies*.

Tinker, A. (1980) *Housing the Elderly near Relatives: Moving and Other Options*, Department of the Environment, Housing Development Directorate Occasional Paper 1/80, London, HMSO.

Tunney, J. (1981) Hammersmith's initiatives: the housing management approach, *Housing Review 30*, 93–95.

Vaswani, N., Parker, C. and Mitchell, J. (1978) *OR Study of Care of the Elderly in Calderdale*, DHSS Operational Research Service Note 41/77. Also *Appendix* to this, by C.J. Parker.

Wright, K.G., Cairns, J.A. and Snell, M.C. (1981) *Costing Care*, University of Sheffield Joint Unit for Social Services Research.

10   Residential Care

In England and Wales in 1980 there were 109,700 elderly people living in homes provided by local authorities, 15,900 living in voluntary or private homes but supported by local authorities and 40,200 others in voluntary and private homes who were not being supported by local authorities. Thus far fewer people live in residential homes than in sheltered housing, but net expenditure on residential care of the elderly by social services departments amounts to about 20 per cent of their total social services expenditure and hence is an important item. According to the Department of Health and Social Security (1977):

> Residential homes are primarily a means of providing a greater degree of support for those elderly people no longer able to cope with the practicalities of living in their own homes even with the help of the domiciliary services. The care provided is limited to that appropriate to a residential setting and is broadly equivalent to what might be provided by a competent and caring relative able to respond to emotional as well as physical needs.*

The exploration of residential care for the elderly was a neglected subject until in 1962 Peter Townsend's *The Last Refuge* burst upon the scene with its depressing revelations about the joyless institutional nature of most old people's lives in statutory residential homes, often in former workhouses. Subsequent concern has been directed towards alternatives to residential care, in the form of sheltered housing and increased domiciliary services, and towards improvements to residential care – in premises, staffing, quality of care and quality of life.

There is little doubt that the physical aspects of residential care for old people have vastly improved during the two decades since Townsend's report. In a recent study (Willcocks *et al* 1982) of a stratified random sample of 100 local authority old people's homes in England, 62 per cent of residents had single rooms. Most homes had lost their forbidding appearance and were found to blend naturally into the neighbourhood, although only one in three had fewer than 40 residents. Over three-quarters of residents were living in homes which were situated in the district in which they used to live.

Notions are gradually taking root that old people's homes should be of domestic scale, where people can feel as much as possible 'at home', and that they should be aimed at the convenience and well-being of the

* Reproduced with the permission of the Controller of Her Majesty's Stationery Office.

residents rather than at the smooth running of the home as an administrative unit. At least, most people pay lip service to such notions. In the survey just quoted, staff in virtually all the homes said that visitors could drop in at any time, and that residents could bring their own pictures and ornaments; and 62 per cent of the homes' residents had a say in the redecoration of their bedrooms.

Most people now shudder at the picture of very old people dozing or staring into space in identical chairs placed around the walls of a large lounge, lining up for toileting and bathing, being dressed by hurried night staff early in the morning and then waiting more than an hour for breakfast. However, homes where such practices can be found are described in at least three recent studies. No elaborate treatises on the impact of residential care are needed to recognise the dehumanising and dependency-creating elements in such practices, although it is important to understand the reasons for their persistence, albeit on a diminishing scale.

Other models of care are increasingly advocated and described. Among these are group unit living, where small groups of old people live together in quasi-domestic units doing as much as possible for themselves and for each other, much as they might have done in their own homes. Another is a modified 'hotel' model: relaxed regimes where people can get up when they like, look after their own rooms as far as they are capable, potter as they might have done at home, come together in small groups for knitting or gossiping, or spend as much time as they like in their bedsitting rooms, have their meals in the restaurant or have them sent to their rooms. Yet another model recently suggested by Willcocks *et al* (1982) is the 'residential flatlet' – 'a larger, more flexibly equipped version of the single room. It would differ from sheltered housing in size, and in that it would remain part of a supportive residential environment. Nevertheless, it would be an unmistakably designated home territory, lockable from the inside, within which the resident would be in complete control'.

In contrast to those who accept a great deal of dependency and passivity among very old people, there are the 'engagement' advocates, who suggest that stimulation and engagement in purposeful activity is generally preferable to passivity, however old and frail residents of a home may be. An apt quotation found in Davies and Knapp (1981) comes to mind: 'Although idleness and meditation may be acceptable for St Thomas and for the gurus of teenagers today, American activity-oriented middle-agers become distraught when Grandpa sits on the porch in his rocking chair for undue lengths of time' (Rosencranz 1974, p. 66). It is worth keeping in mind too that the average age of people in residential homes is now 83, and that a 'home' composed of such very old people is a very 'unnatural' and artificial community.

What can evaluative research tell us about the pros and cons of the many different patterns of communal living for old people – as different in their personalities and attitudes to activity and sociability as other age groups, although their increasing frailty often demands some degree of continuing care? As in other sections of this book, our aims will be to ascertain what has been established so far about aims, needs, inputs and outcomes of various patterns of residential care for the elderly as well as to search for tools and methods which can help practitioners and administrators themselves to evaluate what they are doing and achieving.

As regards methods of evaluation, there are very few controlled experimental studies except those designed to test outcomes of specific forms of intervention, such as reality orientation for the mentally confused or engagement in particular purposeful activities. On the other hand, this is a field par excellence for cross-institutional comparisons where different kinds of outcome can be related to different types of input in terms of physical design, regime and care practices.

The research literature of the last twenty years is vast. While many of the theoretical concepts and measures were developed in the United States, we shall be concentrating mainly on the British studies which have adapted some of these measures for use in the British context. All concerned with research into residential care for old people owe a particular debt to Davies and Knapp (1981), Hughes and Wilkin (1980) and Ward (1980). Davies and Knapp, in their monumental work *Old People's Homes and the Production of Welfare*, have made the theoretical research literature in this field (much of it American) accessible to British researchers and practitioners. Hughes and Wilkin have provided far more than a 'review of the literature', as they entitle their critical discussion of the research material available on admission procedures and the quality of life studies seen from different perspectives in homes for old people. Ward has concentrated his attention on measures of quality of life and quality of the environment. Clearly in this one chapter we can hope only to lift out some evaluative research which has helped to illuminate aims, input and outcome of residential care for old people.

Aims of residential care

Since for many elderly people residential care involves taking up their last permanent residence, the aim most often articulated is that of making it as much as possible 'like home' in which people can continue to do the things they are accustomed to doing, but in safe surroundings with the assurance that support and care are available as and when needed. The crucial question in residential care, as in other forms of social care, is how to achieve the right balance between encouraging activity and helping people to preserve a sense of autonomy over their physical and social life, while at the same time providing sensitive support and care when dependence on others becomes necessary. The DHSS in its *Memorandum of Guidance* on health care in residential homes (1977) has tried to give expression to some of these ideas:

> The organisation and management of a Home should provide an environment in which elderly people may lead as normal a life as they are able, maintaining individuality and dignity and retaining their status as independent adults. Although most new residents are already very old and many have several disabilities, most will, up to the time of admission, have regarded themselves as responsible people able to order their own lives albeit latterly with the help of others, and they lose no more rights or privileges when taking up residence than would any other member of the community on entering such establishments as hotels.
>
> Encouragement of independence and meaningful activity is important to the physical and mental well-being of residents no less than to their personal dignity. The administrative convenience of those in charge of the Home ought not to intrude on this. Residents should be encouraged whenever feasible to have personal effects in their rooms and to pursue their own interests and activities, for example attending a day centre, going shopping or visiting the local pub. They might also, where they are able and willing, help with the running of the Home in such ways as making their own bed and tidying their room, preparing food, gardening, or growing plants indoors. Some Homes have a residents' committee to assist the head of the Home in its management, and voluntary workers can also help residents to involve themselves in providing a satisfying environment.*

Some critics have suggested that the aims might have been expressed in more positive terms, going beyond maintenance towards possibilities of rehabilitation. Elderly people sometimes enter residential care functioning below their potential capacities because they have spent a prolonged period in hospital; or have lived an isolated life in the community and lost some skills of social communication; or they may have lived with relatives who found it easier to do things for them rather than let them exercise what abilities they had.

It is clear that professed aims are moving away from the traditional hospital or nursing model of care, which emphasises good quality physical care in clean and tidy surroundings. Yet a study in 1979 of 124 randomly selected homes in Greater London (93 local authority, 18 voluntary and 13 private) reflected a conventional outlook among the officers in charge:

> The majority of officers in charge and proprietors . . . described their aim as providing care, shelter and comfort for residents. Most

* Reproduced with the permission of the Controller of Her Majesty's Stationery Office.

homes emphasised the need for a homely environment and a sense of security. A sizeable number stressed the protective function and several officers in charge gave priority to good nursing. The encouragement of independence as far as possible was less frequently mentioned and few stressed the need for continued stimulation. Only a handful considered that the task might include a rehabilitative aspect. A not insignificant number of officers in charge were of the opinion that the encouragement of independence, or any programme of rehabilitation, should not be considered as objectives in their establishments. (Briers 1979)

There are, of course, constraints on attainment of more ambitious aims, other than views of heads of homes – although these may be the most important. Besides the views of other staff, such constraints include the design of homes, high levels of physical disability or mental confusion among residents, and the expectations of care held by residents (and their families) on admission. Not to be overlooked, either, is the continued enforcement of habitual patterns by existing residents (Gray 1976; Hanson 1979; Peace and Harding 1980).

Some researchers also suggest that apart from general aims, specific objectives should be worked out for and with every resident on admission, and that these be reviewed from time to time. We will discuss such ideas further in our next section on needs and their assessment.

Need for residential care
The concept of 'need' is even more difficult to interpret in relation to residential than to other forms of social care, since for this most expensive service a strict system of rationing is in operation in most areas. The 'priorities' of need as interpreted by any specific social services department may not necessarily coincide with subjectively perceived needs, or even with objectively assessed needs based on degree of disability, the extent of social and emotional difficulties experienced and the capacity of the potential applicants and carers to cope with these difficulties.

There are many reasons for such discrepancies. The provision of residential accommodation and of other related facilities such as geriatric hospital beds and sheltered housing varies enormously in different areas. Hence – apart from dire emergencies – what is considered a high priority in area A may be deemed an ordinary case to go on the waiting list in area B. Administrative pressures exerted by hospitals for urgent admission may not necessarily reflect an individual's need for residential care, but rather a need for appropriate housing. The provision of extra, almost round the clock, community care or of 'very sheltered' housing may postpone or obviate the need for residential care. Support to carers in the form of short-term admissions, domiciliary services and counselling may be provided in some areas, but may not be available in other districts. Intensive day care may make the difference between frail and very lonely elderly people carrying on a tolerable existence in the community or wanting to give up. Finally, assessment of a client's situation may vary in fullness, expertness and imaginative exploration of alternatives, as we shall see below. Thus 'need' for residential care is a very relative, multi-faceted concept determined to a great extent by the network of services and skills available in different areas as well as by expressed demands arising from potential applicants and their informal and formal carers.

Assessment of needs
In her study of admission procedures to local authority residential homes in Greater London, Neill points to the dilemma of two differing requirements: 'the need to give due weight to the problems and capacities of the applicant, and the need to strike a fair balance between the claims of the differing organisation and individuals such as informal and formal carers who are pressing her case' (Neill 1981). Thus, assessment of the problems of individual elderly people is not the only concern, but also the resolution of conflicts between the different professions, organisations and individuals involved. Such issues are variously resolved through central allocation, panel systems, bargaining between social workers over which client should get in, and different types of rationing and quota systems. Important evaluative questions arise about the impact of these procedures on the clients: for example, do panels result in more considered decisions, or are decisions taken more efficiently by an individual? Which procedures turn out to be of greatest benefit to the client?

Improving allocation procedures may, however, be less important than a prior step: ensuring that only those clearly requiring and wanting residential care are being considered for allocation. Cooper (1981a and b), in an action research project in Essex, found that although staff argued that for many years admission to a residential home had been used only as a last resort, in practice 'the introduction of a more rigorous assessment pro forma and a forceful restatement of County policy' meant that other forms of help were more systematically considered, and the numbers of those placed on the waiting list decreased. Once the wide-ranging needs-oriented rather than service-oriented assessment procedures were in operation, it was expected that a single 'scrupulously controlled' waiting list would contain *only* those clients for whom residential care was the only answer.

Neill, as well as other investigators (Power 1979, Wenger 1981, Willcocks *et al* 1982, Nissel and Bonnerjea 1982) discovered that families who support potential applicants for residential care rarely receive sufficient (often no) statutory domiciliary services. Early thorough-going assessment and appropriate practical and psychological support to care-givers may well obviate, or at least postpone, the crises and breakdown in family relationships which so often precede application for long-term residential care.

Assessments which may lead to important and almost irreversible decisions about an old person's life are often handled by unqualified staff, as was shown in a study in Newham of 55 applicants for residential care (Stapleton 1977). Seventy-one per cent of the cases had been assessed by unqualified staff; the ability to perform domestic tasks had not been assessed in one-third of the cases; alternative forms of accommodation or relief to caring relatives had been insufficiently examined; and absence of an effective priority system for allocation was noted. (Partly as a result of these discoveries, thorough-going assessment procedures have since been established in Newham in relation to day as well as residential care.) Shaw and Walton (1979) in 1976 interviewed 55 people in ten homes; all had been resident for less than a year. They asked about stages in admission, choices offered, preparation for entry (advice, visit to home, etc.), arrival, settling-in and feelings about living in the home. The researchers point to considerable deficiencies in all these areas, noting that since Townsend, despite considerable improvements in physical environments of homes and 'more flexible and less punitive admission procedures', little progress seems to have been made in other areas. Interviews with residents in the national consumer study (Willcocks *et al* 1982) suggested that only about one-fifth had been presented with a choice of home, and just over one-third had visited the home before they took up residence.

Neill highlights the vagueness of concepts which dominate assessment. Since such valid and reliable instruments as the *Crichton Royal* or *Clifton* assessment scales (see Appendices 1 and 2) for determining physical and mental disability are rarely if ever used in assessments, the way is wide open to highly subjective and incomplete appraisals of disabilities and handicaps. For instance, Neill points to the ambiguities over the meaning of words like 'incontinence', 'confusion', 'depression' or 'at risk' which are frequently used in assessment reports. She also points out that assessments are usually conducted in terms of difficulties of applicants and hardly ever contain any information on their interests, ambitions and potential – important items of information if life in a home is to be linked to a person's needs, capacities and interests.

Although there are some social services departments in which comprehensive assessment and allocation procedures have been developed, such practices need to become more general. They would embody already validated scales for assessing physical and mental capacities, a systematic exploration of caring and friendship networks and of alternative options (such as sheltered housing, more intensive domiciliary care, more support to informal carers, and so on). A picture of the applicant as a human being with interests, likes and dislikes, potentialities as well as 'problems' and disabilities is also essential. Cooper (1981b) stresses that implementation of such schemes will be successful only if all staff fully understand the objectives, and his report is intended as a basis for briefing sessions.

Input
Nowhere in the recent evaluative literature have human values related to 'quality of life' asserted themselves more strongly than in the discussion of inputs and intermediate outputs in residential care of both the young and the old. In the battle against the inherent dangers of the 'total institution', responsible for the care of dependent and defenceless very old or very young human beings, with its rules, its close supervision and concern for safety as major objectives, the ordinary values of everyday life have been stressed: these include opportunities for privacy, a degree of choice over daily activities, the preservation of independence and autonomy as far as one's mental and physical capacities allow, and finally the right, especially of those in full possession of their mental faculties, to take risks. It has been suggested that preservation of these qualities of life is more important for the well-being of residents than immaculately clean rooms, regular bathing routines and punctual mealtimes. Much of the evaluative research in the residential field has therefore been directed towards the development of measurements of social and practical inputs designed to bring about such resident-oriented rather than institution-oriented regimes.

The social environment
Goffman's seminal theory of the total institution (1961) has been applied by Hughes and Wilkin (1980) to old people's homes, and summarised as follows:

(i)   All aspects of daily life are conducted in the same place under the same authority.
(ii) Daily activity is carried out with large numbers of others, treated alike and all doing the same thing.
(iii) Daily activity is routinised and fixed to a schedule which is imposed on the inmates by formal rulings and a body of officials.
(iv) The various enforced activities and routines constitute 'a rational plan' designed to fulfil the official aims of the institution.

Most of the pioneers in the evaluation of residential care have attempted to develop hypotheses and measures capable of testing specific components of Goffman's sombre theory. For example, Wing and Brown (1970), in their comparative study of long-stay schizophrenic patients using such measures as routinisation of daily activities, formal rules and lack of personal possessions, showed how the social conditions of the wards contributed to the patients' withdrawal.

King, Raynes and Tizard (1971), the most influential pioneers in exploring the effects of residential care regimes, developed measures of 'inmate management' (derived from Goffman) in homes and hospitals caring for mentally handicapped children. These institutions were classified as tending towards resident-oriented or institutionally-oriented regimes according to four dimensions:

(i)   the rigidity of the routine (inflexibility of management practice – neither individual differences nor unique circumstances were taken into account);

(ii) the block treatment of inmates (regimentation of inmates together as a group before, during or after a specific activity);

(iii) the depersonalisation of inmates (denials of opportunities for inmate privacy, self expression, and personal possession and initiative);

(iv) the social distance between staff and inmates (separation of staff and inmate worlds, keeping their areas of accommodation apart, and limiting interactions between staff and inmates to functionally specific formal activities).

King, Raynes and Tizard's studies showed that in resident-oriented institutions, where the work of staff was geared to meeting the needs of individual residents, where social distance between staff and residents was kept to a minimum and depersonalising aspects of care avoided, children's progress, as measured for example by speech development, was more favourable than in institutionally-oriented environments.

About the same time Pincus in the United States distinguished similar dimensions for describing the institutional environment of *elderly* people:

(i)   the public/private dimension (privacy);

(ii) the structured/unstructured dimensions (regime and the degree of individual choice);

(iii) the resource-rich/resource-sparce dimensions (stimulation and social interaction);

(iv) the isolated/integrated dimensions (communication and interaction outside the home).

Thus Pincus added the important ideas of stimulation and interaction/communication with the outside world to King, Raynes and Tizard's dimensions (Pincus and Wood 1970).

Subsequently Raynes and her colleagues further refined and tested four dimensions of institutional management which can be shown to be either positively or negatively associated with resident-oriented regimes (1979).

Centralisation (the extent to which authority is delegated). Davies and Knapp (1981) quote several institutional studies which show that centralisation is negatively correlated with resident-oriented management practices. The suggestion emerges that some control over their work life seems to encourage staff to give more stimulating care to residents. Barbara Tizard's study (1975) indicating that children's language development in residental nurseries was positively associated with the degree of staff autonomy is pertinent here.

Formalisation (the presence of rules and regulations) also is thought to impede flexible resident-oriented practices. However, research in residential homes in Cheshire (Kimbell *et al* 1974) seemed to suggest that the more structured the routine, the less confusion there was among residents. Thus a framework of reasonable rules and regulations may be beneficial for certain types of disoriented old people.

Communication among staff. Most literature on residential institutions reflects the assumption that good channels of communication between care staff have positive effects on the quality of care. Although the research evidence is equivocal at present, it is reasonable to assume that good staff communication leads to more consistent care practices, particularly when innovations such as group living are being introduced, where a common understanding of aims and methods of achieving them is an important precondition.

Specialisation. King *et al* (1971) found that the clearer the division of labour between direct care staff and supervisor, the more institutionally oriented the care tended to be. Interestingly, Imber (1977) in her study of care staff tasks in old people's homes comes to very similar conclusions: 'in homes where the regime is orientated towards the convenience of the staff and efficient physical care of the residents, staff are more likely to have clearly defined and demarcated sets of task: in homes orientated towards the social and psychological development of the residents, staff role is likely to be more diffuse and there is likely to be more overlap between the activities of different types and grades of staff.' Davies and Knapp suggest another reason for the negative influence of specialisation: when the duties of the supervisor are weighted towards activities which do not directly involve them with residents (which is certainly the case in Britain now) it is more difficult for them to provide a role model for caring.

In summary, the dimensions of the residential social environment which are currently held to affect the residents' quality of life positively are:

(i)   flexibility of management practices;
(ii) individualisation and autonomy for residents;

(iii) opportunities for privacy;
(iv) opportunities for social stimulation;
(v) communication and interaction with the outside world;
(vi) social interaction between staff and residents (in addition to instrumental communication);
(vii) maximum delegation of decision-making to care staff and to residents;
(viii) good communication channels between staff;
(ix) a minimum degree of specialisation of roles and tasks among staff.

Instruments are being developed to measure these dimensions in simple operational ways, the most recent in this country by researchers at the University Hospital of South Manchester Psychogeriatric Unit (Evans *et al* 1981). Their 'Analysis of daily practices' (see Appendix 3) includes such questions as whether residents have a choice of when they are bathed, go to bed or get up in the morning; have control over their money (for example collecting their own pensions, spending their money as they wish); can go out without permission; can retain their own GPs; have privacy in their own rooms; can bring some of their own possessions; have access to tea-making facilities; can undertake everyday tasks such as looking after their own rooms; and so on. In the Manchester study, the schedule was completed independently by each of the two main field workers, on the basis of all the interview and observational data collected over four to six weeks. Where such detailed study of individual homes is not possible, clearly such questions would need to be addressed to residents as well as staff and supported by observations to ascertain whether professed practices are implemented in real life.

Design and physical amenities

We also need to consider other important inputs apart from regime which affect the quality of care and life in a residential community. First is *material resources*, such as structural design and physical amenities of the home. How much importance is being attached to getting the physical environment 'right' is exemplified by the commissioning by the architectural division of the DHSS of a number of studies of accommodation and its relationship to living patterns in old people's homes (Thomas *et al* 1977 and 1979, Willcocks *et al* 1980 and 1982).

The most recent of these studies, carried out at the Polytechnic of North London, was particularly concerned with the reactions of residents of the homes. The researchers at first experienced the usual difficulties of obtaining critical appraisals from the elderly residents dependent on the care provided by the place in which most of them will spend the rest of their lives:

Probing by interviewers on particular aspects of home life proved very difficult. Residents having single bedrooms insisted that they had a preference for single bedrooms; while those occupying double rooms insisted that they preferred to share. Those who eat at a dining table for four insisted that four was the appropriate size; while those who eat at a dining table for six insisted that they preferred six (despite the claim by the officer in charge at this latter home that it is virtually impossible to find six compatible eaters!) At one home residents were asked if they would like television sets in their rooms. The immediate response was that this is not allowed. When asked if they would like one if this *were* allowed the immediate response was: 'oh no, that wouldn't be right if Mr. G. doesn't allow it!' Thus, in response to all probes, they could only approve what they were currently experiencing and very few constructive suggestions emerged. (Willcocks *et al* 1980)

The invention of a visual game in which different physical features were illustrated on cards eventually succeeded in getting residents to make choices. The main impression the investigators gained from the choices expressed (Table 10.1) was that the residents opt for 'the normal, the unexceptional, the non-institutional'. As the table shows, individual control over the immediate environment in terms of opening and shutting doors and windows, and controlling radiators, was very important; so was an ordinary bath, and an appropriate degree of privacy in single bedrooms. Aspects of communal living such as group organisation, shared bedrooms and preparation of refreshments in a small kitchen received low priority. One wonders whether recent publicity about fires in old people's homes accounts for 'safeguard against fire' topping the list.

Staff views were also obtained as part of the study. A common complaint was of wheelchairs or frames being a problem in doorways, and over half the staff pointed to the way in which heavy fire doors inhibit mobility. Dining rooms in the most recently built homes continued to present staff with problems in moving around to serve residents, and in about half the newer homes the space for residents' personal possessions and clothes was judged to be insufficient. Perhaps most disturbing is the evidence that homes still do not provide sufficient and appropriate facilities for the promotion of continence and self-maintenance skills of very old and frail people. Nearly half the staff judged that there were not sufficient lavatories, and about a quarter that they were too far from lounges and bedrooms. A disappointing feature of the most recently built homes is the lack of space generally; thus 53 per cent of the single rooms fell below the minimum size recommended in the DHSS Building Note (ten square metres).

Both staff and residents preferred the provision of several small lounges which facilitate more social interaction, and the majority in both groups favoured large dining rooms with small tables. However,

Table 10.1 Ranked visual game choices: age–sex distribution (first sort)

Score (a)

	Men		Women	
	Under 85 years	85 or more	Under 85 years	85 or more
Safeguard against fire	93	94	92	92
Windows which you can open	85	78	85	82
Easily opened doors	85	79	84	82
A single room	82	80	79	83
Ordinary bath	84	83	79	79
Storage space	81	73	81	76
Views of gardens	75	66	79	76
Receiving friends in bedroom	63	63	73	78
Easily identified rooms	72	63	74	66
A shop selling food/ sweets/stationery	69	53	71	70
Control over bedroom radiators	69	70	69	66
Separate room for confused residents	65	65	67	66
Different types of chair for different people	68	67	66	59
Good sound insulation between rooms	64	58	64	58
A power-point in the bedroom	63	68	62	55
A qupet place for telephoning	61	56	59	55
Lounge areas facing the sun	57	47	61	57
Bedroom facing the sun	52	47	58	53
Medibath	52	52	56	54
Views of streets and roads	57	47	55	50
Hallways with places for relaxing	55	47	53	50
Kitchen for making tea and snacks	49	46	51	44
A low-intensity night light	43	39	45	46
Moveable bedroom furniture	45	39	43	40
Living in groups	38	40	38	39
A shared bedroom	27	32	30	27
Provision of alcohol	37	34	25	25

(a)To base 100
Source: Willcocks, Peace, and Kellaher, 1982, Table 9.1

while just under half the residents expressed their liking for ungrouped chairs placed around the walls, the majority of staff wished to see grouped furniture in their 'ideal' home. (It would be interesting to probe further into the reasons for residents' choices about seating arrangements which possibly suggest desire for a more passive contemplation of life passing by than the activists would allow for. Many other interpretations could of course be advanced.)

Lastly there is the garden, which according to several studies is one of the most neglected facilities. Although most homes in the consumer study were in pleasant grounds, the gardens were often not laid out in attractive ways, nor fenced and appropriately designed to guarantee safety to confused wanderers, nor did they appear to offer facilities to enable frail people to garden, for example by providing raised beds. In this context it should be noted that while just under half the informants used to garden before entering a home, only three per cent did so at the time of the enquiry. The researchers suggest that less than one-third of the homes provides a suitable environment for this activity. This is especially regrettable since gardening emerges in another study as one of the few activities with which seriously confused residents are able to persevere and which they appear to enjoy.

Is there a relationship between design and resident-oriented practices? Not necessarily; staff practices and attitudes can nullify the welfare-enhancing qualities of single rooms for example if there are no locks, if staff intrude at any time, or if the resident is not allowed to use the bedroom in the daytime. A comparative study intended to evaluate the functioning of purpose-built group unit homes showed that even when design was identical marked differences emerged in the way space was used and in the life of the home (Thomas *et al* 1979, Thomas 1981). On the other hand, there are indications that while design is not a sufficient condition to ensure resident-oriented regimes, it may facilitate such regimes. Thomas and his colleagues found that group and semi-group homes were more often 'therapeutically'-oriented in their regimes than non-group homes, and the consumer study reported 'a far higher percentage of group and semi-group homes . . . operating under a liberal regime when contrasted with the non-group homes'.

Conversely the work of Marston and Gupta of the Northamptonshire Social Services Department has shown that physical features of residential homes need not constrain achievement of aims. They were determined to introduce into the county's homes as quickly as possible what they saw as the likely benefits of small group living, self-help and mutual help, although the homes were not designed for group living. Significant resources were devoted to discussions with staff, residents and relatives over many months, but the actual money spent on conversion within the first homes tackled was minimal (Marston and Gupta 1977; Gupta 1979; Marston 1979; Reynolds 1979).

The residents

The second major resource input is the people who make up the residential community.

It is well known that about three-quarters of residents are women, most of whom are widowed. The consumer study found the average age for women to be about 83, and for men 79. The study, like others of aged populations, showed striking differences in physical and mental disability between men and women. While about three-quarters of the men could move about independently, this applied to less than two-thirds of the women. Similar differences emerged in the areas of memory and orientation. The study also confirmed that those most recently admitted had a much greater degree of physical and mental frailty than old people admitted ten or more years before. It is worth noting that, despite this increasing frailty, on average over half the residential population could move about independently, three-quarters could dress themselves, over four-fifths could feed themselves, and more than four-fifths were continent. But the proportion of physically and mentally impaired residents varies enormously between homes, depending on the facilities and resources available.

The most hotly debated questions affecting the quality of life and the well-being of residents as well as the burden on staff is how far relatively able-bodied and very frail residents, the lucid and the confused should be mixed or segregated. Opinions and impressions abound, ranging from those who are fervently against segregation into 'ghettoes' (Meacher 1972) to those who argue that life is better for the mentally infirm if they receive specialist care in homes designed to meet their particular needs. .Recently an empirical study has been completed which was designed to examine how non-specialist homes were coping with different levels of physical and mental impairment in their resident populations. This study was carried out in six residential homes in Manchester, with varying proportions of physically disabled and confused residents (Evans *et al* 1981). The methods of investigation included not only interviews with samples of residents, and most of the staff, but also systematic observation of staff practices, of physical care, of staff-resident interactions and of resident activities. The researchers were surprised to find that when care and supervisory staff were asked which categories of residents were most difficult to care for, only 7 (12 per cent) said the confused and 36 (60 per cent) thought that those who presented non-physical management problems ('mainly the most lucid and physically.able residents') were the most difficult. When asked which categories were easiest to care for, 25 (41 per cent) selected the confused. Staff were more reticent about preferences for working with particular types of residents. However, of the 45 who were willing to say with which groups they particularly *liked* working, 32 ('a startling

71 per cent') said the confused; of the 22 willing to divulge with whom they particularly *disliked* working, 10 said the lucid.

A majority of staff in all the six homes, with varying proportions of physically disabled residents, felt the proportions were tolerable. But staff in the two homes with the highest levels of confusion (36 per cent and 54 per cent) felt that there were too many confused residents. From the residents' side most lucid people (63 per cent) were either tolerant or accepting in their attitudes to confused residents, and only a quarter were clearly rejecting. In general higher levels of physical and mental impairment tended to be associated with more institutionally-oriented practices, and by implication with a poorer quality of care. Nevertheless the authors came to the conclusion that homes for the elderly should include people with a variety of levels of physical and mental functioning, and that the potential advantages, particularly for disabled people, outweigh any disadvantages. Where segregation occurred within homes, the researchers did not observe any substantial improvement in the quality of life experienced by either lucid and able or confused and physically disabled residents. They observed that the general atmosphere in integrated areas of a home was often more lively than in those where residents were segregated. The authors suggest that under present conditions a proportion of around 30 per cent confused residents can be tolerated.

> Such a mix can offer considerable advantages for confused residents in terms of greater stimulation and a more 'homely' environment than would be possible in specialist institutions. For the lucid residents it remains compatible with the maintenance of a satisfactory quality of life. For the staff, it does not impose intolerable burdens upon them.

These conclusions, reached after the most thorough-going interview and observational study yet available in the field of residential care of the elderly, need to be treated with respect and further tested in practice. However, other observations scattered in the literature, as well as personal impressions, suggest that lucid residents have a tendency (where there are opportunities for small groups in separate lounges) to withdraw from the seriously confused and to be critical of their behaviour – for example, their eating habits. In the consumer study separate rooms for confused residents occupied a fairly high place in importance, with rating scores of 65–67 out of 100 (see Table 10.1). The key to these attitudes may well lie, as the Manchester study suggests, in the *proportion* of confused residents which can be tolerated and the number, deployment and attitudes of staff required to ensure adequate attention and assistance to both lucid and confused residents.

Staffing

The staff in old people's homes are usually divided into supervisory, care and domestic staff. The large majority are middle-aged married women, nearly half of whom work on a part-time basis. It is a relatively stable workforce: two of the most recent studies found that about two-fifths of the care and supervisory staff had been in residential work for five or more years. In the consumer study nearly three-quarters (72 per cent) of the care staff and nearly two-fifths (38 per cent) of the supervisory staff said that they possessed no qualifications. One of the obstacles to staff development is the fact that in the majority of residential homes care staff are graded as manual workers, and paid accordingly. Nearly one-third of the supervisory staff had a nursing background, and although only nine per cent had a residential social work qualification a substantial minority had received some in-service social work training. In both the Manchester and the consumer study a considerable proportion of staff expressed interest in further training.

Staff tasks have been succinctly described by Imber (1977) in her study of staffing in residential homes: 'the most significant idea to have emerged from the review was that domestic staff kept the home clean and tidy and care staff provided the same service to the residents, whilst attempting to provide for their soical and psychological needs'. These findings have been substantially confirmed by the Manchester and the consumer studies which suggest that care staff spend a large part of their time on physical care, over a quarter of their time on domestic work and very little on social care. Although the studies report a fairly high degree of work satisfaction, one-fifth of the care staff in the Manchester study disliked the large proportion of time they spent on domestic duties which precluded them from more social contacts with residents, and they also complained that they were expected to care for increasingly impaired old people – a task for which they had little or no training. Willcocks and her colleagues examined a number of different dimensions of staff satisfaction, and related these to regimes, physical characteristics of the homes, and resident characteristics. Overall, female senior staff seemed most satisfied, and male care staff least satisfied.

Although social interaction between staff and residents is considered to be an important ingredient in resident-oriented regimes, most observational studies, and particularly the very detailed observations reported in the Manchester study, show that interaction between staff and residents is largely instrumental, that is to say related to the carrying out of physical tasks that are being undertaken.

Questions have even been raised whether increased social interaction between staff and residents is such a desirable objective, given the present level of training and awareness. For example Fairhurst (1978), who examined staff–resident talk in a geriatric hospital in Manchester, observed four types of talk: *time-out talk* (an alternative to 'real' duties), often taking the form of joking; task-oriented *ceremonial talk* ('it's time to get up'), used to ensure the smooth execution of taks; *superlative talk*, consisting of unwarranted praise such as 'jolly good' and 'wonderful' – often used with the demented; and *persuasive talk*, used to get residents to take unwanted medicines or to participate in activities. Fairhurst suggests that merely allowing staff to spend more time talking with residents would not necessarily improve the character of this talk.

Lipman and his colleagues (1979), who studied and recorded verbal interactions between residents, and between staff and residents, in eight Welsh homes for the elderly, report that 'socio-emotional support exchanged by staff and residents is less than that which residents provide among themselves'. Nor did staff in six of the eight homes offer more emotional support to confused than to lucid residents. The authors see the remedy not in more investment in staff resources, but in greater participation in day-to-day decision-making by the residents, thus reducing the instrumental dominance of staff. Indeed, Lipman and his colleagues (1977) advocate greater separation between residents and staff rather than more interaction in order to enhance mutual helpfulness and self-maintenance skills among the elderly. Thus some observers and researchers cast doubt on the proposition that social interaction between residents and staff is an essential ingredient in the promotion of resident-oriented regimes enhancing the quality of life.

How does one assess quality of care? It is generally assumed that the basic precondition is an adequate level of staffing, which will depend in part on the proportion of mentally and physically disabled people in a home but also on the ways in which staff are deployed. It seems fashionable these days to underplay the physical care functions which are thought to have been over-stressed in the past – residents are toileted, bathed and dressed and so on when they did not really need such comprehensive help – while their social and emotional needs were being neglected. However, the thorough observational studies in the six Manchester homes did not suggest that the physical care being administered by the staff was inappropriate; rather, especially in homes with high dependency ratios, shortage of staff combined with lack of psychological and social skills led to dehumanising block treatment and 'processing' rather than an individualised sensitive and caring type of approach, for instance to continence or to bathing and dressing.

While the amount and type of physical care required by different kinds of residents remains a contentious issue (which, however, is eminently researchable), there appears to be a general consensus that the style of leadership and the attitudes shown towards the care of residents by the officers-in-charge are crucial determinants of the quality of care. Yet no studies similar to those carried out by Sinclair (1971), which pointed to specific characteristics in wardens of hostels for delinquents which were significantly associated with favourable outcomes, have yet been carried out in residential homes for the elderly.

Indeed, apart from the notions emanating from Goffman and from King, Raynes and Tizard that regimentation and block treatment and lack of privacy are undesirable features of care, there appears to be little agreement as to what characterises good quality of care for the very elderly. For instance, as we have already seen, adherents of the mutual help principle discourage too much caring activity and social intervention by staff on the grounds that low visibility of staff stimulates self-help and mutual help. Some innovators advocate that care staff should play an active role in stimulating 'engagement' in all kinds of ways, producing interesting materials and encouraging specific activities, while others feel that this is a highly artificial way of life for a very elderly person.

Quality of care will be perceived differently by different types of elderly people with different kinds of expectations: some, when they finally get to 'a haven of rest', want to put their feet up and expect to be waited on for a change, while others wish to retain their independence for as long as possible. Hence it is the *fit* between individual characteristics and the social situation which is of importance rather than stereotyped prescriptions with ideal types in mind – be they grandads in rocking chairs or mutually helpful busy bees.

Quality of care thus emerges as a flexible construct, built on the accurate assessment of capacity for self-care, social and emotional needs and expectations of the elderly resident, the living arrangements available which most closely fit the resident's capacities, needs and expectations (for instance group unit living, semi-hotel style, nursing home type, etc.) and the skills and attitudes of the staff. Hence monitoring devices need to be developed to spot and respond to changes in any of the three spheres of individual needs, social provision and caring skills.

Monitoring requires adequate records, as well as sensitive observation. Individual social records (as distinct from medical records, often meticulously kept) are as yet poorly developed in residential care for the elderly, and the introduction of internal assessment and review procedures – sometimes involving residents and their relatives – is only slowly gaining ground. Briers' study of a sample of London residential homes for the elderly (1979) suggests that there is no consensus as yet among officers-in-charge and other staff about the desirability of formal review procedures, many considering that daily long-term contact with residents makes such procedures unnecessary. However, clinical experience and evaluative research indicate that periodic objective reviews are essential in order to assess progress, particularly in long-term care in which the carers are closely involved with those cared for.

Training of staff is held to be another important contributory influence to the quality of care. Training spans a whole spectrum, from full-time qualifying residential social work courses to informal discussions on the job. While a general consensus appears to be emerging that at least one of the supervisory staff in any home should have a residential social work qualification, the general training needs of care staff are still not clear. The Manchester researchers advocate the provision of short training packages which should include 'medical and social aspects of ageing, the sociology of institutions and applied psychology, as well as training in the provision of physical care'. Briers' study revealed little agreement among supervisory staff as to the kind of staff and type of training needed for residential work with the elderly. The majority of officers stressed basic nursing skills in training and care for the mentally infirm. Others felt that a regrading of care assistants and a professional course of training in residential social work was needed. These views possibly mirror the tension between the two currents of thinking about residential care – the need to respond adequately to higher levels of dependency, and the move towards more self-care and self-determination by residents. The field appears to be wide open to experimentation and evaluation before training criteria become crystallised. It is also worth noting that Davies and Knapp, in their diligent search for empirical evidence of the effect of staff training on the quality of life of residents, found very little, if any, such evidence. Indeed, one American study found no evidence of a relationship between the proportion of highly trained professionals in American nursing homes and either the quality of care or the well-being of residents (Kart and Maynard 1976).

Life in the home

Lastly, the most important social input is what actually goes on in the home. One of the aspects of life in the home which has attracted considerable attention is the activities of residents. Originally, attempts to counteract the apathy of elderly people who sat for most of the day arranged around the walls of a large room, doing nothing, consisted of encouraging games, craft work, or outings. With the move towards helping residents retain more control over their lives has come a new emphasis on ordinary activities of daily life. The disjunction between the skills necessarily exercised even by very frail elderly people when they are living at home, and the inactivity often encountered as soon as they enter residential establishments, is marked. Gray (1976) has pointed out that 'two vital elements of everyday life are lost':

(i)   They lose the physiotherapy of everyday life: turning on the gas, opening milk bottles, lifting saucepans. All use similar muscles, joints, and control systems as dressing, undressing, shaving and all the other skills of personal independence.

(ii) They lose the occupational therapy of everyday life. Decision-making (for example, deciding how brown the toast should be, if they can afford a lamb chop or whether they should buy beans or macaroni) uses skills and nerve circuits which function in such personal decisions as deciding to remain continent. Although it may be dreadful that many elderly people spend so much time worrying about fuel bills, the complex calculations of domestic budgeting have many beneficial spin-offs.

As mentioned earlier, some of those who enter residential care come from hospital, and may already have lost some of these skills. To those coming from their own homes, residential care may have been presented as an easing of responsibilities, and they – and their relatives – may need convincing of the value of retaining skills (which they may not have recognised as such). Staff, too, may need much convincing of the value, and possibility, of an enabling role; they may well have entered such work in order to provide a particular kind of care for elderly people, and may resist being party to the problems and pains of self-care on the part of the residents. They may also have difficulty relinquishing such accepted criteria of outcome as well-scrubbed, well-brushed, tidily-dressed old people in clean and tidy rooms. Additionally, engagement in 'ordinary' activities means greater 'risk' to residents (the idea of providing kettles and toasters has aroused some storms), and this again requires new thinking by staff – and all others with responsibilities for residential care. Where headquarters staff responsible for development, or heads of homes, have been able to convince the carers of the value of the more 'natural' approach to activity, however, both care and domestic staff are said to have found their new roles more demanding, but more satisfying.

For confused residents, there has been a development in recent years of the use of reality orientation, designed to prevent, halt, or reverse signs of disorientation and memory loss; it can take the form of 'class reality orientation', a small group activity run by a therapist for about 30 minutes a day, or '24-hour reality orientation', where the emphasis is on the attitudes, expectations and behaviour of all those who come in contact with the confused person, and on reorganisation of procedures and of design to provide greater stimulation and simple orientation aids. In a sense, this latter technique is informed by the same principles as the emphasis on ordinary activities described above. Hanley *et al* (1981), in describing the use of reality orientation in a geriatric ward and an old people's home in Scotland, noted that

The attractive thing about RO is that every interaction with an old person suddenly has potential. For many staff their job becomes more interesting as they are presented with a rationale for dealing constructively and personally with the residents they care for. The procedural aspects of care no longer assume absolute priority and an improvement in atmosphere and morale, unfortunately a difficult thing for a researcher to measure, seems to develop.

Marston has suggested that staff who have grasped the principles of group care in residential homes, and have been able to adapt their behaviour accordingly, should have little difficulty in further adapting to the use of reality therapy or behaviour therapy, which he describes as 'a shift of emphasis, not of basic attitudes and objectives'. He is engaged on a quasi-experimental action research project (supported by the Mental Health Foundation) to test the application of specific reality orientation techniques to a group of confused residents of a Northamptonshire home purpose-built for group unit living. The group is compared with a similar one not receiving this treatment.

Another type of activity which has been seen as an important aspect of life in the home is participation of the residents in decision-making: not just about the time they will get up, the way they will spend their day, when they will have a bath, the time they will go to bed (all of which are, of course, of great importance) but also in decisions about group activities or the functioning of the home more generally. The DHSS *Memorandum of Guidance* (1977), as noted earlier, suggests the possibility of a residents' committee, and some authorities have experimented with regular discussions within homes, meetings of residents from several homes, and so on; a number of researchers have instituted discussion groups as part of studies of quality of life. Where residents feel relaxed and 'at home', and have satisfying relationships with individual members of staff, viewpoints are likely to be continually canvassed and offered in a less formal way, perhaps more appropriate to the frail state of many residents.

Other uses of homes

Some homes provide short-stay in addition to long-term care. Only fragmentary evidence had until recently been available about this form of care, and its use for purposes other than relief of caring relatives; a large-scale study for the DHSS now provides more information about its extent, and its effects on the lives of residents and on the functioning of homes (Allen 1982). As noted in Chapter 7, day care is provided in some residential homes, and again, there is little evidence as yet about its extent and its effects, although a number of possible advantages and disadvantages have been listed by researchers. Some homes provide other services, such as meals-on-wheels; and the use of homes as 'neighbourhood resource centres' for the elderly is being developed in some areas.

All these ways of using homes are likely to influence the lives of residents. Just how is not yet clear although Allen recommends caution in expecting that homes for long-stay residents can easily be used as a base for a variety of other services. One of her major findings was that officers and staff regarded their prime function as making a 'home' for long-stay residents, and that short-stay residents and day care attenders were regarded as extra. Many homes were found to be operating under some stress with increasing proportions of very dependent long-term residents, and found it difficult to cope with any additional responsibilities.

Outcome

In the residential field it is even more than usually difficult to draw the boundary between input and outcome. For instance, many people would consider client-oriented regimes sensitive to the needs for autonomy, privacy and so on of residents as desirable aims or outcomes in their own right. Others (and we incline to this view) might consider resident-oriented regimes as inputs, or *intermediate* outputs which in themselves do not as yet tell us about the ultimate welfare benefits as they affect the individual residents. There are fashions in client-oriented regimes, as in everything else; for many reasons some changes instituted with the best of intentions may not, in practice, work out to the residents' benefit, as already indicated: the uncertain effects of intensive staff/client interaction, or stress on engagement and mutual help with people who want to 'sit and think' and put their feet up. Or again, while a certain amount of mixing of lucid and mentally infirm residents may *overall* work out to the benefit of both, there may be an appreciable minority of lucid residents whose well-being is grossly impeded by the presence of severely confused residents.

Hence it seems safer to regard the non-regimented, non-routinised, socially stimulating, enabling residential environment as an input or precondition for the achievement of desirable outcomes in terms of residents' physical and social functioning and subjective well-being, rather than as an end in itself. Objectively observable as well as subjectively felt outcomes are likely to vary in relation to individual needs, expectations and capacity of residents on the one hand and the opportunities offered by the social environment, staff skills and attitudes on the other.

What can evaluative research tell us about outcomes as understood in the above sense? As yet comparatively little, although promising foundations are being laid by a well-planned succession of evaluative studies in several research centres.

Mortality

One inevitable outcome in such an aged population is death. There is cumulative evidence that mortality is particularly high during the first three months of admission, due to a variety of factors, not necessarily associated with the residential environment; many old people are admitted at a point of breakdown or crisis and others appear unable to survive the shock of leaving their accustomed environment. However, we are not aware of any studies of mortality trends in residential care following the first three months after admission and how they compare with survival rates of populations of similar age and dependency levels living in the community. Suggestions arising from investigations carried out by Pattie and her colleagues at Clifton Hospital suggest that disability scores are by and large predictive of mortality wherever old people find themselves (Pattie *et al* 1979).

Social functioning: morbidity

How is psychological and physical morbidity related to pre-institutional capacity, relocation and the subsequent residential environment? The much-quoted work of Tobin and Lieberman (1976) has stressed the adverse effects of relocation. Their thesis is that poor adjustment to the *idea* of moving into an institution accounts for many of the noxious effects often attributed to *living* in one. Hence the importance of careful preparation and preservation of as much continuity as possible, such as relocation in the same neighbourhood, enabling residents to bring furniture and other belongings which symbolise their own past.

Further work by Pattie and Gilleard (1979) suggests that the negative relocation effect has possibly been overstressed and is mainly confined to a particularly vulnerable group which shows an immediate negative effect after admission. For the majority of newly admitted residents, the effect was not evident – they either showed a steady functional decline throughout the year of observation, congruent with the level of health and disability on admission, or if initial disability was minimal it remained so throughout the year. The authors suggest that further research is needed to identify the characteristics of the vulnerable group which reacts very negatively to relocation, in order that alternative ways of support can be tried.

Apart from morbidity a number of other observable features of social functioning have been used as criteria of outcome among old people in residential homes. Such criteria are activity rates, interaction with residents and staff, aspects of self-care and mutual help as well as observable moods and expressions of feeling. These measures can either be used for monitoring purposes to assess progress or deterioration under fairly constant conditions of regime and staffing, or as indicators of results brought about by deliberate changes in structure, regime and staff functions, as we shall see below.

. . . engagement

This is a comparatively easily measured criterion of social functioning which has received a great deal of research attention, especially by the Health Care Evaluation Research Team under the direction of Kushlick. Engagement theory postulates that an engaged person is usually mentally healthier and happier than a passive, inactive person. Felce and Jenkins (1979) of the Health Care Evaluation Research Team have defined a resident as engaged in activity if 'she is interacting with another person or is interacting with any material which may be used in self-care, work, domestic or recreational activities'. They have reported several illuminating behavioural experiments in old people's homes showing a substantial rise in activities on days when materials for activities were provided by professionals or volunteers, compared with days when such materials were not available.

In another context a time graph of the day showed significantly different levels of engagement in two lounges, one of which provided newspapers, a knitting session twice a week and television programmes, while the other lounge had little to offer. In yet another experimental study a tray of simple materials was offered to residents, most of whom were disabled and confused. The researcher helped the residents to begin the activity, expressed interest and helped when they got into difficulty. The results showed that on the days when no materials were provided an average of 6 per cent of the people were engaged in any activity, while on the days when materials were available an average of 37 per cent of those present were engaged. Even when staff involvement was reduced engagement levels were still high. A gardening experiment led to similar results. The researchers conclude that the level of activity observed in elderly people in residential and hospital care is affected by the opportunities and assistance provided to them and not only by irreversible factors like ageing and disease. The authors suggest that staff and managers should create opportunities for engagement for all elderly residents, preferably in the spheres in which they had been active before entering a residential home. They also consider that since the introduction of small amounts of stimulation and opportunities leads to increase in engagement of some very disabled people, far greater changes could be brought about with more far-reaching environmental and organisational rearrangements. Unfortunately plans for more extensive experimental work have not materialised. A great deal is still to be learned about the optimal balance between engagement and disengagement for different types of residents in different environmental conditions, and how engagement relates to subjective feelings of pleasure, satisfaction and well-being. In the United States experiments in nursing homes, stimulating greater self-responsibility and participation in decision-making among residents, also led to substantial improvements in activity and functioning. However, it is suggested that such opportunities will have to be offered early in residential experience, since otherwise the pervasive phenomenon of 'learned helplessness' and hopelessness induced by over-protective caring and corresponding passivity may have taken root and be difficult to dislodge (Mercer and Kane 1979).

. . . participation

Other aspects of social functioning which have attracted much research and experimentation are those associated with interaction among residents, mutual help and preservation of independent self-care. The main input has been the introduction of small group living where residents can participate in the everyday domestic activities of living and self-care much as they used to in their own homes. Although some interesting observational studies are available on the process of introducing group unit living in homes, there are as yet few rigorous outcome studies which compare residents' functioning and well-being in group living situations with less active and less participatory living arrangements.

Some information about the changeover to group living and its short-term effects on the behaviour and attitudes of both staff and residents is available in the report of the DHSS Social Work Service Development Group exercise on patterns of care for the elderly, carried out in conjunction with East Sussex Social Services Department (DHSS 1980). In Leicestershire, a study group within the social services department examined the functioning of two homes which had recently changed to group living, one with apparently considerably more success than the other (Leicestershire SSD 1979). Accounts of the methods adopted in the homes were prepared with the officers in charge, followed by interviews with residents and staff asking what they understood by group unit living, what difference the change had made, and their opinion of the method. The study group drew certain conclusions about the extent to which this form of care allowed 'for the development of personal freedom and choice within establishments', and the importance of preparatory work in achieving these aims. They thought it probable that many of the improvements noted could be related to the process of preparation and resulting changes in attitudes, rather than to group living itself. This clearly is a hypothesis well worth investigating further.

Both these studies of process, as well as writings by Gupta and Marston, emphasise the importance of staff preparation and develop-

ment, since the group living experiments depend partly for their success on a change in the roles of the care staff who become enablers, with
residents as active participants rather than as passive recipients of care
and service.

The first researchers who attempted to measure outcome of group
living arrangements more systematically were Hitch and Simpson
(1972), who compared residents' daily activities and self-care abilities
in three homes with different architectural designs and regimes. One,
recently designed, was divided into five self-contained flats with unob-
trusive staff playing a generally supporting and enabling role; the other
two were more traditional in design and functioning. The study is based
on a cross-sectional design with observations and comparisons at one
point in time, rather than on an experimental design with assessments
of residents before and after the change towards group living. It was
assumed that the disability levels of the residents in the three homes
were similar since selection criteria were similar, but an attempt was
made to control for length of time in the home and for male/female
ratio. The ages and the sample size were also similar in the three homes.
Residents' activities and interaction in the three homes were assessed
on the basis of ratings made by staff and systematic observations by the
researchers. The researchers found that the techniques they used were
not necessarily appropriate for describing and assessing the innovative
home – the number of those doing craft work is irrelevant if purposeful
ordinary activity is aimed at; and where residents are free to be in their
bedrooms whenever they wish, observation of activities in public
spaces will be inadequate.

While it is very likely that the physical structure and facilities as well
as the regime were decisive elements in the higher levels of activity and
interaction in the group home, this might in part be explained by
unexplored selective factors, since no base line data are available comparing the residents' behaviour and disability levels in the three homes
before the group living experiment started.

A more sophisticated study by Peace and Harding (1980) did adopt a
quasi-experimental design in which residents in two homes were assessed before one home went over to group living, catering for five groups
of residents, while the other home did not undergo any planned change.
This study is bedevilled by different shortcomings: the time scale was
very short – the follow-up had to take place (for reasons outside the
control of the researchers) only six months after the change – and only
12 residents in the experimental home had both pre- and post-change
interviews; in the control home the numbers were 17. Hence it is not
surprising that some of the results are puzzling: for instance, in the
group unit home there was a marked decrease from pre- to post-test in
neuroticism as measured by the Eysenck Personal Inventory. Yet this

230 Social Care for the Elderly

decrease is not mirrored in other measures referring to worries and anxieties. On indices of physical health and mobility, however, the respondents in the group home reported substantial changes in the direction of greater ability to participate and interact in the home. Respondents in the control home showed no change on these measures. Again one has to take into account that there was a more active policy of encouraging residents and giving them appropriate facilities to do things for themselves at the group home. This apparently led to renewed attempts to get about the home by themselves, to feed themselves, to cut their own toenails, get in and out of chairs alone and so on.

Interestingly, there is also an indication in this study that where change in the direction of greater self-determination is instituted, residents' aspirations rise and so does their dissatisfaction with those aspects of life in the home which do not improve sufficiently or fast enough.

Both these attempts to assess the impact of physical arrangements and regimes which encourage interaction and participation of residents are instructive and valuable pilot runs which pave the way for more comprehensive experimental comparisons of different patterns of residential living and regimes.

Social and psychological well-being

How does one assess what finally matters most – the subjective feeling of well-being and life satisfaction among residents and how such feelings are related to their activities, their social functioning and the social environment? We have already discussed how difficult it is to obtain critical views, judgements and choices from residents, although the recent consumer study introduced a novel way of encouraging choices through use of a visual game. Various life satisfaction measures have been devised in the United States, and some of these have been tried out in this country. A team at the Polytechnic of North London has, for example, explored the feasibility of a number of measures with residents of 16 homes (Peace *et al* 1979).

Lawton's Philadelphia Geriatric Center (PGC) Morale Scale (1972 and 1975), although not specifically designed for the residential context, seems the most satisfactory instrument so far, since it focuses upon the measurement of morale in the very old. Several British studies of elderly people living in the community have used the scale, which tests three dimensions of morale among frail elderly people: depression, anxiety/frustration, and negative experience of ageing (Challis and Knapp 1980 – see Appendix 4). It is easy to administer, but it needs sensitive handling since it touches on difficult and painful areas of experience in old age. How far such instruments can elicit what people are actually experiencing still remains an open and controversial question. Power's study (Power *et al* 1982) raised many doubts in this direction. One would like to see results obtained from the administration of morale scales tested further by systematic and careful observation and unstructured interviews before relying on their validity. One also hopes that the more relaxed modern regimes which encourage choice and self-expression, together with sensitive methods of consumer research, may enable even very elderly people to express their choices and feelings – both positive and negative – more freely.

Cost

Finally, at what cost are these various patterns of care achieved? Information is as yet sparse. The study of purpose-built group unit homes carried out by Thomas and others (1979) attempted to grapple with some of the difficult questions involved in comparing costs, and more substantial work on costs has been carried out at York University (Wright *et al* 1981) and the Kent University Personal Social Services Research Unit. (e.g. Knapp 1981).

A pilot study for the current Personal Social Services Research Unit (PSSRU) survey of a national random sample of residential homes in the public, voluntary and private sector included factors associated with running costs (Darton and McCoy 1981): intermediate output, such as number of places provided, day places, meals for outside consumption, and so on; level of dependency of residents, resident turnover; and structural features of the home. Contrary to expectations, running costs did not seem to be associated with the location of homes, which the researchers thought would be affected by the price of labour and consumables. Heavily dependent residents clearly increased staff costs. (However, Knapp [1979] found in an earlier analysis that residents 'of appreciable dependency' may place greater demands on care staff than those 'of heavy dependency': as they are more mobile they may actually require *more* supervision and care.) A large number of day places also appeared to be raising running costs per resident place. Good designs which enable residents to be more independent of staff were found to be associated with lower running costs. Size of home was also an important factor. Up to a certain size larger homes tended to be cheaper, but above 60 places the average cost per place rose again. Thus it seems possible that the creation of nursing homes for those chronically disabled (who do not need hospital care but demand too much nursing and supervisory care to be suitable for residential homes) and the creation of well-designed homes in which residents can be as independent as possible, may well lead to a decrease in running costs of residential homes for the elderly. However, the whole subject clearly needs a great deal more investigation and attention, which it will receive in the national census planned by the PSSRU.

Conclusions

(1) Evaluative studies in the field of residential care are increasing in sophistication and scientific rigour and are producing a growing body of useful information which can inform the planning and practice of residential care for the elderly.

(2) Our previous discussions on community, day care and various forms of special accommodation for old people indicate that the aims and effectiveness of residential care in meeting needs in any one area can only be evaluated realistically in comparison with the functions and extent of provision of other complementary services. There is little evidence as yet of attempts at more comprehensive evaluation of a network of services and their interaction in one defined area.

(3) The need for developing more standardised assessment procedures emerges clearly, not only in order to clarify aims and priorities of allocation in individual cases but also to enable those responsible for administering residential care to adapt their caring arrangements to the needs and potentialities of their newly admitted residents.

(4) Evaluation studies of the impact (including comparative cost effectiveness) of different types of structural and social caring arrangements on old people of differing physical and psychologically dependency levels are essential so that both the quantity and proportion of different types of residential care can be planned in relation to different kinds of needs. Otherwise there is a danger that fashions will dominate certain types of provision almost irrespective of their appropriateness to different users.

(5) Impact studies which combine observation of staff practices and resident behaviour with residents' subjective reactions to these practices are needed to test the appropriateness and effectiveness of different types of training of staff.

(6) The development of more regular formal review or monitoring procedures in relation to both individual client progress and institutional practices emerges as an important issue if more than lip service is to be paid to the pursuance of some degree of rehabilitation and in order to adapt type of care and support to changing resident needs.

(7) Practice wisdom, imaginative experimentation along the lines of Felce and Jenkins' and Marston's behaviour therapy designs, and studies of consumer opinion are needed to tell us more about what *kinds* of activities are enjoyed and felt to be satisfying by what kind of people in what circumstances. Otherwise 'activity' may become as meaningless and empty as the prevailing inactivity among many residents of old people's homes.

Appendix One

Modified* Crichton Royal Behavioural Rating Scale

MOBILITY	0	Fully ambulant including stairs
	1	Usually independent
	2	Walks with supervision
	3	Walks with aids or under careful supervision
	4	Bedfast or chairfast
MEMORY	0	Complete
	1	Occasionally forgetful
	2	Short-term loss
	3	Short and long-term loss
ORIEN-TATION	0	Complete
	1	Oriented in ward, identifies people correctly
	2	Misidentifies but can find way about
	3	Cannot find way to bed or toilet without assistance
	4	Completely lost
COMMUNI-CATION	0	Always clear, retains information
	1	Can indicate needs, understands simple verbal directions, can deal with simple information
	2	Cannot understand simple verbal information *or* cannot indicate needs
	3	Cannot understand simple verbal information *and* cannot indicate needs; retains some expressive ability
	4	No effective contact
CO-OPERATION	0	Actively co-operative
	1	Passively co-operative *or* occasionally unco-operative
	2	Requires frequent encouragement or persuasion
	3	Rejects assistance, shows independent ill-directed activity
	4	Completely resistive or withdrawn
RESTLESS-NESS	0	None
	1	Intermittent
	2	Persistent by day *or* night
	3	Persistent by day *and* night
	4	Constant
DRESSING	0	Correct
	1	Imperfect but adequate
	2	Adequate with minimum of supervision

*The modifications include a few changes in wording, and the addition of 'Memory' and 'Bathing'.

	3	Inadequate unless continually supervised
	4	Unable to dress *or* to retain clothing
FEEDING	0	Correct, unaided at appropriate times
	1	Adequate with minimum of supervision
	2	Inadequate unless continually supervised
	3	Requires feeding
BATHING	0	Washes and bathes without assistance
	1	Minimal supervision with bathing
	2	Close supervision with bathing
	3	Inadequate unless continually supervised
	4	Requires washing and bathing
CONTINENCE	0	Full control
	1	Occasional accidents
	2	Continent by day only if regularly toiletted
	3	Urinary incontinence in spite of regular toiletting
	4	Regular or frequent double incontinence

Source: Wilkin and Jolley 1979.

Appendix Two

Clifton Assessment Procedures for the Elderly Behaviour Rating Scale

Please ring the appropriate number for each item

1 When bathing or dressing, he/she requires:
- no assistance — 0
- some assistance — 1
- maximum assistance — 2

2 With regard to walking, he/she:
- shows no signs of weakness — 0
- walks slowly without aid, or uses a stick — 1
- is unable to walk, or if able to walk, needs frame, crutches or someone by his/her side — 2

3 He/she is incontinent of urine and/or faeces (day or night):
- never — 0
- sometimes (once or twice per week) — 1
- frequently (3 times per week or more) — 2

4 He/she is in bed during the day (bed does not include couch, settee, etc):

          – never   0
          – sometimes   1
          – almost always   2

5 He/she is confused (unable to find way around, loses possessions, etc):

          – almost never confused   0
          – sometimes confused   1
          – almost always confused   2

6 When left to his/her own devices, his/her appearance (clothes and/or hair) is:

          – almost never disorderly   0
          – sometimes disorderly   1
          – almost always disorderly   2

7 If allowed outside, he/she would:

          – never need supervision   0
          – sometimes need supervision   1
          – always need supervision   2

8 He/she helps out in the home/ward:

          – often helps out   0
          – sometimes helps out   1
          – never helps out   2

9 He/she keeps him/herself occupied in a constructive or useful activity (works, reads, plays games, has hobbies, etc):

          – almost always occupied   0
          – sometimes occupied   1
          – almost never occupied   2

10 He/she socialises with others:

          – does establish a good relationship with others   0
          – has some difficulty establishing good relationships   1
          – has a great deal of difficulty establishing good relationships   2

11 He/she is willing to do things suggested or asked of him/her:

          – often goes along   0
          – sometimes goes along   1
          – almost never goes along   2

12 He/she understands what you communicate to him/her (you may use speaking, writing, or gesturing):

          – understands almost everything you communicate   0
          – understands some of what you communicate   1

- understands almost nothing of what you communicate   2
13 He/she communicates in any manner (by speaking, writing or gesturing):
- well enough to make him/herself easily understood at all times   0
- can be understood sometimes or with some difficulty   1
- can rarely or never be understood for whatever reason   2
14 He/she is objectionable to others during the day (loud or constant talking, pilfering, soiling furniture, interfering with affairs of others):
- rarely or never   0
- sometimes   1
- frequently   2
15 He/she is objectionable to others during the night (loud or constant talking, pilfering, soiling furniture, interfering in affairs of others, wandering about, etc.):
- rarely or never   0
- sometimes   1
- frequently   2
16 He/she accuses others of doing him/her bodily harm or stealing his/her personal possessions – if you are sure the accusations are true, rate zero, otherwise rate one or two:
- never   0
- sometimes   1
- frequently   2
17 He/she hoards apparently meaningless items (wads of paper, string, scraps of food, etc.):
- never   0
- sometimes   1
- frequently   2
18 His/her sleep pattern at night is:
- almost never awake   0
- sometimes awake   1
- often awake   2

Eyesight: (tick which applies)
- can see (or can see with glasses)
- partially blind
- totally blind

Hearing: (tick which applies)
- no hearing difficulties, without hearing aid
- no hearing difficulties, though requires hearing aid
- has hearing difficulties which interfere with communication
- is very deaf

Anyone interested in using the scale should contact Hodder and Stoughton Educational-test Department. © 1979 A.H. Pattie and C.S. Gilleard. Reproduced by permission of Hodder and Stoughton.

Appendix Three

Analysis of Daily Practices

Aim: to judge particular organisation practices or features according to their tendency to facilitate or limit resident freedom, to facilitate administrative efficiency at the expense of resident needs, to regiment residents and subject them to block treatment, to depersonalise residents by eroding individual differences or limiting decision-making powers, to maintain social distance between resident and staff.

Coding: within each category, the extent to which that practice is institution-oriented or resident-oriented is assessed on the basis of observations and interviews with resident staff. Each question is to be answered according to what happens generally in the home. For each question, Yes = 0 and No = 1. Total 78 questions.

1 Resident Care (21 questions)

1 Do residents have a choice of when they are bathed?
2 Do residents have a choice of who bathes them?
3 Can able residents bathe without permission?
4 Can residents bathe in private (apart from a necessary staff helper)?

1 Are residents toileted according to their individual needs? (Routine toileting at set times, code 1)
2 Are residents toileted in private (apart from staff helper?)
3 Are males/females toileted in separate facilities?

4   Is each toileted resident attended throughout the procedure by only one staff member? (Conveyor belt system, code 1)

1   Is there a choice of meals?
2   Do residents receive food as soon as they sit down? (If residents have to wait until everyone is seated, code 1)
3   Can residents eat with whom they wish?
4   Do staff eat regularly with the residents?
5   Are there facilities for the disabled to feed themselves?

1   Can residents choose when to go to bed?
2   Do staff attend promptly when resident needs help retiring?
3   Is there extensive use of sedation? (yes = 1, no = 0)

1   Can able residents choose when to get up?
2   Can disabled residents choose when to get up?
3   Are residents brought tea if they wish it?
4   Do staff routinely dress many residents? (yes = 1, no = 0)
5   Is breakfast available for residents as soon as they get up?

2   Resident autonomy (21 questions)
1   Do residents choose what to wear each day?
2   Do residents choose the new clothes allowed them by the Local Authority?
3   Are facilities provided for residents to buy/order additional clothes if they wish?
4   Are clothes generally kept in a good state of repair?

1   Can residents choose a private or shared room?
2   Can residents visit their own room at will?
3   Is there reasonable privacy for residents in their own room? (if observation windows/staff don't knock, code 1)
4   Have the majority of residents personalised their own room? (pictures and photographs don't count; evidence must consist of furniture, rug/bed cover or many smaller personal items together)

1   Do residents collect their own pensions?
2   Can all residents spend their money as they wish? (If money controlled by matron, or if restrictions are placed on certain residents, code 1)
3   Do staff help the disabled/mentally infirm residents to buy what they wish?

1   Are ambulent, lucid allowed to go out of Home without permission or without informing staff?
2   Can residents stay out as long as they wish? (If curfew, code 1)
3   Do staff often accompany disabled/mentally infirm residents?

4   Are relatives freely allowed to take out residents?

1   Do residents have access to tea making facilities?
2   Do residents have control over communal TV/radio?
3   Do residents have access to telephone?

1   Are all communal areas available to all residents? (If segregated, code 1)
2   Are other areas (e.g. kitchen) open to residents?
3   Can residents choose where to sit in lounges?

3   Resident–staff interactions (9 questions)
1   Does matron/deputy regularly chat to residents?
2   Do residents discuss personal matters with staff?
3   Do staff regularly communicate with residents for social purposes? (If communication mainly instructive/informative, code 1)

1   Are residents generally addressed only by their Christian names? (yes = 1, no = 0)
2   Is matron known to most residents by her name? (If title only, code 1)
3   Do most able residents know the names of some staff?

1   Do staff among themselves display accepting respectful attitudes to residents? (If critical, hostile, or distant, code 1)
2   Do staff avoid generalised terms for categories of residents (e.g. the 'babies', the 'incontinents')?
3   Do staff avoid demonstrating infantilisation of residents in their attitudes to them?

4   Organisational practices and features (27 questions)
1   Are pre-admission visits by prospective residents a general occurrence?
2   Does matron/staff generally visit prospective residents at home?
3   Are new residents introduced to staff and other residents?

1   Does a residents' committee exist?
2   Do staff and residents meet to discuss issues?
3   Are issues brought for decision to residents by matron?

1   Are there regular staff meetings?
2   Are care staff involved in admissions, case conferences, etc.?
3   Do staff control their daily work routines?

1   Does a formalised complaints procedure exist?
2   Does an informal opportunity for complaining exist?

3 Can residents complain to SSD management without acting through matron?

1 Can residents freely retain their own GP?
2 Do residents see VMD by appointment or on request? (If *en masse* or with group regimentation, code 1)
3 Is there evidence that minor medical problems are properly treated? (e.g. if ill-fitting dentures, inadequate spectacles, hearing aids, etc., code 1)

1 Are the furnishings pleasant and varied? (If furnishings uniform, regimented, code 1)
2 Are facilities adequate for disabled residents? (e.g. adequate hand-rails, room for wheelchairs, colour coded doors, lift, etc.)
3 Are pleasant gardens surrounding the home?

1 Are visiting times unrestricted?
2 Is the number of visitors unlimited?
3 Are there facilities for residents to see visitors privately?

1 Are regular outings/functions a feature of the home (at least once a month)?
2 Do residents organise any functions themselves?
3 Are residents consulted before outings/functions are decided upon?

1 Do residents undertake tasks in the home (e.g. cleaning, own small laundry)
2 Do many residents undertake individual activities?
3 Are facilities/materials/teaching regularly available to residents (e.g. library service, visiting teachers, etc.)?

Source: Evans *et al* 1981, Appendix 1h.

Appendix Four

Adapted version of Philadelphia Geriatric Center Morale Scale
1 Do things keep getting worse as you get older?
2 Do you have as much energy as you did last year?
3 Do you feel lonely much?
4 Do you see enough of your friends or relatives?
5 Do little things bother you more this year?

6   As you get older do you feel less useful?
7   Do you sometimes worry so much you can't sleep?
8   As you get older are things better than expected?
9   Do you sometimes feel that life isn't worth living?
10 Are you as happy now as you were when you were younger?
11 Do you have a lot to be sad about?
12 Are you afraid of a lot of things?
13 Do you get angry more than you used to?
14 Is life hard for you most of the time?
15 Are you satisfied with your life today?
16 Do you take things hard?
17 Do you get upset easily?

Source: Challis and Knapp 1980.

*   *   *

References
Allen, I. (1982) Short-stay residential care for the elderly, Unpublished report to DHSS, London, Policy Studies Institute.
Briers, J.M. (1979) *Residential Care for the Elderly in London*, London, DHSS Social Work Service, London Region.
Challis, D. and Knapp, M. (1980) *An Examination of the PGC Morale Scale in an English Context*, Discussion Paper 168, University of Kent at Canterbury Personal Social Services Research Unit.
Cooper, M. (1981a) Alternatives to residential provision for the elderly, Essex Social Services Department Research Section.
Cooper, M. (1981b) Needs assessment of elderly clients: new operational procedures briefing, Essex Social Services Department Research Section.
Darton, R.A. and McCoy, P.V. (1981) Survey of residential accommodation for the elderly, *Clearing House for Local Authority Social Services Research* 1981:2.
Davies, B. and Knapp, M. (1981) *Old People's Homes and the Production of Welfare*, London, Routledge and Kegan Paul.
Department of Health and Social Security (1977) *Residential Homes for the Elderly: Arrangements for health care. A memorandum of guidance*, London, DHSS.
Department of Health and Social Security Social Work Service Development Group Southern Region and East Sussex Social Services Department (1980) *Growing Old in Brighton*, London, HMSO.
Evans, G., Hughes, B. and Wilkin, D. with Jolley, D. (1981) *The Management of Mental and Physical Impairment in Non-Specialist Residential Homes for the Elderly*, University Hospital of South Manchester Psychogeriatric Unit – Research Section, Research Report No. 4.
Fairhurst, E. (1978) Talk and the elderly in institutions, Paper presented to the Annual Conference of the British Society of Social and Behavioural Gerontology, September 1978.
Felce, D. and Jenkins, J. (1979) Engagement in activities by old people in residential care, *Health and Social Service Journal*, 2 November.

Goffman, E. (1961) *Asylums*, New York, Doubleday Anchor Books.

Gray, J.A.M. (1976) Will old people's homes be swamped by the confused elderly? *Residential Social Work 16*, 265–267.

Gupta, H. (1979) Can we de-institutionalise an institution? Part 2, *Concord 13*, 47–57.

Hanley, I., Cleary, E., Oates, A. and Walker, M. (1981) In touch with reality, *Social Work Tcday*, 7 July.

Hanson, J. (1979) Residential homes for the elderly – survey of provision. Dorset Social Services Department. Unpublished report by Director to Social Services Committee.

Hitch, D. and Simpson, A. (1972) An attempt to assess a new design in residential homes for the elderly, *British Journal of Social Work 2*, 481–501.

Hughes, B. and Wilkin, D. (1980) *Residential Care of the Elderly: A review of the literature*, University Hospital of South Manchester Psychogeriatric Unit – Research Section, Research Report no. 2.

Imber, V. (1977) *A Classification of Staff in Homes for the Elderly*, DHSS Statistical and Research Report Series No. 18, London, HMSO.

Kart, C.S. and Maynard, B.B. (1976) Quality of care in old-age institutions, *Gerontologist 16*, 250–256.

Kimbell, A., Townsend, J. and Bird, M. (1974) Elderly persons' homes: A study of various aspects of regime and activities . . . and their effect upon the residents, Cheshire Social Services Department Research Section.

King, R.D., Raynes, N.V. and Tizard, J. (1971) *Patterns of Residential Care*, London, Routledge and Kegan Paul.

Knapp, M. (1979) On the determination of the manpower requirements of old people's homes, *Social Policy and Administration 13*, 219–235.

Knapp, M. (1981) Cost information and residential care of the elderly, *Ageing and Society 1*, 199–228.

Lawton, M.P. (1972) The dimensions of morale in D.P. Kent *et al* (eds) *Research Planning and Action for the Elderly*, New York Behavioural Publications.

Lawton, M.P. (1975) The PGC Morale Scale: A revision, *Journal of Gerontology 30*, 85–89.

Leicestershire Social Services Department (1979) Study of group living in homes for the elderly, Unpublished report.

Lipman, A. and Slater, R. (1977) Homes for old people: towards a positive environment, *Gerontologist 17*, 146–156.

Lipman, A., Slater, R. and Harris, H. (1979) The quality of verbal interaction in homes for old people, *Gerontology 25*, 275–284.

Marston, N. (1979) Can we de-institutionalise an institution? Part 1, *Concord 13*, 27–45.

Marston, N. and Gupta, H. (1977) Interesting the old, *Community Care*, 16 November.

Meacher, M. (1972) *Taken for a Ride*, London, Longman.

Mercer, S. and Kane, R.A. (1979) Helplessness and hopelessness among the institutionalised aged: an experiment, *Health and Social Work 4*, 91–116.

Neill, J.E. (1981) Some variations in policy and procedure relating to Part III applications in the GLC area. Unpublished paper, London, National Institute for Social Work.

Nissel, M. and Bonnerjea, L. (1982) *Family Care of the Handicapped Elderly:*

Who pays? PSI Report 602, London, Policy Studies Institute.

Pattie, A.H. and Gilleard, C.J. (1979) Psychological assessment in the care of the elderly, *Social Work Today*, 31 July.

Pattie, A.H., Gilleard, C.J. and Bell, J.H. (1979) *The Relationship of the Intellectual and Behavioural Competence of the Elderly to their Present and Future Needs from Community, Residential and Hospital Services*, York, Clifton Hospital Department of Clinical Psychology.

Peace, S.M., Hall, J.F. and Hamblin, G.R. (1979) *The Quality of Life of the Elderly in Residential Care*, Polytechnic of North London Department of Applied Social Studies, Survey Research Unit Report No. 1

Peace, S.M. and Harding, S.D. (1980) *The Haringey Group-Living Evaluation Project*, Polytechnic of North London Department of Applied Social Studies, Survey Research Unit Report No. 2.

Pincus, A. and Wood, V. (1970) Methodological issues in measuring the environment in institutions for the aged and its impact on residents, *International Journal of Ageing and Human Development 1*, 117–126.

Power, M. (1979) The home care of the very old, University of Bristol Social Care Research. Unpublished report to DHSS.

Power, M., Clough, R., Gibson, P., Kelly, S., with the assistance of Kaul, E. (1982) Helping lively minds – a volunteer experiment in residential care of the elderly. Unpublished report to DHSS, University of Bristol Social Care Research.

Raynes, N.V., Pratt, M.W. and Roses, S. (1979) *Organisational Structure and the Care of the Mentally Retarded*, London, Croom Helm.

Reynolds, D. (1979) Getting them back on their feet, *Community Care*, 24 May.

Rosencranz, H.A. (1974) Sociology of ageing, in W.C. Bier (ed), *Ageing: Its Challenge to the Individual and to Society*, Fordham University Press.

Shaw, I. and Walton, R. (1979) Transition to residence in homes for the elderly, in D. Harris and J. Hyland (eds) *Rights in Residence*, London, Residential Care Association.

Sinclair, I.A.C. (1971) *Hostels for Probationers*, Home Office Research Studies No. 6, London, HMSO.

Stapleton, B. (1977) A survey of the waiting list for places in Newham hostels for the elderly, *Clearing House for Local Authority Social Services Research*, 1977:5.

Thomas, N. (1981) Design, management and resident dependency in old people's homes, in E.M. Goldberg and N. Connelly (eds) *Evaluative Research in Social Care*, London, Heinemann Educational Books Ltd.

Thomas, N., Gough, J. and Spencely, H. (1977) *A Report on the Provision of Residential Accommodation for the Elderly Mentally Infirm*, London, DHSS.

Thomas, N., Gough, J. and Spencely, H. (1979) *An Evaluation of the Group Unit Design for Old People's Homes*, London, DHSS.

Tizard, B. (1975) Varieties of residential nursery experience, in J. Tizard, I. Sinclair and R.V.G. Clarke (eds) *Varieties of Residential Experience*, London, Routledge and Kegan Paul.

Tobin, S.S. and Lieberman, M.A. (1976) *Last Home for the Aged*, San Francisco, Jossey-Bass.

Townsend, P. (1962) *The Last Refuge*, London, Routledge and Kegan Paul.

Ward, P. (1980) *Quality of Life in Residential Care*, London, Personal Social Services Council.

Wenger, C. (1981) The elderly in the community: help and helpers. Unpublished draft paper, University College of North Wales, Bangor, Department of Social Theory and Institutions.

Wilkin, D. and Jolley, D. (1979) *Behavioural Problems among Old People in Geriatric Wards, Psychogeriatric Wards and Residential Homes 1976–78*, University Hospital of South Manchester Psychogeriatric Unit – Research Section, Research Report no. 1.

Willcocks, D.M., Cook, J., Ring, J. and Kelleher, R. (1980) *PSS: Consumer Study in Old People's Homes Pilot Report*, Polytechnic of North London Department of Applied Social Studies, Survey Research Unit Report No. 6.

Willcocks, D., Peace, S. and Kellaher, L. (1982) *The Residential Life of Old People: A study in 100 local authority homes*, Polytechnic of North London Department of Applied Social Studies – Survey Research Unit Reports No. 12 (Vol. I) and No. 13 (Vol. II).

Wing, J.K. and Brown, G.W. (1970) *Institutionalism and Schizophrenia: A comparative study of three mental hospitals*, Cambridge, Cambridge University Press.

Wright, K.G., Cairns, J.A., and Snell, M.C. (1981) *Costing Care: The costs of alternative patterns of care for the elderly*, University of Sheffield Joint Unit for Social Services Research.

Part Four
Conclusions

11   Comments and Reflections

We have come to the end of our laborious journey in which we tried to explore the state of the art of evaluating social care – illustrated by care for old people – and to draw out some of the emerging issues. The ground we traversed proved very uneven: some of the terrain was well cultivated, some rather patchy, and some pretty bare with a tree here and there. Did the exploration teach us anything? The answer is yes: the shape of the landscape of social care for the elderly has become clearer with its promising heights and neglected troughs.

Above all, this exploration kept raising fundamental questions about realistic aims in relation to people whose image of themselves and whose attitudes to others has long been established, and who look back over their lives rather than forward to new ventures; about the balance between active involvement and independence and contemplation and disengagement; about the benefits between segregation and 'mixing' in all kinds of contexts – housing, leisure, residential care. These questions do not lend themselves to any definite answers but perhaps call for a sharper awareness among social carers of the individual and social contexts which help to shape people's lives, and of the fact that there are no recipes for social care that are generally 'right'.

In this last chapter we do not wish to repeat in detail the conclusions and issues which we have summarised in relation to specific social care services. Nor do we wish to reiterate in detail the importance of evaluating the effectiveness of social care since the case was made explicitly in Chapter 2 where we gave as the main reasons: public accountability; the search for rational and as far as possible equitable deployment of resources; the assessment of the impact of services on users; cost effectiveness; and finally as a safeguard against fashion and enthusiastic and uncritical belief in 'the new'.

What we will do is reflect on the state of the art of evaluative research in the social care of old people, including the tools and methods that have been developed. We hope to highlight both the difficulties and the gaps as well as the progress made, and point towards further developments which are well within our reach now.

Finally we wish to return to some of the major issues and questions emerging, some of which need further research and enquiry, and some of which are policy issues to be decided in a continuing dialogue between the users and potential users of services, the carers and service providers and policy-makers.

The state of the art

Descriptive studies
Many readers may have been surprised by the preponderance of descriptive studies containing few *comparative* features which could assist one in saying 'this method of care or organisation of services appears to be able to achieve greater well-being among these kinds of clients than that method'. There are several reasons for this. Some fields are so new that full analytic descriptions are essential before one can start to compare and contrast. For example, when the National Day Care Study was started no-one knew how many day care facilities there were in the country, how they were distributed, what went on in them, what types of clients attended which kinds of centres, how often and so on. Even less was known about the number, types and distribution of neighbourhood care schemes, which thus demanded a descriptive account in the first place. Incidentally, in both instances the imaginative researchers went far beyond head counting and began to outline contrasting patterns of provision in relation to different social contexts and in relation to more idiosyncratic factors such as social characteristics and experiences of service providers and clients. Thus both these investigations set us well on the way towards asking more specific questions about the feasibility and effectiveness of different types of day care provision or neighbourhood care schemes, and both studies abound in intriguing hypotheses about what 'mixes' of provision in what social contexts result in what kinds of outcomes.

Another reason for the preponderence of descriptive studies is that many useful *ad hoc* surveys have been carried out – often with very small resources – in response to questions about the working and appropriateness of specific services provided by local authorities. For example, what do recipients think about meals, home helps, or the environmental features of residential care? What are their dependency levels in relation to types of help received? What do home helps do and how does this relate to the home help organisers' prescriptions? Other questions addressed the problem of equity in the distribution of resources, seeking to relate 'needs' found among recipients to the amount and type of services received. If many of these enquiries revealed discrepancies and maldistribution of resources this should not discourage us unduly, since so often the reason for calling in the research officers is suspected malfunctioning and inadequacy of services, and hardly ever the confirmation of suspected good practice!

These numerous local enquiries have repeatedly thrown up similar issues in many different spheres of social care: the mismatch between needs and resources, the inadequacy of appropriate initial assessment and the lack of monitoring and review procedures leading to even greater discrepancies and inappropriate resource allocation; lack of co-ordination between the various services not only at field level but at the policy level too. Thus the cumulative effect of these studies makes a considerable contribution to the evaluation of services. Some of the findings could lead directly to changes in policies and practices without further study. For example, the finding that home help organisers did not achieve (as they claimed) optimal geographical programming for their home helps and were not contributing significantly to the matching of client and helper; or that the needs of many recipients of meals on wheels were for shopping rather than a ready cooked meal; or that what residents in old peoples' homes desired greatly was individual control over their immediate environment such as being able to open and shut doors and windows and turn radiators on and off. Yet other issues emerging from these surveys demand the development of tools and guidelines: guides to assessment procedures, relevant and easily applied monitoring devices and so on.

Other suggestions need further study and testing in order to arrive at sound policy decisions. For example, how will the hypothesis emerging from the researches in Manchester old people's homes, that both staff and lucid residents are able to tolerate up to 30 per cent mentally confused residents, stand up to wider cross-sectional comparisons between homes of different kinds, or to experimental testing? Many similar questions arise in day care. For example, in what circumstances is it beneficial to mix frail and disturbed old people with more vigorous young-olds, or is it helpful to distinguish more strictly between day *care* provision for the frail and very old and 'senior citizens centres' for mobile, less disabled people? What about the cost implications? What are the advantages and disadvantages (including costs) for clients and service providers of setting up specialised information and advice sections within or without the social services departments rather than making these functions part of social workers' tasks? Is purchase of service – for example in the home care service – more cost effective and equally useful and acceptable to clients as direct service? Are tasks such as fetching pensions, shopping and escorting people to hospital appointments most satisfactorily and reliably carried out by home helps despite the cost involved, or are they the very tasks that neighbours, volunteers or semi-volunteers like and could do just as well? What are the consequences of splitting the administrative aspects of home help organisers' duties from their management, supervision and assessment roles?

Action research of an experimental kind would also be desirable to test the hunches arising from several studies that many families caring for mentally confused relatives need skilled social work support rather than voluntary or relatively unskilled help, at any rate for a time.

This is only a small sample of questions and hypotheses that descriptive and monitoring studies have raised and which require further cross-sectional comparisons between different agencies or quasi-experimental action research to assess relative effectiveness (including cost-effectiveness) of different types of service and methods of delivery.

Experimental outcome studies
The relatively few quasi-experimental and cross-sectional comparative studies are of great interest because they throw a sharper light on outcome, that is to say on the effects that specific types of social care have on the well-being of clients, the satisfaction of care givers and at what cost. And it is the final outcome after all – how different ways of giving care affect the lives of clients and those closest to them and perhaps even the neighbourhood – that is the main aim of evaluation.

The harvest is as yet small, but that should not discourage us since the numerous surveys and follow-up studies have either already shown quite decisive results as discussed above, or done the necessary ground work by specifying relevant questions and meaningful hypotheses which are now ready for testing. What is more, these studies have also prepared some of the appropriate methods and tools for doing the job, as we shall discuss below.

In the community care field the Thanet experiment which devolved budgetary responsibility to field level and allowed social workers to 'buy in' services and help from sources other than the local authority has shown the most encouraging results of any experimental study known to us. They indicate that packages of service, imaginatively tailored to individual needs and carefully monitored, not only 'keep very vulnerable old people out of institutional care' but significantly improve the quality of their lives and apparently serve to prolong life as well compared with a similar control group receiving conventional services. Perhaps most important, these researchers are well on the way to answering one of the most vital questions which group comparisons often mask: to which clients under what kinds of circumstances is a particular scheme of intervention more beneficial and cost effective compared with existing provision? The researchers are beginning to disentangle the chain of inter-relationships between level of dependency, informal support available, attitudes to help, outcome and cost. The methodological progress, together with the practical demonstration of greater autonomy of social workers not only as mobilisers of resources but also as resource holders and co-ordinators of care services, has far reaching implications well beyond the specific client group with which this experiment is concerned.

Compared with these striking results, Power's findings in his volunteer experiments both in the community and in the residential environment seem very modest. But again they may have far wider significance. Although the old people living in their own homes or in old people's homes enjoyed the relationships with their volunteers, who gave them a good deal of practical help and/or steady support, and although many friendships ensued in both settings, the final outcome indicators did not register much difference between the old people who had voluntary support and those who did not. There are possibly several reasons for these contrasting findings between the two studies which are of general importance when assessing the significance of experimental results. While the Kent researchers dealt with a very disabled group who received a great deal of intensive daily help and support, Power in his community volunteer project had a mixed group of old people ranging from those with no particular welfare needs to some who were very frail; and of course the inputs of the volunteers were very much less – usually one weekly contact except in emergencies. Thus the chances for 'improvement' were potentially much greater among the very frail Kent clients who received so much additional help compared with Power's sample. Among the residential clients one outing or good chat for a couple of hours a week, however pleasant, is probably a drop in the ocean of unfilled time in a residential home. Even more important, the rather global life satisfaction index adopted to measure social and psychological change could not hope to capture the pleasure that the residents might have experienced on the *day* they saw their volunteers, which did not necessarily mean that their underlying attitudes to life in general had changed significantly. Thus this study raises starkly the question of realistic aims and appropriate measurements.

Promising beginnings have also been made in small controlled experiments in residential settings, stimulating interest by providing lounges with reading materials, and knitting and gardening sessions. These activities raised the level of engagement among very old people quite considerably in contrast to the days when such stimulation was not provided. It is regrettable that through lack of funding plans for more extensive experimental work have not materialised. For so much needs to be learned about the optimal balance of engagement and disengagement among different types of residents in varying social environments and how involvement in a range of activities and personal relationships relates to subjective feelings of pleasure, satisfaction and well-being;

the mere measurement of activity rates does not tell us nearly enough about their meaning for particular people.

Valuable pilot experiments have also begun to assess the impact of different types of social arrangements – for example group living which can further social interaction among residents, mutual help, and preservation of self care. But again more comprehensive cross-sectional studies now need to be designed to assess the effect of different patterns of living which are being developed in residential homes and their effect on the social functioning and well being of different kinds of residents and staff. Such studies are particularly desirable in order to guard against two potential dangers: fashion, and thinking of 'old people' as a homogeneous group. People who have always lived in family groups, and those who have lived alone for a long while, those who have always been fiercely independent and know their own minds and those who are used to depending on others for most decisions will thrive in very different social environments whatever the pundits consider to be progressive care for 'the elderly'.

Developing tools and methods of investigation

We came across many promising developments in clarifying concepts, in forging research and practice tools, and in refining methods for surveying, monitoring and evaluating different aspects of social care in community and residential settings. Some of the instruments and methods not only further research, but are also of immediate use to practitioners.

Evaluative research has developed tools to monitor flows of clients in and out of the caring systems – those who walk in and out in rapid succession through the revolving doors of the social services departments and those who are becoming almost permanent fixtures in the welfare system; those who consume many resources and those who consume few, and so on. Similarly it is becoming possible to describe more succinctly what the carers are up to, whether in fieldwork, in day care or in residential settings. Hence fieldworkers, management and (potentially) the general public can learn 'who gets what' and roughly with what results. In conjunction with area studies using indicators of potential needs, monitoring systems can identify gaps or overlaps in provision and indicate where shifts in the distribution of resources may be desirable. At present these developing instruments are freely adapted by different groups of researchers and practitioners for various specific purposes. But if policy-makers are to take serious notice of the ensuing results and if comparisons between areas and regions are not to be misleading there is an urgent need to carry out reliability and validity studies of these instruments.

Provided that a monitoring instrument has undergone sufficient testing in different field situations and makes sense to a variety of practitioners it can easily be tested further in a wider national context: copies of case descriptions, and the monitoring forms and instructions for use can be sent to practitioners in different parts of the country in order to assess their agreements and disagreements on the classifications of 'problems' and the fieldwork processes. Such studies have been successfully carried out in the difficult field of mental ill-health on an international basis, and need not consume very substantial financial resources.

In the areas of day and residential care, the seminal work leading to the concepts of client-centred and institutional-centred regimes begun by Goffman in mental hospitals and prisons, and modified by Tizard and his colleagues in institutions for mentally handicapped children, is now being further developed and adapted to settings caring for old people. These developments are a shining example of the imaginative transfer of knowledge from one field to another. The visual game techniques created by the researchers at the North London Polytechnic in order to elicit old people's preferences in conditions where choices are severely restricted are another promising beginning. Similarly measurements of life satisfaction and 'morale' are being gradually adjusted to the limited life experiences and expectations of the very old, and may eventually be able to tell us something 'real' about their feelings of well-being, depression or disappointment; but these instruments too need to be validated more rigorously by direct observation and interaction with old people over time in order to be fully convincing and useful. Various tested measures of disability and dependency have been developed, for example the modified Crichton Royal Behavioural Rating scale and the Clifton Behaviour Rating scale which appear as appendices to Chapter 10. These tools enable practitioners to assess potential and actual residents and to monitor their progress. Finally the checklist of daily practices (also appended to Chapter 10) developed by the Manchester researchers should prove invaluable to practitioners and other researchers. It could also provide a useful guide to social services committee members and other people with responsibility for the quality of services.

In relation to methods of investigation we have travelled a long way from the few interesting, not to say exotic, case descriptions, full of interpretative insights by the care giver (with the voice of the client hardly perceptible) to the sober if duller accounts of representative samples of clients. Attempts are made to distinguish between the many problems and worries that beset them (and may interest the care giver) and those that seem important to the *clients* and which *they* want to tackle; similarly to specify more clearly what care givers are doing in response, and occasionally to ask the consumers what they make of it all. This is not to say that case studies are unimportant. On the contrary, they are vital in generating insights, hypotheses and speculative theories, but except for rare occasions it is not possible to generalise from them. Methodologically we have experienced great leaps, from case descriptions with over-optimistic generalisations, to random experiments with inadequate tools and disappointingly negative results (discussed in Chapter 3), to experimental research based on more specific hypotheses with limited aims and using common and at least partially tested tools. But what is perhaps most encouraging, and denotes slow knowledge-building at last, is the triangulation of methods which is being adopted in most major evaluative studies of field practices and methods of service organisation and delivery. Firstly, referral routes, clients and their problems are described in ways that can be compared across authority boundaries, and the important distinction is being observed between incidence (new cases arising) and prevalence (current or ongoing cases at a certain point or period in time). Secondly, the care givers' activities are being described more concretely, as are their contacts with other agencies or networks. Thirdly, workers' satisfaction and their interpretation of outcomes is distinguished from evaluation by consumers and independent assessments by outside observers.

In the residential field casual impressionistic observations are giving way to systematic observations sampled on a time basis. The many ingredients that make up 'residential care' are being disentangled into physical environment, regime, client/staff interaction, client satisfaction and staff attitudes, and related to each other. The configurations most conducive to a reasonably satisfying life for all actors still largely elude us. But certain hypotheses are emerging – as we have already discussed – for example, about the proportion of confused elderly people that lucid residents are able to tolerate. And certain simple design features are clearly preferred by the majority of a representative sample of residents. Even in the as yet little explored field of voluntary action systematic study is beginning to distinguish certain patterns of relationship between types of statutory authorities and types of neighbourhood care systems. Hypotheses are being formulated about the factors that appear to be associated with relative success and failure in neighbourhood care.

Some policy issues

Assessment

Throughout this review we have encountered the service-oriented or 'welfare tray' approach to need assessment, and it has been suggested that assessments should be more broadly based, asking what this particular person in her particular situation needs or wants and would find acceptable – obviously within the framework of available resources. But what are these resources? Several studies suggest that service providers often overlook possibilities at hand, such as neighbourly support, liaison with volunteer groups and local voluntary organisations, appropriate support to relatives, who may not always live *with* the clients, but may be closely involved in their care. It has even been suggested by practitioners and researchers that imaginative service providers should see themselves also as creators of resources, starting informal day care or a special group in outlying districts, for example. Another important problem arises in relation to assessment: how not to over-complicate a simple request made by a sensible old person who knows what she wants, and on the other hand to ensure that frontline workers learn to recognise the signs which indicate that more than a simple bath aid is at stake. Much thought and experiment will have to be devoted to possibilities of in-service training and developing guidelines so that clients are not deprived of their freedom to decide what they need and want and yet ensuring that difficulties are spotted before they explode into a crisis.

Domiciliary services

Despite the shortcomings that have repeatedly been shown to limit its effectiveness, the home help service remains the basic domiciliary service. Far more doubts have been raised about the appropriate uses of home-delivered meals services.

The most important issue facing the domiciliary services is how their resources should be distributed and what considerations should go into achieving the right balance between providing intensive domiciliary support and social care for the increasing numbers of very frail and very old people, and giving basic domiciliary support to the many old people who cannot manage heavy housework any more. As the overhead and running costs rise in the big bureaucracies we call social services departments, there is a strong case for devolution in the shape of patch-based service delivery, or neighbourhood service centres with budgetary responsibility. But there are also possibilities for contracting out the simpler domestic jobs to the voluntary or private sector, with the social services department still responsible for assessment, review and holding the purse strings, thus providing some guarantee for upholding standards. Would such arrangements be more or less cost effective, and would they enable the service to expand more rapidly? Experiments comparing effectiveness, accountability and cost as between direct service (both patch based and more centralised) with contracted-out service are called for.

If the social services department is to concentrate more on providing home and personal care services to the older physically and mentally frail people, will home helps need more training? What should such training comprise? Basic nursing skills? Knowledge about the ageing process, and particularly how to cope with mentally confused people? Should these special home helps have at least a basic idea of welfare rights so that they could refer people on? How much do such duties overlap with district nursing services, as happened in the Coventry project? Should one aim at intentional overlapping and would such collaboration constitute a case for joint funding with the health services? How do these intensive personal support services relate to the substantial number of very old handicapped people who are looked after by their families, or rather by their daughters and daughters-in-law? According to the evidence emerging from several exploratory studies such family carers are often almost totally unsupported by domiciliary or personal care services apart from day care one or two days a week – and this only for a small proportion of cases.

How should this intensive home care service (which is bound to have to shoulder increasing workloads till well into the middle 1990s) relate to the rest of the fieldwork team and to the primary health care team? Here we have encountered evidence that the present state of affairs is unsatisfactory. In many authorities the home help service is quite separate from the rest of the social services team, not to mention the primary health care team. In particular we noted poor or non-existent communication with social workers, and yet a two-way traffic would be desirable in the interests of the clients: social workers could be of help as resource persons and advisers to home helps, and occasionally as counsellors to the old persons and their informal carers when difficulties become apparent with which the home care assistant does not feel able to deal. Conversely the intimate day-to-day knowledge the home help has might prove invaluable to a social worker or doctor who may also be involved. Communication via an already overburdened home help organiser seems to create an unnecessary barrier between fieldworkers.

This brings us once more to a consideration of the role of the home help organiser. Some studies have raised serious doubts about the viability of her current role; she is partly a personnel manager and partly a social service worker assessing and reviewing people in need of domiciliary services. Should the home help organiser be merged more wholeheartedly into area teams, either retaining her personnel functions and giving up her assessment functions; or passing the personnel functions to suitably equipped administrators and retaining her social service functions, becoming a home care specialist within the social services team? The latter would make a great deal of sense if some of the domestic home help functions were to be contracted out, which would require expert assessment and reliable supervision. A home care specialist within the social services team would also facilitate close co-operation with social workers, which would be essential if the Kent community care model were to be adopted for the care of the very frail elderly.

Collaboration between social and health services
The next question is how better communication and collaboration is to be brought about between the social service teams and the primary health care and hospital teams. Would the creation of community teams for the elderly along the lines of the developing community mental handicap teams be a possibility? Would more part time attachments of social workers to primary health care teams with specific duties vis-à-vis the older patient population be another desirable route? How is the detection of the myriad of minor – often remediable – miseries of the aged to be tackled which are at present not reported to either district nurse, general practitioner or social worker? Two possibilities suggest themselves. The first is clearly more awareness on the part of the professionals of the cumulative effects of these many unreported discomforts. The other is to create more and better opportunities for those in close touch with old people, such as home helps, neighbourly volunteers and deliverers of meals to report back to the professionals; or to encourage elderly people themselves to bring their minor troubles to the relevant professionals.

Social work
The evaluative studies surveyed indicate the changes in roles and functions that would be necessary if social workers are to make a more central contribution to the social care of the old people. Their skills are badly needed in the assessment of complex situations, as enablers and resource persons to ancillary statutory workers and volunteers, as case workers in specific problem situations and as community workers helping to start or support community and neighbourhood initiatives. It is questionable whether their expertise is equally suited to information and advice giving on a broad scale which they often attempt at present. Nor is it feasible for them to act in general as direct long-term supporters rather than supporting caring networks.

Should social workers dealing with old people be specialists in 'ageing'? We doubt it, on two grounds: if generic training equips social workers to tackle problems associated with childhood, adolescence and family functioning, why should it not prepare them to deal with problems of old age at a time when 15 per cent of the population are 'senior citizens'? Secondly, if either through community teams for the elderly or other mechanisms close collaboration and consultation with geriatric specialists develop, then a thorough grounding in social work skills (which in future will have to include the indirect resource and community function) will be more helpful than specialisation in gerontology. These arguments do not exclude the postgraduate option some social workers are already choosing of becoming specialists in the care of the elderly, particularly if they are in senior positions and can make their expertise freely available to other colleagues.

Transport
Looking beyond the domiciliary services, the provision of suitable transport is arguably the most serious stumbling block to the optimal use of care resources. We saw that those who were most disabled and most dependent on transport received less day care than those who were able to get about. The pilot study of a small sample of 22 families by Nissel and Bonnerjea confirmed this state of affairs. Almost all of the families would have liked more, and more flexible, day care, and so would a substantial minority of the 150 families seen by Levin who were looking after mentally confused relatives. Lack of transport was also one of the impediments mentioned by 20 per cent of neighbourhood care schemes. At the same time day centres are not fully used – the occupancy rate in Carter's national study was 70 per cent. It seems that the problem of transport needs to be tackled in a radical manner, beginning with a detailed scrutiny of the current use of transport resources. Here we should remember the inefficient use of transport resources in Cumbria, where home helps were shown to travel back and forth over their areas. How many social workers and other social services department officials do likewise? Small patch-based area teams running more localised services may contribute in some part to the solution.

Autonomy
The next issue that seems to permeate implicitly if not always explicitly much of the evaluative research and writing generally about the social care of old people is the failure to aim at maintaining their independence and autonomy rather than to encourage passivity and dependency, partly for administrative convenience and partly from the motivation of helpfulness. This issue is most prominent in residential care, but also raises its head when ready-cooked meals are provided to people who could manage to cook if someone got their shopping, or if home helps do light dusting which many old people can do. It is also possible that more frequent use of occupational therapists advising home helps and old people may enable more of the latter to cope successfully with domestic jobs. In residential care one needs to remember that the average age of residents is over 80 and that many of them are very frail and confused. Yet, as the visual game suggested, some old people in

residential homes, even if they are very frail, would like to exercise more control over their lives. But allowing more choice, more autonomy, and more independence is probably more costly in terms of well-trained sensitive staff and involves a higher degree of risk-taking on their part.

There are many roads that lead to Rome
When trying to draw general conclusions from selected evaluative studies in such a multi-faceted endeavour as social care which ranges from income maintenance, food and shelter to counselling, it is difficult to avoid the impression of imposing generalised prescriptions. This is not our intention. Old people differ in their personalities and coping abilities as much as other people, as we stressed at the beginning. Willcocks and her colleagues in their sensitive consumer study highlight these differences: men often expressed different preferences from women; some people preferred to be where the action is in a residential home – in the entrance lobby – while others liked small cosy lounges. Though most valued privacy and a single bedroom, some did not mind sharing, and so on. Power will show in his publication on the volunteer experiment in old people's homes that some people thought residential care was marvellous – the best thing that ever happened to them, security, good food, company, and so on. Others were resigned to it, and yet others resented and deplored their fate bitterly, however long they had been residents. All these attitudes could be encountered in one and the same environment.

Similarly what the caring services have to offer can vary greatly and the way in which they are put together also varies: where a policy of building very sheltered housing is instituted fewer residential homes and long-term hospital beds may be needed. Where a vigorous day and domiciliary care programme is pursued the need for residential care may be diminished (though not necessarily the need for hospital beds). Where a policy of building half-way houses between residential homes and long-term geriatric wards is instituted, hospital admissions will become rarer. Where a widespread system of warden supervision has been instituted, as in Sheffield, it may be possible for very frail people to stay at home, feeling reasonably secure that even if they have a fall help will be available very soon. In one London borough in which many upper-class widows of restricted means reside, a great deal of residential care in the private sector has been supported by the social services department and comparatively few intensive home care services have been available.

Thus the balance of care can vary between areas not only according to the resources that are available, but according to the history of an area, the social class mix and the prevailing customs. It would be encouraging to think that these variations would take into account not only 'needs' as seen by professionals and councillors, but also people's preferences and choices, of which we still have only a hazy idea. A beginning has been made in Stockport's comprehensive survey of old people's needs in relation to the distribution of health, housing and social services resources in 1976. This survey led to considerable shifts in service provision which are now being evaluated after five years. This incidentally is one of the very rare examples of survey results leading to change and further evaluation; we very much hope that Stockport's example will be repeated in many other areas.

Implementation

Although the type and balance of care in any area will depend on many factors, one of them will be or should be tested knowledge and practice. The field of social care is still short of such contributions to policy. Even where evaluative research has shown fairly hard evidence about how practice could be improved, there is resistance to change or a tendency to ignore the findings and repeat the exercise. There is a modest accretion of knowledge and practice, some of which we have tried to capture in this book. But this is not enough. We need continuing and clearly established channels of communication on the results of significant research and practice presented in a language that everybody from social work assistants to scholars will find acceptable.

How to translate even freely accessible knowledge into policy and practice still remains one of the hardest nuts to crack. More resources need to be invested in the *development* and adaptation of research-based findings if the effectiveness of social care is to be enhanced.

Index